Kindergarten Screening

Kindergarten Screening

Early Identification of Potential High Risk Learners

By

SHIRLEY ZEITLIN, Ed.D.

Director, Child Study Center
Associate Professor of Educational Psychology
State University College
New Paltz, New York
Formerly, School Psychologist
Beacon City School District, New York

CHARLES C THOMAS • PUBLISHER
Springfield • Illinois • U.S.A.

Published and Distributed Throughout the World by
CHARLES C THOMAS • PUBLISHER
Bannerstone House
301-327 East Lawrence Avenue, Springfield, Illinois, U.S.A.

© *1976, by* CHARLES C THOMAS • PUBLISHER
ISBN 0-398-03574-1
Library of Congress Catalog Card Number: 76-12416

With THOMAS BOOKS *careful attention is given to all details of
manufacturing and design. It is the Publisher's desire to present books that are
satisfactory as to their physical qualities and artistic possibilities and
appropriate for their particular use.* THOMAS BOOKS *will be true to those
laws of quality that assure a good name and good will.*

Printed in the United States of America
R-2

Library of Congress Cataloging in Publication Data

Zeitlin, Shirley.
   Kindergarten screening.

   Bibliography: p.
   Includes index.
   1. Prediction of scholastic success. I. Title.
LB1131.Z44   372.1'2'64   76-12416
ISBN 0-398-03574-1

to Norman

PREFACE

KINDERGARTEN screening is one small part of a ground swell movement which recognizes the importance of educators becoming involved with the child at a young age in order to prevent or reduce failure in school and in life.

When I first became interested in screening, many viewed kindergarten and prekindergarten as too early to get so involved with the child. In approximately a ten-year period, the emphasis for early identification of high risk children and the prevention of failure has shifted to younger and younger children. Head Start has focused on the three- to five-year-old child. Burton White at the Brookline Early Education Center has focused on the eight- to eighteen-month-old child. Some in the medical profession are screening infants, pre- and postnatal.

These emerging trends are still in their infancy and affect a small number of children. Kindergarten screening has the potential to reach almost all children because the school is the one place that has access to them. There is only a small percentage of the population that is so severely handicapped that it never becomes involved with the school.

This book developed from personal experience working with children as a school psychologist, and involvement with many screening programs. The development of the Zeitlin Early Identification Screening (ZEIS) stemmed from the frustrating search for an adequate screening instrument. As my knowledge and interest grew, I started collecting information about, and corresponding with many people who were also involved in program development. In the late 1960's and early 1970's research and other literature started to appear in the journals and other publications.

My learning has grown with the writing of this book, and at its completion I have personally found some answers to the many problems and concerns about screening, but have also raised many other questions that I'm still working on. I am totally convinced of the value of kindergarten screening as a first step for early identification and educational planning for potential high risk children.

This book strives to find the balance between being a "how to" cookbook and raising the issues and exploring the processes that need to be considered before the reader uses the cookbook.

The book is organized so that the reader, depending on his need, can read it from beginning to end or can read only those chapters that relate to his need. As knowledge of screening is only in the developing stages, the author would appreciate hearing from people who are involved in developing or already have functioning screening programs.

In referring to children and teachers it was difficult to choose an appropriate pronoun to use which would recognize the equality of the sexes. Because the English language does not have a personal pronoun which recognizes both sexes, it would have been cumbersome to continuously write he/she or some other similar combination.

I have arbitrarily referred to the student as "he" and the teacher as "she," but the intent is to refer to both sexes.

This book could be useful for people who have an interest in young children getting off to the best educational start. Included in this group are parents, teachers, paraprofessionals, college students, administrators, physicians, educational specialists, member of boards of education, and special interest community groups.

There are many people whom I want to thank most especially because their help and support were vital to the writing of this book. Terri Cohen gave me the initial encouragement that this book could and should be written. Margaret Casson encouraged and supported the book through my experiences with her as a master teacher of young children and her critical feedback as she read the book. Lois Nichols, the coauthor of the personalized learning model, helped clarify many points. Sadie Caram typed the first drafts and struggled successfully with reading my handwriting, and Alice Wendover typed the final manuscripts. Patricia Milano typed the endless correspondence. Mary Barrett did the editing of the book and made many constructive suggestions regarding the format. Joan Gallagher and her students, Roger Coutant and Denice Carter, did the statistical work for the ZEIS.

A most special thanks to all the members of the faculty of the van den Berg Learning Center who were participants in the development of the ZEIS and the personalized learning model, and to the many project directors throughout the United States who took the time to correspond and share materials and ideas. Many students and teachers helped by giving feedback and raising questions about their experiences with kindergarten screening.

Most important was the love, support, encouragement, and endless hours of reading and listening given by my husband.

Shirley Zeitlin, Ed.D.

CONTENTS

Kindergarten Screening

Chapter One

WHY SCREEN?

WHAT is kindergarten screening, and why and how do we do it? This is a question being asked in many schools and communities. For some, screening is perceived as the opening of a door to more positive learning experiences; to others, it is one more threat and infringement on the rights of individuals. Screening and other early assessment programs are a first step in an educational process that focuses on success in school. It begins with early identification of those children who, because of problems of development and/or experience, may be least able to meet the typical expectations of the school. For these children school is often an unhappy, failure-ridden experience. Many of them can be identified at a young age and given help to prevent failure. They cry out for help, begging to be heard. It is far more humane to help them succeed by identifying and capitalizing on their strengths, and at the same time working to eliminate their difficulties than it is to just let them fail. Kindergarten screening programs are one way of accomplishing this.

As a school psychologist, the author became involved in pre-kindergarten screening out of frustration and anger. All too often, when the author saw a child in the upper primary grades or higher, the author found the cumulative records showed that often there were indications of the problem as early as in kindergarten. Only when a child had failed or acted up was his cry for help heard. The author thought how economical it would be both in human resources and dollars and cents if it was possible to find these children before they get into trouble. Therefore, the author devised a screening instrument and found that one could identify many of the children who potentially had severe problems. Once involved in a screening process, the author searched for more information and found that many people shared her interest and concern. Relevant data about programs and instruments existed,

3

but they had to be searched out. Her searching was the seed for this book.

When popular education began approximately 100 years ago, those children who were difficult to educate did not attend school. Today, however, more attention is being turned to the task of educating those who are more difficult to teach: the handicapped, the disadvantaged, and others who for a variety of reasons need more help than the schools currently offer.

The expanding role of the school has had positive implications for many children, but for others it has spelled failure. Evidence of this failure is seen in such statistics as the lower age of delinquents, high rate of dropouts, retentions, and lower reading scores. The average age of the juvenile delinquent today is 13.5. In 1969, 39 percent of all arrests were persons under twenty-one years of age, with 22 percent being committed by persons fifteen years of age and younger (Mauser, 1974). Despite an average IQ of 91 for black delinquents and 94 for white delinquents there was a two-to four-year discrepancy between actual achievement and achievement potential (Mauser, 1973). Fifty percent of the juvenile delinquents referred to the courts had a specific learning disability (Poremba, 1967). In 1969, one out of every four pupils nationwide had significant reading deficiencies. About half of the unemployed youth in New York City ages sixteen to twenty-one were illiterate. Any community in the country can develop its own statistics to demonstrate the whole continuum of failure. Failure is represented not only by the extremes of poverty, crime, unemployment, and alienation but also by far too many children who struggle with learning they cannot comprehend or by others who are bored by teaching which does not challenge their greater ability.

Individual differences in rate and pattern of development influence a child's readiness to learn. Estimates of the problem population vary greatly. In 1966, it was estimated that approximately 25 percent of children entering school show some signs of developmental deviation (statistical abstract of the U. S., 1966). In the 1972-73 school year, the Association of Children With Learning Disabilities estimated that 15 percent of students can be expected to show some sort of mild learning disability requiring help, while another 3 to 5 percent would have more severe problems. Another statistic is that 40 percent of all children have problems which can seriously interfere with their learning or adjustment in the primary school years (Rogolsky, 1968). These problems, which can be identified as early as kindergarten, show up in children as emotional disorders, intellectual defects, learning disabilities, and visual-motor and sensory defects. These difficulties have a major impact on the personal and vocational adjustment as the student moves through school and into the adult world. The psychology of failure becomes a vicious cycle. "I'm not learning, therefore I feel inadequate. When I feel inadequate, why should I try to learn because I'll only fail again and feel still more inadequate." Success, on the other hand, encourages learning and the willingness to try.

Cultural differences foster different early experiences and expectations for learning. Poverty creates the problem of poor nutrition for the child. It limits his learning opportunities at home, and gives him little or no understanding of what the public school system will expect and demand. There are some hopeful movements which may mitigate the situation. Militant minority groups and parent groups of children with special needs such as the Association for the Help of Retarded Children and Council for Exceptional Children are bringing these problems to public attention and are actively involved in working toward solutions.

In education, there are specific stages when intervention is more likely to be effective. The federal government, too, recognized the importance of early educational intervention. The Head Start project, started in 1965, had by 1973 spent approximately 2.5 billion dollars in an effort to give four to five million preschool children from poor families a better chance at the education starting line. A five-year study of children with learning disabilities by Koppitz (1971) concluded that extremely immature and vulnerable children should be identified at time of school entry and be given special consideration before they develop serious learning and emotional problems. Her study showed that most children with learning disabilities tend to have difficulties in school beginning with the primary grade. She recommended that "all children should be screened prior to their enrollment in kindergarten." Such a recommendation is particularly important because early school years are very difficult for some. The results of being placed in an inappropriate environment or being held up to unrealistic expectations may have catastrophic and lifelong ramifications for a child.

In 1970, the Joint Committee on Mental Health of Children published a report entitled *Crisis in Child Mental Health: Challenge for the 1970's*. The document is a plea for this country to reaffirm its concern for its young through meaningful actions and programs. Legal, medical, and educational reforms are advocated in an attempt to diminish inequality in justice, care, and opportunity. The report included a model for delivering services to children and families. This model included the screening and assessment of young children in school for early signs of dysfunction.

In 1972, the President's Committee on Mental Retardation supported screening and assessment programs which they saw as a preliminary stage to a general program of prevention and remediation (Meier, 1973).

The American Academy of Pediatrics in November 1973, through their Council on Child Health, made a statement supporting the establishment of early identification programs in each community. These programs would follow children considered as potential high risks because of their past history or their unusual behavior which might interfere with normal learning at home or in the school environment.

In 1975, the State of California placed its emphasis on massive expenditure and expansion of resources to the very young on the theory that it is better to diagnose and correct learning problems during a child's first few years of school than to provide costly remedial programs later.

DeHirsch (1966), a pioneer in the field of early identification, found that there is a close link between a child's maturational status at kindergarten age and his reading and spelling achievement several years later. She felt that the educator cannot afford to wait passively for maturation to occur, nor should the child be exposed to a kind of instruction that is clearly inappropriate at his particular stage of growth.

In 1958, the Human Relations Service of Wellesley, Inc., a privately supported mental health agency in a middle class suburban community, initiated a free, confidential preschool check-up program which was conducted in the spring and early summer for families of children expecting to enter kindergarten in September. The check-up consisted of interviews of parent and child, and was intended to detect children who would later show evidence of poor school adjustment. The agency worked closely with the schools and was the forerunner of a funded pilot program that ran from 1968 to 1970 called "Project of Early Identification of Children with Potential Learning Disabilities." The goals of this project were to identify and examine those children who showed signs or symptoms of developmental delay or deviation, to initiate a program of compensatory education focused upon parent counseling, to train parents to help their own children, and at the time of school entry, to plan appropriately and provide special services to children if needed. It was hoped that such early identification and training of "high risk" children would contribute to the prevention of school failure in later years.

During the two years of the program many problems were identified which might interfere with learning (see Table I).

This project, referred to as the Wellesley project, gave impetus to many schools to initiate their own programs.

While all children, because of their unique developmental patterns, have special educational needs, screening is most concerned with the children who are at the two extremes of the continuum of learning competence: the so-called "high risk" child who may have difficulty with the learning process and the so-called "high potential" or gifted child. It is the child who may have difficulty who is the focus of most screening programs and is the prime concern of this book.

Screening is not a one-shot miracle solution to the problems of education, but a process of early identification and follow through program. It is a step toward "humanizing education." What could be a more human approach toward the teaching-learning process, than to gather information and design specific objectives of learning for the child at his own developmental level? There is a need to refocus on how we educate and what we

TABLE I

Types of Developmental Problems Encountered
in Wellesley preschool project*

	Percent of Cases	
	1968-69	*1969-70*
Behavior and emotional dis-orders (mild to severe)	10.8%	10 %
Speech and language disorders	7 %	9 %
Multiple problems: Language disorder, restlessness, hyperactivity, short attention span, poor motor coordination	5 %	5 %
Possible hearing problems, hearing test recommended	3 %	2.5%
Markedly poor motor coordination	1.9%	2 %
Mental retardation	1.2%	0.6%
	Fall 1969	*Fall 1970*
No. children entering kindergarten	399	396
	1968-69	*1969-70*
No. families reached through preschool project	226 (56.6%)	291 (73.5%)

*Wellesley Public Schools - Title VI Project Final Report

expect from young children.

Early identification programs are in their infancy. Most educators support the concept but many have concerns about what programs are most effective and the potential for abuse inherent in the concept.

This book is not a definitive last word on the subject — all the answers are not known nor has everything that has been done in the field been researched. It is an effort to bring together information, research, and criticism relating to kindergarten screening from many sources, and to try to organize and clarify it. The book has two goals:

1. to describe the various aspects, implications and directions

of prekindergarten and kindergarten screening, diagnosis, and related programs, and

2. to facilitate the development of screening programs appropriate to the needs of educational institutions.

Early identification programs are based on the assumption that no two children are alike, because they differ in what they bring to school in both their experiences and pattern of growth. They also differ in the skills, feelings, and behaviors they develop in school. The goal of screening is not to stereotype children through labeling, e.g. slow learner, but rather to set appropriate expectations for all children and to design appropriate experiences so that they may have success in the classroom as they move toward acquisition of the basic skills necessary to function in our society.

Chapter Two

DEFINITIONS, MODELS AND USES

THE definition of a word or concept can often determine or strongly influence the programs which subsequently develop. Key words, such as "screening," "diagnosis," "high risk," and "personalized learning" have been explained in different ways.

Screening

Screening is defined in the dictionary (Barnhart, 1963) in eighteen different ways including "Matter separated out with a screen [and] to sift by passing through a screen." In the field, screening has been defined as measures which can be used with groups of children as contrasted with individually administered procedures (Rogolsky, 1968); as early detection procedures for handicaps which employ simple and reliable techniques which are applied routinely to a large number of children (Egan, 1969); or as a process that separates children into those who have no apparent problems from those who do (DIAL, Learning Disabilities/Early Childhood Research Project, 1972).

Meier (1973) uses an analogy to describe the screening process. He says one of the primary concerns of a large screening system is the yield factor. He compares the screening to sorting oranges. If, for example, oranges are being sorted according to size, an initial screening can be done by one screen which prevents only the grossly oversize oranges from passing through. These extraordinarily large and relatively rare oranges can then be subjected to careful analysis (diagnosis) in terms of the causes and prevention of their oversizeness, assuming that they are undesirable for marketing, packaging, and other reasons. He sums up his analogy by saying that "it is important to maximize the efficiency of a massive screening procedures to be carried out with large numbers of oranges in order to sort out the grossly abnormal from the normal at Stage I, with provisions for successive and more refined stages of screening, assessment and differential diagnosis of both the grossly abnormal and the borderline cases."

In this book screening is defined as a short procedure to identify those children who might have the characteristics of high risk learners. This possibility is confirmed or rejected by diagnosis. It is a technique for educational planning, not predicting. Screening is the first step of a process which is called the *screening program*. Lessler (1972) differentiates the two terms as follows: Screening is a technique for acquiring information about a large number of people, which may have significance in their lives; a screening program does something about the problems that have been identified.

Diagnosis

Diagnosis is often confused with screening. It is also frequently associated with health and medicine. The dictionary (Barnhart, 1963) defines diagnosis as "the process of determining by examination the nature and circumstances of a diseased condition." The implication is that a single procedure (examination) or set of procedures is engaged in and then a pronouncement is made about a negative (diseased) state of being. The medical definition of diagnosis is too constraining for educational use.

In this book, diagnosis is defined as the identification, collection, and interpretation of data relevant to a specific objective. The objective can be to detect a problem condition, for example the characteristics of high risk learners, and it can also be used to determine a strength or to describe development and/or the present state of a student. Diagnosis starts with the identification of those variables that need to be known to reach the objective. The next step is to collect the data which will provide the information related to the identified variables. The collection of the data can take many forms such as testing, observing, interviewing, examining records, and so on. This part of the process may be as simple or as complex as the objectives require; for example, it can consist of one variable such as an eye examination or be as complex as a diagnostic kindergarten year. When the data is collected, it is interpreted or analyzed. Diagnosis is part of a

process, and like screening, has value only in relationship to the
total process. The total educational process of which diagnosis is
part involves prescription, implementation, and evaluation. Prescription is defined as the specifications of instructional objectives and strategies. Implementation is the process of carrying out
the prescription, and evaluation is the assessment of the effectiveness of the prescription. All parts of the process are interdependent and interrelated.

The differentiation between screening and diagnosis is criti-
cally important because in many existing programs screening is
used as if it were diagnosis and diagnosis is used where screening
would be adequate. Because the techniques and tools of screening
and diagnosis are not precise, further confusion results.

High Risk Learners

The term *high risk child* is not only emotion packed but is also
difficult to define.

The Leadership Training Institute in Learning Disabilities,
which coordinated the federally funded Title VIG programs researched this problem. McCarthy and Kirk (1975), members of the
Institute, reported that an answer had not been found. Projects
describe high risk groups as ranging from 5 to 40 percent of the
population and design their programs accordingly. In the development of the DIAL screening instrument, Mardell (1975) defined the high risk child as one who, statistically speaking, seems
to be seriously behind those like him (same age, sex, location) and
for whom further observation is necessary. She operationally defined this population as the lowest 10 percent of screening scores.
Hainsworth (1974) says that children entering kindergarten with
learning efficiency skills in the lowest 40 percent or those who
refuse testing are children who we should observe further and be
prepared to help. He says that 10 to 20 percent of these children
most likely do not have the skills to cope easily and readily with
the traditional public school curriculum. Mackie (1969) estimated that 10 percent of the school population had some handicapping condition which may or may not be specifically related
to learning. He includes mental retardation, speech, vision and

hearing handicaps, and severe physical and emotional problems. High risk children are those whom we fear may become school failures.

As the child is just starting school we are hypothesizing on the basis of experience and research that children with certain characteristics will have difficulty unless certain interventions are planned. Young children vary greatly in their developmental pattern. To differentiate between a specific problem and an immature developmental pattern is quite difficult. Regardless of the cause, children at the low end of the continuum almost always require special help to feel successful in school.

In this book, high risk is defined as those children who, because of problems of development and/or experience, are least able to meet the expectations of the school unless the teaching/learning expectations are modified or changed. A child has success in school when there is a match between what he is asked to do and what he is able to do. There are two components to high risk: what the child brings to the school and what the school requires of the child. There are some children who, because of their problems, can only meet success through very special programs such as those for the severely retarded and the neurologically impaired; others can successfully function in the mainstream if there is flexibility and support in their programs. It is to this latter group that most screening programs are directed.

In a screening program the word "potential" is used with "high risk." If early identification and programming are successful, the risk of failure may be greatly reduced or eliminated.

Personalized Learning Program

In the broadest terms there are two types of programs relating to the education of young children that are based on assessment: screening programs and personalized learning programs. Screening programs focus on the children who may have special educational needs. Personalized learning programs are for all children.

Educational planning grows from basic philosophies about curriculum. One philosophy is to match the child to the curriculum. There is the expectation that a single curriculum will meet the needs of all children and that successful students will function on grade level. A variation of this philosophy is to individualize instruction, that is, to allow each child to progress through the same curriculum at his own pace. This philosophy assumes that some children will be successful and others will fail because of a defect within the child. The defect often is given a label, and the child is expected to function within the constraints of the label. Personalized learning is based on the philosophy of matching the curriculum to the child within the framework of the school structure and expectations. Personalized learning is flexible and can utilize the whole range of teaching and learning strategies which can facilitate successful learning experiences for each child. The teacher may have common goals for all of the children. The priorities and the methods will vary according to the child's needs. For example, the goal may be for each child to learn to read, but how and when each child reaches this goal will vary.

Personalized learning is defined as matching the curricular

TABLE II

A SCREENING PROGRAM

Screening of all children

Diagnosis of identified
potential high risk
children

Personalized curriculum for specific   Referral for identified problems be-
children in areas of identified need.   yond resources of school

Evaluation

expectations for a child to his development and experiences by utilizing a range of teaching strategies and learning experiences to achieve common educational goals.

A screening program includes personalized learning for the children identified as being potential high risk and is described in Table II.

A personalized learning program would start with diagnosis of all children to determine where they are in their development and experience and is described in Table III.

TABLE III

A PERSONALIZED LEARNING PROGRAM

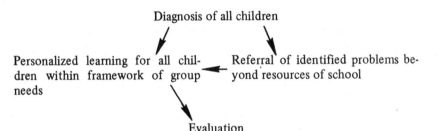

Diagnosis of all children

Personalized learning for all children within framework of group needs ← Referral of identified problems beyond resources of school

Evaluation

To clarify the differences and commonalities between screening and initial diagnosis, let us examine their uses.

Uses for Screening
1. to identify children who may have special learning needs;
2. to refer identified children for further assessment;
3. to identify children who may need to be observed over a period of time to determine if they need special help or are just immature in their development;
4. to give an overview of the developmental range of the screening population;
5. to facilitate reexamination of existing programs.

Initial screening should *never* be used for placement or exclusion of children.

Uses of Initial Diagnosis
1. to create a developmental profile for each child which identifies areas of strength and weakness, preferred or problem modality, learning style and special talents;
2. to develop personalized learning prescriptions for each child;
3. to refer to outside agencies for further diagnosis and possible remediation of problems beyond the resource of the school;
4. to provide an overview of a class for planning personalized learning programs;
5. to provide baseline data for record keeping;
6. to help set appropriate expectations for each child so that he may have successful learning experiences;
7. to facilitate appropriate placement of children;
8. to facilitate reexamination of curriculum, expectations and educational planning.

Uses in Common for Screening and Initial Diagnosis
1. to provide data and incentive for inservice training of educational personnel;
2. to provide information for communicating and interacting with parents;
3. to provide data for research.

Some existing programs have characteristics of both screening programs and personalized learning programs. An ideal program would screen for existing or potential problems in the prekindergarten years and then involve all children in a personalized learning program.

The descriptions of screening and personalized learning programs can be used as guidelines. The development of a sound program is long and arduous. It requires the coordinated efforts of many people who may have different perceptions of a program. Of necessity, there will be much trial and error learning by everyone in the process.

Kindergarten screening programs appropriately vary in different communities. Table IV provides a model which may facilitate the development of a screening program. The next four chapters will discuss each step for the process.

Models and definitions are a help to start the process, but the

TABLE IV

A KINDERGARTEN SCREENING PROGRAM

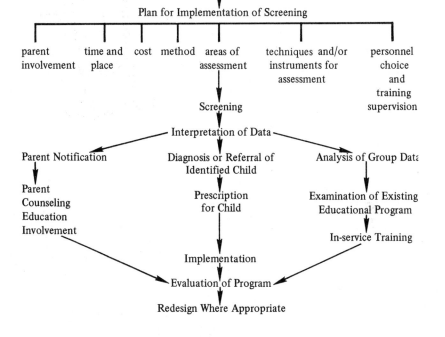

when Eddy was four years, eight months. His results showed him to be the least successful of any child in the group, and he was referred for diagnostic study.

His nursery school teacher described his behavior as friendly, cooperative, but hyperactive. "He loses focus easily and frequently even in a self-chosen activity. He does a lot of horsing around." She observed that his gross motor skills were very good,

Figure 1. Human figure drawing. Eddy, age 4 yrs. 10 mos.

but his fine motor skills were almost nonexistent. The screening, among other things, showed a lag in verbal skills and analogies. Figure 1 shows his first figure drawing.

As the psychologist, the author observed Eddy several times in the classroom and tested him twice at a four-month interval. Young children are very variable in their behavior, and the author felt it was necessary to have many samples. Stanford Binet IQ scores were 87 at age four years, ten months, and 86 at age five years, two months. The clinical analysis of the tests as well as much other data convinced the author that Eddy was not a slow learner. From the initial screening, the parents were involved. The background history indicated that Eddy was an adopted child and had had some very traumatic experiences at a very young age when he had been in a foster home. Eddy did not start to talk until age three.

Eddy was referred to a pediatric neurologist who found evidence of minimal neurological dysfunction and to an optometrist who found Eddy's eyes healthy but perceptually functioning at a level two to three years below his chronological age.

The initial prescription in the nursery for Eddy was to help him manage in a group — to be able to appropriately interact with the children and his teacher and to have some one-to-one help with visual-motor skills. Much time was spent with both the parents and the teacher to help them understand and accept Eddy with his disability. In kindergarten Eddy was put into the resource room program where he worked with a college student for a half hour, five days a week. Sometimes he was cooperative and sometimes he was very difficult to work with. The tutor often became discouraged because what he seemed to know one day, he completely forgot the next.

The prescription included work on auditory and visual memory, discrimination and sequencing, and language development. Learning experiences were through informal interaction with the tutor, music, games, use of the tachistoscope, work on the chalkboard, and use of some published material such as the Frostig program. In the kindergarten year he took Thorazine®, a medication which was prescribed to control his hyperactivity. It was discontinued at the end of the first year, when he began to control his behavior reasonably well without it. In first grade his resource room program was extended to include recognition of symbols through Sounds and Letters®, by Stern Structured Readings and an Introduction to SRA Linguistic Series in Reading®. The classroom teacher included Eddy in all activities. The program was flexible enough for him to have many experiences appropriate to his development. Some days were very frustrating for all concerned, but a lot of support was given the teacher by the child study team and Eddy's parents. At the time of this writing, Eddy functions well in the mainstream but there is the expectation that Eddy will need resource room support throughout elementary school. In second grade, he "cracked the code" and I don't know who was prouder he or I when he came to visit me to read "A Duck is a Duck"© (Preprimer, Ginn 360). He reads with difficulty and does not always remember the words, but he feels very good about himself and so does everyone who works with him (at least most of the time).

This short synopsis leaves out the daily highs and lows working with a child who has very special needs. Eddy functions in the mainstream. His figure drawings over four years are one indicator of his growth (see Figure 2). Even though much time and effort has been directed toward helping Eddy, it is much more economical than the cost of supporting a nonfunctioning adult in our society, which he might become if we did not help him now. Since our program was started, we have seen it make a difference to many children.

In this chapter, definitions and uses were given for screening, diagnosis, high risk, and personalized learning program. The appropriate use of these terms is basic to program examination and development. The model for the screening program in Table IV outlines the procedures which will be described in detail in the next four chapters.

Draw-A-Person, Eddy, age 5 yrs.

Draw-A-Person, Eddy, age 8 yrs. 1 mo.

Draw-A-Person, Eddy, age 6 yrs. 2 mos.

Figure 2.

Chapter Three

WHY AND HOW TO START PLANNING
A SCREENING PROGRAM

SCREENING programs are started for many reasons. For a program to be effective, much planning is necessary. The first step is to form a multidisciplinary committee. This committee will develop appropriate goals and objectives that give direction to the program. A theoretical framework provides a base from which to make choices in all phases of the program: initial screening and subsequent diagnosis, what to assess, how to assess, and finally the educational program to be developed.

Many states have laws which mandate education for handicapped preschoolers and a few have laws which mandate screening for early identification of educationally handicapped children at the time of school entrance. (See Appendix A for a description of state laws for education and screening of handicapped children, 1975.) Early childhood and special education programs supported by federal funds often include screening. Some states have guidelines for screening but no law mandating it. More than half of the states have some pilot program (usually federally funded) relating to early identification of educationally handicapped children.

When there is no mandate or guidelines, kindergarten screening can be started within a school or district by the efforts of interested people. The initiators can be administrators, teachers, specialists, parents, parent groups, or community agencies. What seems most important to getting started is the dedication of one or a few people to the idea. This interest is necessary because sometimes long and hard work is required to convince others that a kindergarten screening program is a priority for a particular school system. Along with the interest is the need for authority or power to implement the program. This power ultimately comes from the superintendent of schools or supervising principal and/or the board of education. The involvement and support of the elementary school principals is critical to the success of any program.

A good screening program requires input from many disciplines; therefore, program development is best done by a committee. When the committee works well together, it becomes a support group for the emerging program.

Committees should be representative but not too large. They may include an administrator, school psychologist, reading, speech and curriculum specialists, the physical education teacher and nurse/teacher, parents (school doctor and social worker if these are available), and always, the kindergarten teacher. When the leader of the committee has knowledge of how a group develops and functions, the task is made easier.

Development of Goals and Objectives

The next step toward the development of a screening program is the clarification of what the program is to accomplish, i.e. the goals. The efforts to achieve these goals are the objectives. A goal is a statement describing a broad or abstract intent or condition. A goal is written "to describe specific outcomes that, if achieved, will cause you to agree that the goal is also achieved" (Mager, 1972). One goal may require several objectives to make all of its implications explicit. In this sense, the relationship between goal and objective is analogous to that between whole and part.

Objectives are concrete and explicit, spelling out the details in observable behaviors or end products. Objectives are necessary to clarify the procedure and direction of the program but create a dilemma.

The dilemma is based on the assumption that there is precise knowledge of how a particular behavior is acquired and that there is a precise tool to measure the behavior. There is not a commonly agreed-upon single body of knowledge which describes exactly how children learn and in what sequence of observable behaviors. Children learn in a variety of often idiosyncratic ways. It is not necessary to be proficient in each facet of a learning process to achieve an end product. Reading is a good example. Reading is a mastery of the whole, the learning of a new gestalt (Goodman, 1972). Failure in reading does not necessarily stem from inability to master one or more subordinate kinds of skills (Jansky, 1971).

A committee should be aware of the limitations of goals and objectives, but should nevertheless recognize that they are tools for clarification and evaluation. They set the stages for the development of the program.

In Chapter Two we noted that existing programs often confused screening and diagnosis. The goals of seven screening programs are copied exactly as written in their program description. When looking at these goals, the reader should keep in mind the definitions previously given, noting the importance of having a clear and appropriate goal.

Program 1.   GOAL — to identify needs of children before they enter school. This goal would imply initial diagnosis of all children and no plan for follow through.

Program 2.   GOAL — to enhance a child's first experience in school. This goal would imply a personalized learning program.

Program 3.   GOAL — to identify children with potential learning problems and develop a plan for intervention. This goal would imply a screening program.

Program 4.   GOAL — to learn as much as possible about the children before they enter school so that the curriculum should be set up to meet their individual needs. This goal would imply a personalized learning program.

Program 5.   GOALS — a) to identify and examine those children who showed signs or symptoms of developmental delay or deviation, b) to initiate a program of compensatory education focused upon parent counseling and training of parents to help their own children, and c) to plan appropriately, at the time of school entry, and provide special services to children if needed. These goals imply a screening program.

Program 6.   GOAL — to prevent school failure through early identification and remediation of developmental learning deficiencies in kindergarten children, deficiencies that would adversely affect their school performance. This goal would imply a screening program.

Program 7. GOALS — a) to identify the learning style of each youngster entering kindergarten by assessing his strengths and weaknesses, and b) to identify those children who may require special educational planning and possible placement in special education classes. Goal "a" implies an initial diagnosis while goal "b" may be initially met through a screening.

Program objectives are the steps necessary to reach the goal and are the second step in program development; they describe the procedures to be used to accomplish the goals.

An example is the Peotone, Illinois (Title III, ESEA, 1971) program which has both goals (see goal 6) and the following program objectives:

1. to screen all kindergarten children during the summer prior to their initial enrollment in school in order to identify learning problems that could adversely affect school performance;
2. to provide professional services to all children who are enrolled in regular kindergarten classrooms;
3. to provide consultant services to teachers in regular kindergarten classrooms;
4. to provide special educational services for children identified as having moderate or severe learning problems through the development of Model Learning Disability Classrooms.

Objectives which specified the criteria for evaluation were not included in most programs. One program had fifteen pages of behavioral objectives which then became the basis of their kindergarten program. Goals and objectives are used to establish the criteria for assessment of the individual child and the total program.

The majority of forty programs which were examined by the author did not specify goals or objectives. They described an assessment instrument and a procedure for screening. In a few programs there was a rationale for the particular choice. There were no statements of how the results were to be used or any procedure for evaluation of the program. There seemed to be a concentration on data collection without clear understanding of why the particular instrument was chosen and what specific value or use the data would have when collected.

To translate the goal to program objectives, i.e. to behavior or product objectives, requires an analysis of the task. The primary criteria of the objectives is that they make sense as being ways of showing that the goal is being achieved. For screening programs, the questions that need to be answered are: What does the successful learner look like? and What process will identify the presence or absence of those behaviors and characteristics which describe the successful learner?

The description of the successful learner will depend on the philosophy and expectations of a particular community. In one school, success may mean reading on grade level, or making continuous progress, or may be defined in cognitive and affective terms, etc. If one goal of the screening program is to "filter out for further study" those children who may have great difficulty being successful, then it is necessary to assess those characteristics or behaviors that are related to achieving this success. Screening programs are based on the assumption that if information is known about a child's development and behavior, appropriate educational experiences could be designed to help the child learn more effectively. Difficulty lies not only in the uncertainty of what specific information is most relevant but also what educational experiences best facilitate the desired learning.

Assessment Models

Screening is the first step toward identifying those characteristics which are associated with children who have the greatest difficulty learning in school. These difficulties have been ascribed to immaturity, problems in development, breakdowns in the ability to process information, and the impact of the child's interaction with the environment. There are four models for assessment of one or more of these problem areas which are based on different learning theories. These models describe what would be assessed to determine a child's potential learning ability.

In the *developmental model,* the five major areas of a child's development are considered. This model is based on the assumption that if the pattern of strengths and weaknesses of a child's development is known, then an educational prescription can be made which reflects the uniqueness of that particular child.

The second model is the *behavioral model,* which is only interested in observable behavior. It is based on the assumption that you can only measure and change what you can see.

The *information processing model* is based on how the child receives, interprets, and transmits information. A breakdown or an unusual strength will influence the whole process.

The fourth model is the *interaction model,* which is based on the assumption that children learn through the interaction of their development and their experiences in the environment. In this model, in addition to knowledge about the child, information about the people and the environment that may influence the child's learning are sought.

The Developmental Model

The child's development is categorized in five major areas: physical, perceptual-motor, cognition, speech and language, and social-emotional. These areas are interrelated and interdependent. Each category has many components which influence how a child learns. Some of the components are assessed in screening, others in diagnosis. In total they describe the child. This listing is to make the reader aware of the complexity of the child, to define the terms, and to serve as a checklist for screening and diagnosis (see Table V).

I. *Physical* includes physiological and health-related functions. The condition of the body is basic to growth and learning.

Physical intactness exists when all body parts are whole.

General health is the presence or absence of illness or other debilitating factors. Diabetes and asthma are examples of diseases that have been related to learning problems.

Activity level is part of the behavioral style of the child. It is the motor component of the child's function and is measured by the

TABLE V

Major Areas of Development Related to Learning

I. *Physical*

    a. physical intactness
    b. general health
    c. activity level
    d. vision
    e. hearing
    f. nutrition - eating patterns
    g. neurological structure
    h. endocrine balance

II. *Perceptual Motor*

    a. gross motor - large muscle coordination
    b. fine motor - small muscle coordination
    c. body image - identification of body parts
    d. laterality
    e. directionality
    f. perception of space relations
    g. figure-ground perception
    h. visual motor coordination
    i. auditory discrimination
    j. visual discrimination
    k. perceptual constancy
    l. dominance or sideness

II. *Cognition*

    a. IQ
    b. thinking processes
    c. concept formation
    d. memory - auditory, visual
    e. sequencing
    f. classifying
    g. creativity

IV. *Speech and Language*

    a. communication - receptive and expressive language
    b. rhythm
    c. syntax (grammar)
    d. vocabulary

V. *Social Emotional*

    a. self-concept
    b. motivation
    c. adaptive behavior - coping style
    d. social skills - interaction patterns
    e. level of maturity (psychosexual development)
    f. dependence - independence
    g. aspiration level (self-expectation)
    h. nervous tendencies

proportion of active and inactive periods during the daytime.

Vision is the act of seeing with the eye. The eyes sense information but do not interpret it. Since a child receives information via the senses, any disruption of this sensory input would seriously affect the learning process.

Hearing is the act of receiving and discriminating sounds.

Nutrition and eating patterns may relate to learning problems. Recent research linked problems of learning and behavior to high or low blood sugar (hyper and hypo glycemia), allergic reactions to food dyes, and other groups of foods. Diet may be used as a remedial factor.

Neurological structure may indicate a defect or dysfunction in neural transmission to, from, and in the brain. Assessment of neurological structure should be made by a pediatric neurologist.

Endocrine balance relates to the hormones which the endocrine glands secrete directly into the bloodstream. The secretions of the endocrine system are essential to normal brain development, maturation, and intellectual function. Assessment should be made only by a competent medical specialist.

II. *Perceptual-Motor Behavior* is the reception, integration, and expression of sensory data. Perception supplies the information upon which behavior is based. Motor responses supply the movements which are the overt aspects of the behavior. Perceptual motor behavior relates to automatic or habitual behaviors.

Gross motor skills involve movement of the whole body, particularly arms and legs, in activities like throwing, catching, running, and jumping.

Fine motor skills involve movement of the fingers and hands in activities like grasping objects, drawing, using eating utensils, and handling tools.

Body image is the awareness of one's own body and the relationship of the body parts to each other and to the outside environment.

Laterality is knowing that there are two separate sides to the body, the left and the right, and being able to identify them and move them.

Directionality is being able to relate movement from a fixed position (perhaps one's own body) to, away, under, over, into, and out of.

Space relations is the perception of the positions of objects in space.

Figure-ground perception is the ability to attend and distinguish an object from the background surrounding it.

Visual-motor coordination is the ability to coordinate vision with the movements of the body or parts of the body.

Auditory discrimination is the ability to discern the differences between sounds. In language it is the ability to recognize the fine differences that exist between the phonemes used in speech.

Visual discrimination is the ability to discern the difference among objects or symbols and to distinguish one from another.

Perceptual constancy is the ability to perceive the invariant properties of objects such as shape, position, size, etc., in spite of the variability of the impression these objects make on the senses of the observer.

Dominance or sideness is the preferred side of the body. Dominance is seen in the eyes, hands, and feet.

Perceptual-motor development proceeds through stages in which the child learns to match the information received through his senses with the motor responses. Delayed motor learning may be a significant factor in the identification of children with learning problems.

Perceptual functions develop maximally during the period from approximately three and one-half or four to seven or seven and one-half years.

III. *Cognition* is symbolic or representational functioning and consists of many different skills and abilities.

IQ is one measure of intelligence or cognitive functioning. It is a test score which reflects the person's performance relative to other people his age. The cognitive abilities measured vary with the particular IQ test. IQ scores generally correlate with academic success as defined by the middle class culture. Because of this, the use of IQ tests have sometimes been seen as discriminatory.

Thinking processes is another way of defining intelligence. According to Piaget, "intelligence is a general human capacity through which the person organizes his environment. This can take place as well in one modality as in another, provided an individual has at least a minimum amount of normal contact with the world through his sense and body activities." (Furth, 1974) Thinking processes develop through successive stages from sensorimotor learning to abstract thinking.

Memory is the ability to associate, retain, and recall experiences. Memory assumes awareness of time and ability to sequentialize experience.

Auditory memory is the ability to store and recall what one has heard.

Visual memory is the ability to recall visual stimuli in terms of form, detail, position, etc.

Concept formation is the ability to classify and categorize ideas and thoughts.

Sequencing is the ordering of events on the temporal scale.

Classifying is the ability to categorize information.

Creativity is defined as fluency and flexibility. Fluency is the ability to develop fluent productions and process familiar information, produce and elaborate upon information, and fluently produce original information. Flexibility is the ability to recognize the identity of an object or processes seen from different viewpoints, produce reinterpretations and redefinitions of known information.

IV. *Speech and Language* are the symbolic tools of cognition and communication. There is an increasing body of literature stressing the need to check the linguistic performance of preschool and kindergarten children. It is language ability that permits communication and interaction for further cognitive development and is critical in learning to read. A study in Edinburgh found that independent of IQ, 75 children from high income groups whose linguistic development at the age of four years was at least eighteen months behind failed in reading several years later (Mason, 1967-68).

Communication requires receptive and expressive language.

Receptive language is the process of understanding verbal symbols.

Expressive language is the process of producing spoken language.

Syntax refers to the grammar system of language — the way the words are strung together to form sentences.

Rhythm refers to the flow of speech. The most serious problem involving the flow of speech is stuttering.

Vocabulary is all the words a speaker is capable of using in communication.

V. *Socio-emotional* refers to feeling-related behavior and development. School learning is largely a group activity. The ability of a child to adjust to a group, relate to his peers, and interact with adults is basic to social competence. There is a positive relationship between emotional problems and learning problems.

Self-concept consists of all the different ideas the child has about himself. Self-concept reflects the feedback that one gets from interaction with others.

Motivation is the willingness to become involved.

Adaptive behavior or coping style is the characteristic way of responding to various situations.

Social skills or interaction patterns describes how one behaves when interacting with others.

Level of maturity describes the level of psychosexual development. Erikson (1963) describes eight stages of man. The first four, trust versus mistrust, autonomy versus shame and doubt, initiative versus guilt and identity versus inferiority are relevant to the understanding of the social-emotional development of the young child.

Dependence-Independence is the degree to which the child is able to make decisions and care for his own needs.

Aspiration level describes the child's expectations for himself.

Nervous tendencies are nonfunctional behaviors which utilize a large amount of psychic energy. Examples are bed wetting, unusual fears, tantrums, extreme withdrawal, or excessive moods or depression.

The Behavior Model

The behaviorist is concerned only with observable behavior and is not interested in causes. Objectivity is stressed and the assumption is that, only by observing and responding to those aspects of human functioning that are clearly describable and thus measurable, can valid or reliable conclusions be reached. Emotional or subjective data is not seen as relevant.

Learning is a stimulus-response process, and behavior can be conditioned through types and schedules of reinforcement. Screening tools for this model would be observations and checklist. The author supports the use of behavioral techniques as one of many tools for a screening program. When it is used as the basis for an entire program, the results tend to be mechanistic and lead to checklist curriculums. By not seeking the causes of an observable behavior, a child can be embedded in a failure-producing situation.

An example of this would be a child who was observed to have difficulty with auditory discrimination. A description of three children with auditory discrimination difficulties demonstrates the fallacy of prescribing just from the observable behavior.

One child has poor auditory discrimination due to a lack of attending. This child needs work in learning to attend, not practice in discriminating different sounds. The second child has a language problem because he speaks only Spanish at home and at play and does not have enough experience in listening to English sounds. He needs practice in hearing English. The third child does have a physiological discrimination problem and needs help to improve his auditory discrimination.

Information Processing Model

The Information Processing Model is based on neobehaviorist information processing theory which refers to "the way in which a child uses his eyes, his ears and his body to attend to and to gather information from the world around him — how he relates this information to past experiences — and how he expresses his knowledge and ideas through his speech and his body movements" (Hainsworth, 1969). The model in Table VI analyzes this process by outlining the five stages of information processing and the three basic modalities through which learning occurs.

A breakdown in any one of the stages within or across any of the modalities may affect the child's learning and/or behavioral

TABLE VI

AN INFORMATION PROCESSING MODEL

	Visual-Perceptual-Motor	Language	Body Awareness and Control
Orientation		Focus of Attention Selection of Appropriate Cues From Background	
Intake		Discrimination for Form, Space and Time Cues	
	Visual	Auditory	Kinesthetic
		Retention of Pattern and Sequence of Information	
Integration		Set Selection Association to Previous Learning Retrieval of Relevant Information	
		Selection of Appropriate Sequences For Outgoing Information	
Output		Execution of Precise and Controlled Movement Patterns	
	Eye-Hand	Articulation	Body Control
Feedback		Immediate Response Monitoring Relevance of Response to Overall Goals	

Denhoff, 1971.

efficiency.

Orientation is to be able to focus and attend to the task at hand without being unusually distracted by either internal or external events.

Intake involves the rapid discrimination and assimilation of complex sensory (auditory, visual, kinesthetic, tactile) information from the world around him.

Integration involves the ability to sort, order, sequence, store, organize, categorize, associate, present information with past experiences, and plan appropriate actions in a logical manner.

Output involves the expression of knowledge and ideas through the production of appropriate behaviors (responses) expressed through one or more of the basic motor systems.

Feedback is the information from the environment (both internal and external) which is returned to a child regarding the consequences of his own behavior.

The Interaction Model

The interaction model which is most favored by the author recognizes the interrelationship between the child's development, his ability to integrate and process information, and the influences of the environment. A substantial number of school learning problems may be attributed to the interaction of the child and the learning situation, yet influencing factors in the home and school environment are not often investigated.

In this model the child is seen as a naturally active, seeking, and adapting organism who constructs his understanding of and competence in coping with the world through continual transaction with it. These transactions are carried on through a repetoire of various kinds of developmental tasks or "operations;" different types of these are more important at successive stages of development. There are five main sets of influences on development:

1. maturation — including genetic factors;
2. experience and environment;
3. developmental tasks — individuals carry on transactions with the environment;
4. consultations with other people who share the world with them;
5. interactions among all the preceding.

Assessment might include the five areas of development, the ability to process information, and knowledge of the child's environment.

What to Assess in Screening

The examination of the literature shows lack of common agreement on what is most important to assess in a screening program.

DeHirsch (1975) and Ilg and Ames (1946) said that the facets in child development related to school achievement were language, cognition, and sensory, perceptual, and physical motor development, Leydorf (1970) reviewed the literature and found that medical and physical motor predictions yield few child characteristics which provided a solid basis for the prediction of school success or failure. Rogolsky (1968) said that Koppitz's work with the Bender Gestalt test suggested that the visual-motor abilities are strong predictors of success. Longitudinal studies (Keogh, 1963 and Keogh & Smith, 1967) based primarily on the Bender Gestalt test, demonstrated that although there are consistent statistically significant relationships between Bender scores in kindergarten and later school achievement, one cannot predict with certainty the meaning for a particular child.

Hainsworth (1969) uses the information processing model as the base for his work in early identification at the Meeting Street School in Rhode Island. Ames (1972) said that "poor visual-perceptual skills are the 'most common causative factor in cases of reading disability' ". De Hirsch (1966) and Haring and Ridgway (1967) indicated that gross motor disabilities are not predictive of learning problems. Money (1966) said that disability in laterality and directionality has frequently been cited as either contributory to or associated with reading disability. Belmont and Birch (1965) say that it is doubtful if questions about directionality would be applicable to kindergarten or first grade children.

Rogolsky (1968) said that since the etiology of learning problems is so unclear, a screening program should use a variety of measures which tap visual, perceptual, and verbal fields. Haring and Ridgway (1967) indicated eight areas for assessment of children with learning disabilities: visual perception, eye-hand coordination, auditory discrimination, visual attention span, directionality, auditory attention span, large muscle coordination, and general language development.

Bernstein (1964), Bloom (1965), and Hodges (1967) saw testing in the following five developmental areas as providing a means for early identification and discrimination by quantifiable measures of learning disabilities. They are: verbal, cognitive, motor, sensory, emotional, and neurological. They felt that the concept of profile analysis in which an array of developmental skills are measured would be a viable approach to early childhood assessment.

The American Academy of Pediatrics (1973) said that in a screening, information should be obtained about the child's present physical, mental, and social-emotional development in addition to formal sampling of: visual acuity and perception, auditory acuity and perception, tactile acuity and perception, language comprehension and expression (including the primary language of the home), cognitive-associative-conceptual skills, and motor integration (gross and fine) and development.

The factors identified by DeHirsch and Jansky (1966) as significantly associated with later performance in reading are: presence or absence of hyperactive, distractible, uninhibited behavior; fine motor control; graphomotor ability; human figure drawing (body image); visual-motor integration; receptive language skills; expressive language; visual perception; integration of intersensory information; ego strength; and work attitude.

A panel of experts in New York state (1973) who were consulted, when a mandatory screening bill was written, thought the following were most important: general behavior (background history), motor and sensory integration, laterality, directionality, visual and auditory acuity, conceptual skills and language development, and previous academic experience.

Satz (1974), in a long-range study of the most valid predictors of problems in reading, developed a battery of twenty-two predictor variables. He found that the finger localization test had the highest discriminable ranking, with recognition-discrimination, day of testing, and alphabet recitation ranked second, third, and fourth respectively.

The author, in the development of the ZEIS (see Chapter 4) used questions that related to language, cognitive development, auditory and visual memory, gross motor, visual-motor, body image, directionality, and laterality.

The range of information that may contribute to the knowledge of how or why a particular child learns is overwhelming. Even in a comprehensive diagnosis it would be impossible to know everything about a child. Screening starts the process of raising questions about those particular aspects of the child which we need to know more about. The research indicates that a definitive answer is not known. The goals and objectives of the program will help clarify the areas of choice.

In this chapter, the first steps in the planning of a screening program were described. Four models were presented as a base to help make choices of what to assess to determine if the child is a potential high risk learner.

Screening Program

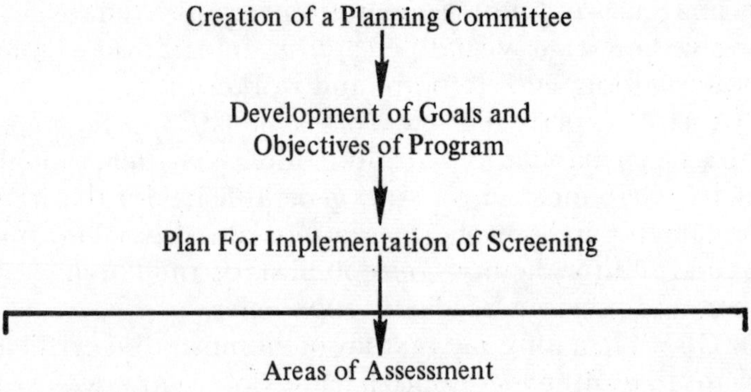

Creation of a Planning Committee

↓

Development of Goals and
Objectives of Program

↓

Plan For Implementation of Screening

↓

Areas of Assessment

Figure 3.

Chapter Four

TOOLS FOR SCREENING

$\mathbf{A}$ SCREENING program consists of many different tests and techniques to assess each child's special educational needs. The choice of test is influenced by many factors, including the following:

1. the goals of the screening program;
2. the objectives by which the goals are reached:
3. age of children to be assessed;
4. staff available for assessment;
5. whether the initial assessment will be screening, diagnostic, or a combination of both;
6. what characteristics of the child are to be assessed;
7. expectations for the reliability and validity of the instrument;
8. where and when assessment is to take place.

Once the goals and objectives for the screening program have been set, the next step is to consider the various tools for screening in detail.

Test Versus Observation

Tests and observation are two major approaches for screening. Testing is based on the belief that all development and behavior is quantifiable and that screening and diagnostic tests may be designed to measure individual variations. This viewpoint recognizes the limitations of tests and their imperfect state of development, but feels that their value is more positive than negative. Those who support the observation or behavioral approach argue that enthusiasm for standardized tests has obscured the importance of other sources of information. How a child approaches a learning task, his strategies for solution, his sensitivity to various kinds of reinforcement, and his ability to sustain attention and persist may all be important indicators of his likelihood

39

of success in school. They feel that systematic observation of children's behavior in the educational setting provides useful information and that teacher assessments are generally quite accurate. Haring and Ridgway (1967) found teacher ratings far more effective than test batteries in predicting learning disability.

Feshback (1974) found that classroom observation could predict first grade success as adequately as diagnostic testing, but questioned whether it was as fruitful for developing learning prescriptions.

Parent questionnaires as well as teacher observation have been used for assessment. Although Wyatt (1970), in the Wellesley project, used parent questionnaires, she assumed parents would be biased. On the other hand, McCleod (1969) and Denhoff (1971) found that parents can give accurate descriptions of their children's behavior in many areas.

Problems of Measurement

There are many strengths and problems associated with assessment. Extreme bias for either the test or observation approach limits free and open exploration of appropriate tools.

When a technique or instrument is chosen with an understanding of its values and limitations, there is a greater likelihood that it will be used appropriately.

The state of knowledge varies both between and within the general areas of human growth, development, learning, and behavior. For example, more is known about the chemistry of growth than about the chemistry of learning. More is known about cognitive development than about social-emotional development, and more is known about language development than cognitive development. More is known about physiological development than learning behavior, and more is known about disease than personality. Within any given area the same pattern is found. In language, more is known about vocabulary development than about concept development. In social-emotional development, more is known about aggressive behavior than withdrawal behavior, and more about competition than cooperation, and more about peer assessment than self-concept.

The instruments and techniques reflect these variations in the state of knowledge. In addition, measurement, in itself, is a complex field of study. The issues of validity and reliability, test items, standardization, administration, analysis, etc. force those in measurement to limit themselves in the production of tests. Behavioral observation can be very subjective and reflect the bias of the observer. Sometimes a generalized assessment of the child is made from a particularized measure. For example, a statement about the functioning of the whole child may be made based on assessment in one field such as medical, psychological, learning, language, intellectual, physiological, or neurological. A whole child is not an IQ, a self-concept, a disease, or a maladaptive behavior.

Consideration of validity and reliability with both assessment approaches helps avoid some of the inherent dangers of testing. Validity asks the question, "Are you measuring what you say you are measuring?" There are two ways of determining validity: logical and empirical. Logical validity refers to a judgment about the adequacy and appropriateness of the content. The content and format of a test is inspected to see if the test looks as though it is measuring what it is supposed to measure — to see if the content is appropriate. Empirical validity is determined through various statistical procedures; researchers determine if a test or evaluation device measures what it is intended to measure. For example, if test "A" is thought to measure intelligence and test "B" is also thought to measure intelligence, then children should get similar scores in both tests. Generally, a newly established test is compared with an established test which is assumed to measure the same trait or ability. If the new test yields a similar score as the established test, the new test is said to have validity.

Another way of testing the validity of the test is by determining how effectively this information can be used to predict a particular outcome. This presents a methodological paradox. If early identification and diagnosis were insightful, and remedial implementation successful, the preschool or kindergarten child would receive the kind of attention and help which result in successful school performance. In essence, he would no longer be high risk and instead would be a successful achiever. Predictive validity of the identification instruments would therefore be low. Research on the development of predictive tools is thus limited by ethical considerations. Having identified a child as high risk, the researcher is obligated to intervene, thus limiting examination of the long-term predictive validity of the instruments.

Reliability refers to the accuracy (consistency and stability) of measuring a skill, ability, or behavior. An evaluation device or test is reliable if the results are repeatable. If a child does not learn from taking the same test, and hasn't learned it anywhere else, he should get the same score each time he is tested. There are several types of reliability and several ways of deriving estimates of reliability. Two most relevant types are test reliability and observer reliability. Test reliability is determined through research procedure. Observer or inter-rater reliability is the degree to which two people agree in their observations of a particular child or phenomenon.

Information pertaining to the reliability and validity of an instrument is usually included in the test manual. Many screening instruments have been criticised for lack of data in this area.

In children younger than six, development is uneven. It is not unusual to see very verbal kindergarteners who are immature in their perceptual-motor functioning and vice versa. There is not a clear-cut formula of how much development in each area is necessary for optimal school learning. Research and experience negate the statement that each child need be equally proficient in all areas of development to learn effectively, but children who are very uneven or who have specific problems in one or more areas are more likely to have difficulties in a typical school environment. There are few clear one-to-one relationships between specific preschool characteristics and specific school learning. It is the total pattern of interaction which is significant.

One area which is least adaptable to screening procedures is social-emotional development. There has been opposition to screening in this area because of the difficulty in establishing a set of norms which could be universally accepted. Personality development and adaptation vary between subcultures and change with time. To establish a set of norms would impose a rigidity on behavioral expectations which would be detrimental to the perception of, and analysis of the behavior of the child.

Walker (1973) says that the greatest problem in socio-emotional measurements is the lack of adequate socio-emotional developmental theory. She says there is a mismatch between the need for socio-emotional evaluations and an existent technology.

Tools for Assessment

Within the two broad categories of assessment, many types of instruments and techniques can be used.

<u>Tests</u>
    Standardized — norm referenced — national norms
                                             local norms
                    criterion referenced
    Informal — descriptive — no norm
<u>Behavioral Reports</u>
    Interviews — parent — child
    Checklists
    Rating scales
    Anecdotal reports
    Observations
<u>Other</u>
    Questionnaires — background history — expectations
    Self reports
    Physical examinations

Testing and behavioral reports are useful for both screening and diagnosis. Their value depends on the instrument used. Screening instruments can be less precise as they are meant to be a filter and to detect gross deviation. Behavioral reports are usually dependent upon observation over a period of time. For the preschool child, parent observation may be used. In school, the classroom teacher is most often the one who makes the behavioral observations. In many screening programs more than one type of assessment or instrument is used. Often, an assessment battery is developed by the committee which uses parts of published tests and/or informal assessment techniques devised by the specialists. In a survey of thirty screening programs, eighteen used devised tests which may include parts of published tests; eleven programs had devised tests plus one or more published tests or total subtests in their battery. One screening program used only published tests. In the thirty programs, two used checklists devised by teachers as their initial screening (see Table VII).

Criteria for a Screening Instrument

Batteries or instruments are often devised by schools or other agencies because assessment tools vary greatly in their ability to be responsive to local needs. They also vary in their ability to measure what they say they do, the amount of training necessary to give the test, and the amount of time required to take the test. Many assessment tools only measure one dimension of the child's development. Suggested criteria for a screening instrument or battery to identify potential high risk learners are:

Procedure
  1. short screening procedures of not more than a half-hour duration;
  2. objective scoring — scoring of an instrument based on observable behaviors, rather then subjective judgments;
  3. training procedures for examiners should be clear and not too complex;
  4. screening should be administered to each child individually;
  5. movement of child should be allowed for.

Content
  1. multidimensional — should cover several areas of development;
  2. noncategorical — only identify potential high risk children regardless of the reason for the potential learning problem;
  3. items in battery should be appropriate to age range to be assessed;
  4. cultural difference — items should not reflect any one culture;

TABLE VII

	Screen	Initial Diagnosis	Vision	Hearing	Devised + Parts Published	Devised + Published	Published Only
Alaska, Anchorage	1				1*		
Connecticut, Fairfield		1			1		
Georgia, Gwinnett	1	1					
Hawaii	1					1	
Illinois, Peotone	1		1	1		1*	
Evanston			1	1			
Maryland	1				1*		
Massachusetts, Wellesley	1		1	1	1		
Hanover	1		1	1	1		
Michigan, Detroit	1		1	1		1	
Missouri, Ferguson	1		1	1	1		
New Jersey, Cherry Hill	1		1	1	1		
New York, Horseheads	1		1	1		1	
Beacon	1		1	1	1		
Wappingers	1	1	1	1			
N. Bellmore	1		1	1		1	
New Paltz	1		1	1	1		
Arlington	1		1	1	1		
Middletown	1				1		
Carmel	1					1	
Hilton	1	1				1	

	Screen	Initial Diagnosis	Vision	Hearing	Devised + Parts Published	Devised + Published	Published Only
Ohio, Columbia County	1		1	1	1		
Grove City	1		1		1		
Oregon, La Grande	1				1		
Central Point	1						1
Washington, Tacoma	1		1	1	1		
Wisconsin, Oconomowoc	1					1	
Green Bay	1		1	1	1	1	
Appleton	1		1	1			
Waupun	1				1		
Total: 30	28	4	14	14	18	11	1

*Checklist. See Appendix for names and addresses of surveyed projects.

5. should be paced to hold the attention of the child.

Many programs have been called screening programs on the basis of the administration of a group readiness test. In a national survey of 980 school districts, 55 percent responded saying they did some type of screening for readiness for academic instruction. Thirty-six percent of the districts responding used one measure, the Metropolitan Readiness Test (Hildreth, Griffith and McGauvran, 1969) which is a group test (Feshback, 1974).

By individual administration of the screening instrument you can have some sense of whether the child is not responding because he does not know the answer or because he does not know what is expected of him. Group testing adds to the existing difficulty of getting a representative sample of a kindergarten child's performance. Observation of hundreds of five-year-olds suggests that they are not particularly testwise; many cannot give a good indication of what they know if left by themselves to work in a group test using pencil and paper. A number of children who will become good readers are still preoccupied or distracted by the effort required for graphomotor expression. On the other hand, in working with the child on a one-to-one basis, the examiner has the opportunity to observe and comment upon behaviors of concern which may not be part of an objective assessment. For example, the child may articulate poorly or exhibit some other atypical behavior that would seem essential to study further.

Normative Data

Studies of child development are usually based on normative data, that is, how a child or one aspect of his development compares to other children at a similar age or stage. Normative-based tests measure children in relation to each other. In using normative-based tests, it is important to note whether the population used to develop the data was similar to the one being tested. This is a problem particularly in testing minority groups or handicapped children. These tests may give results that are detrimental to the child being tested. The normative sample should include a wider age range than the one for which the test is constructed. The sample should include various geographic areas, racial and ethnic groups, and types of schools.

Some communities construct tests and assessment procedures for their own use. This has both advantages and disadvantages. The local development can result in a list of criteria which indicate success, both of the children and of the program. Careful development or selection of these criteria would require a complete review of the program and its goals and objectives. The planning and program review activities may result in significant and positive side effects for the assessment program.

There are, however, some serious problems associated with local development of tests and assessment procedures; perhaps the most serious is the absence of training for most program personnel in the areas of evaluation procedures and test construction. Furthermore, there is no basis for evaluating performance of children and personnel when tests are developed locally, unless they are only evaluated internally. That is, there is no external reference for comparison of program results. The absence of apparent references can be treated in at least two ways. First, criteria for performance can be based upon a set of goals and objectives which are directly related to external goals and objectives. These external goals and objectives might be those of federal, regional, state, or local agencies which provide services to children such as those in a local program. Evaluation, then, can be done in terms of contribution to the accomplishment of goals and objectives of some larger system. Second, the specific indicators of change (the test items) can be selected to be similar to those of some recognized tests or procedures.

Farrald and Schamber (1973) in their ADAPT program describe what they call the "last car child." They derive that name from the Verbal Absurdities Question, Age XI in the Stanford-Binet (LM) IQ test which says "When there is a collision, the last car of the train is damaged the most, so they have decided that it will be best if the last car is always taken off before the train starts. What is foolish about that?" In each community we have "last car children." They may be different in each community but the need for help is the same. This may be a rationale to look at that percentage of the screened population that is consistent with the percentage of failure generally experienced throughout the grades in that school district. It may vary from 3 to 5 percent in some communities and up to 20 percent or more in others. When the percentage of failing children is consistently high, it may signal a need to look even more closely at the curriculum than at the children.

Criterion referenced tests measure progress toward specifically defined objectives. A problem of criterion referenced tests is that when the criteria are known, there may be a tendency to teach for the test.

Screening Instruments

There are over a thousand instruments which are available for screening and diagnosis of young children, and new ones appear in the literature regularly. A sampling of these instruments is given to acquaint the reader with the range of what is available. It is not meant to imply that the described instruments are the very best but rather that they meet most of the criteria for screening instruments. Some major sources for information on screening and diagnostic tools are:

Buros, O. K. (Ed.): Seventh Mental Measurements Workbook. Highland Park, New Jersey, Gryphon Press, 1972.

Guthrie, P. D.: Head Start Test Collection. Princeton, New Jersey, Educational Testing Service, 1971.

Hoepfner, Ralph, Stern, Carol and Nummedal, Susan (Ed.): CSE-ECRC Pre-School Kindergarten Tests Evaluations. Los Angeles, California, UCLA Graduate School of Education, 1971.

Walker, Deborah: Socio-emotional Measures for Preschool and Kindergarten Children. San Francisco, Jossey-Bass Publishers, 1973.

Evaluation Bibliography, Tads Evaluation Bibliography, Tadscript #2, Technical Assistance Development System (TADS), Chapel Hill, North Carolina, 1973.

The screening instruments and techniques which will be described are in six categories: published tests, teacher observation instruments, parent surveys, information-gathering questionnaires, physical examinations, and devised tests which includes the ZEIS.

Published Tests

The published screening tests are summarized according to the areas of development they measure and whether they are also

Kindergarten Screening

TABLE VIII

Published Screening Instruments

Name of Test	Physical Motor	Perceptual	Cognitive	Speech & Language	Social Emotional	Can be used for Diagnosis
		Areas of Assessment				
ABC Inventory		X	X			
Bannatyne System		X	X	X		X
Basic Concept Inventory			X			
Beery Buktenica Developmental of Visual Motor Integration		X				
Daberon		X	X	X		
Dallas Preschool Screening Test		X	X	X		
Denver Developmental Screening Test		X		X	X	
DIAL		X	X	X		
Draw A Person - Koppitz		X			X	X
Echoic Response Inventory		X			X	X
Gesell Developmental Kit		X	X	X	X	X
Goldman Fristoe Test of Articulation				X		X
Goldman Fristoe Test of Auditory Discrimination		X				X
Jansky Modified Screening Index		X	X	X		
KELP		X	X	X	X	
Kindergarten Auditory Screening Test		X		X		
K-Q Kindergarten Questionnaire	X	X	X	X	X	
Meeting Street School Test		X		X	X	
Northwestern Syntax Screening Test				X		
Peabody Picture Vocabulary Test			X	X		
Pre School Inventory - Rev. Ed. 1970		X		X		
Pre School Screening System	X	X	X	X		
Riley Pre School Developmental Screen Inventory		X		X	X	
Screening Test for Auditory Comprehension of Language				X		
Slosson Intelligence Test		X				X

Name of Test	Physical Motor	Perceptual	Cognitive	Speech & Language	Social Emotional	Can be used for Diagnosis
		Areas of Assessment				
Token Test			X	X		X
Yellow Brick Road		X	X	X		
Vallett Developmental Survey	X	X	X	X	X	X
Vane Kindergarten Test		X	X	X	X	X

suitable for use as a diagnostic tool (see Table VIII). A short description is given of each test. The names and addresses of the publishers are in the appendix. All tests are individually administered unless specifically indicated.

These tests were selected because they seemed to meet many of the criteria for a screening instrument or because they might be useful to take parts from for a devised test, i.e., Kindergarten Evaluation of Learning Potential (KELP) and Vallett. Many language-related screening instruments are included because of the increased awareness of the relationship of language and effective school learning. They range from tests with standardized scores to tests which classify abilities according to strength or weaknesses.

ABC Inventory (1965)

The ABC Inventory is designed to identify children aged four to six who are likely to fail in kindergarten or who are not likely to be ready for grade one. Items relate to drawing, copying, folding, counting, memory, general information, colors, size concepts, time concepts, etc. The Inventory is paced, and takes about nine minutes to give. No special training is needed to administer the questionnaire.

Basic Concept Inventory (1967)

The Basic Concept Inventory provides a broad checklist of basic concepts involved in new learning situations and used in explanations and instructions in the first grade. It is primarily intended for culturally disadvantaged preschool and kindergarten children, slow learners, emotionally disturbed children, and mentally retarded children. The inventory is criterion-referenced and uses basic concepts, sentence repetition and comprehension, and pattern-awareness tasks. It is paced, and requires about twenty minutes. If the inventory is to be used as a basis for remedial instruction, it may be given by the classroom teacher. If, however, it is to be used diagnostically as the basis for special treatment or special placement, a trained examiner should administer the instrument.

Daberon (1972)

The Daberon surveys knowledge of body parts, color and number concepts, functional use of prepositions and plurals, ability to follow directions, general knowledge, visual perception, gross motor development, and the ability to categorize. Developmental age levels are indicated for most of the 124 items on the test, ranging from eighteen months to six years. The test takes about twenty minutes to administer and some training is necessary.

Denver Developmental Screening Test (1968)

The Denver Developmental Screening Test is a simple, clinically useful tool designed to assist in the early detection of children with serious developmental delays. It may be used with children from age two weeks to six years. Although the test contains 105 tasks, a child of any given age will usually be tested on about twenty items. The DDST evaluates the following areas: gross motor, fine-motor-adaptive (use of hands, ability to solve nonverbal problems), language (ability to hear and talk), and personal-social (tasks of self-care, ability to relate to others). Task norms which indicate the age at which 25, 50, 75, and 90 percent of boys, girls, and all children successfully complete each item are available. It takes about twenty minutes to administer. A programed training manual is available.

Dallas Preschool Screening Test (1972)

The Dallas Preschool Screening Test evaluates skill development in these areas: information, counting, noun association, memory, color naming, matching, copy forms, picture description, and gross motor. Developmental age levels are given for each test item, ranging from three to six years. The test takes about fifteen minutes and some training is necessary.

Developmental Test of Visual-Motor Integration (Beery-Buktenica, 1967)

The Developmental Test of Visual-Motor Integration assesses the degree to which visual perception and motor behavior are integrated. It consists of a series of twenty-four geometric forms which the subject is asked to copy without erasures or corrections. The test is for ages two to fifteen years, and scores provide a visual-motor integration-age equivalent. It takes about ten minutes to administer, and minimal training is necessary.

DIAL (1974)

The DIAL is multi-dimensional and assess gross motor, fine motor, concepts, and communication. It is administered by a trained team of one coordinator and four operators and takes twenty to thirty minutes. The test is for ages two and one-half to five and one-half years.

Draw-A-Person — Koppitz Scoring System (1968)

The Koppitz scoring system of a figure drawing is objective and based on the expected number of body parts drawn at each age by a normative sample. Thirty developmental items are categorized as "expected," "common," "not unusual," and "exceptional" for ages five to twelve. Thirty-eight items are classified as emotional indicators and are classified according to age. No experience is necessary to administer.

Human figure drawings reflect primarily a child's level of development and his interpersonal relationships, that is, his attitude toward himself and significant others in his life.

Echoic Response Inventory for Children (1969)

The Echoic Response Inventory screens auditory discrimination, articulation, language, and school readiness. It takes about fifteen minutes and is used for children aged three to six. No training is necessary to administer.

Gesell Developmental Kit (1964)

The Gesell kit includes the name and address test; date; numbers; copy forms; right and left test; incomplete man test; Monroe Visual Test; and naming animals, home and school preferences. It is for children age five to ten. It requires a trained administrator and takes twenty to thirty minutes to give.

Goldman Fristoe Test of Articulation (1969)

The Goldman Fristoe Test of Articulation provides a method of assessing an individual's articulation of consonant sounds. There are three subtests. The Sounds-in-Words Subtest utilizes thirty-six stimulus pictures of familiar objects; the examiner records the child's articulation of speech sounds. The Sound-in-Sentences Subtest consists of two stories read aloud by the examiner and illustrated by sets of pictures. In order to approximate speech production of ordinary conversational speech, the child is asked to recount each story in his own words using the pictures as memory aids. The Stimulability Subtest asks the child to pronounce a previously misarticulated phoneme, given both visual and oral stimulation. The test is designed for children aged two and over, with the results to be recorded on a form which graphically portrays the child's articulatory profile. It takes about ten minutes to administer and training is required.

Goldman Fristoe Woodcock Test of Auditory Discrimination (1970)

The Goldman-Fristoe-Woodcock Test of Auditory Discrimination uses a tape-recorded stimulus and pictures which the child is to select. There are three parts to the test: a training procedure, a quiet subtest, and a noise subtest. Each of the two subtests includes six words from each of the categories: voiced plosives, unvoiced plosives, voiced continuants, nasals, and unvoiced continuants. The age range is three years, eight months through adult. It takes fifteen to twenty minutes to administer and some training is required.

Jansky Modified Screening Index (1973)

The Jansky Modified Screening Index consist of several subtests, some of which are adapted from other instruments. It includes letter-naming, picture-naming from the Peabody Auditory Memory, word-matching, and copying of figures from the Bender Gestalt Test. It can be given individually or in a group of children aged five to seven. Some training is necessary to administer.

Kindergarten Evaluation of Learning Potential (KELP) (1963)

KELP predicts school success in the early grades based on the learning that a child actually achieves in kindergarten. It is designed as both a teaching and evaluation instrument. KELP items include skipping, color identification, bead design, bolt board, block design, calendar, number boards, safety signs, writing a name, auditory perception, and social interaction. The latter nine items are rated at three levels: association, concept formation, and creative self-expression. The items are taught by the teacher, who observes and records the accomplishment of the tasks over the entire kindergarten year. Parts of the KELP may be used in devising a screening test.

Kindergarten Auditory Screening Test (1971)

The KAST contains three subtests: auditory figure ground, phonemic synthesis (sound blending), and auditory discrimination of word pairs. It requires no special training to administer and is fully recorded on a 33 1/3 rpm record. It takes twenty minutes to administer.

K-Q: Kindergarten Questionnaire (1972)

The K-Q Questionnaire is designed to screen children prior to kindergarten in order to identify specific strengths and weaknesses in the areas of language, emotional-social development, motor development, and health. The instruments include: Child Tasks Questionnaire, which consists of drawing, copying, balancing, and memory tests; Parent Questionnaire, which elicits parental perceptions of the child; and Individual and Summary Data Cards, which are designed to collate information. Minimal Training is required.

Meeting Street School Screening Test (1969)

The Meeting Street School Screening Tests is based on the information processing model. It assesses language, visual perception, motor, school readiness, and self concepts. It takes approximately thirty minutes to give and requires a trained administrator. It is for children age five to seven.

Northwestern Syntax Screening Test (1969)

This test was designed as a structured screening test for deficits in both expressive and receptive use of syntax for children three through eight years of age.

The test consists of a series of pictures. The procedure is structured for both the comprehension and production portions. It takes approximately twenty minutes to administer, and requires training to give.

Peabody Picture Vocabulary Test (PPVT) (1959)

The PPVT is assumed to measure recognition (hearing) vocabulary by having a child identify correct pictorial representations (from among four alternatives) in a series as the examiner speaks a word corresponding to each picture. Items are arranged from simple to complex. This test is suitable for use with children of preschool age and beyond and is easily administered. The PPVT requires little special training for scoring and interpretation.

Preschool Inventory — Revised Edition (1970)

The Inventory is an individually administered screening measure of achievement in areas considered vital to success in school. General factors assessed are: personal-social responsiveness (knowledge about the child's own personal world and his ability to get along with and respond to communications of another person); associative vocabulary (ability to demonstrate awareness of the connotation of a word by carrying out some action or by associating to certain intrinsic qualities of the underlying verbal concept); concept activation-numerical (the ability to label quantities, to make judgments of more or less, and to recognize seriated positions); and concept activation-sensory (the awareness of certain sensory attributes — shape, size, motion, color — and to be able to execute certain visual motor configurations).

This Inventory was originally referred to as the Preschool Achievement Test. It is suitable for children aged three to six years and requires training to give.

Preschool Screening System (1974)

The Preschool Screening System is in a field trial edition. It is by the authors of the Meeting Street School Test and is directed to children aged three to six. The test assesses information processing skills in language, visual motor, and gross motor areas, plus two supplementary subtests; Draw-A-Person, and verbal reasoning. The parent fills in a developmental questionnaire covering behavioral characteristics of the child at home plus a short medical and developmental history. It takes fifteen to twenty minutes to administer and requires minimal training.

Riley Preschool Developmental Screening Inventory (1969)

The Riley Preschool Developmental Screening Inventory includes visual perception, motor, school readiness, and self concept. It has a design score, and Make-a-Boy (Girl) score. It requires some training to administer and takes from three to ten minutes to give. It is for children aged three to six.

It was designed to quickly identify children with serious behavioral problems. It was developed and used in Head Start programs in poverty areas. It provides an index of the child's developmental age and self-concept.

Screening Test for Auditory Comprehension of Language (STACL) (1973)

STACL is a screening device designed to assess oral language comprehension independent of language expression and to establish the child's dominant language. STACL is derived from the Test for Auditory Comprehension of Language (TACL) and may be used to identify children who require more complete testing of auditory comprehension with the TACL. Instructions are provided in both English and Spanish. It requires minimal training to give. The test is for children age three and up.

Slosson Intelligence Test for Children and Adults (SIT) (1961)

The Slosson assesses mental ability in infants, children, and adults. One item is available for each one-half-month interval for infants up to two years of age, one for each month for ages two to five, and one for each two months for ages five to sixteen. The examinee proceeds with items until he has missed ten in a row. The resultant score is the examinee's mental age. The test is untimed, individually administered, and paced. Testing time is ten to twenty minutes. It requires no training to administer.

The Token Test (1962)

The Token Test consists of tokens in two shapes (circles and squares), two sizes (big and little), and five colors. The examiner gives increasingly complex commands relating to the tokens. The test assesses receptive language disorders and auditory processing. Minimal training is necessary to administer, and it takes five to ten minutes to give.

The Yellow Brick Road (1975)

The Yellow Brick Road consists of twenty-four game-like tests following the Wizard of Oz theme. It has a motor, auditory, and language battery. It requires four to eight examiners and is given individually at different stations. It is designed for easy administration and immediate scoring and is for children age three to six years.

Vallett Development Survey (1966)

The Vallett Developmental Survey evaluates various developmental abilities of children between the ages of two and seven, to aid in planning individualized learning programs. It consists of 233 tasks in the areas of motor integration and physical development, tactile discrimination, auditory discrimination, visual-motor coordination, visual discrimination, and conceptual development. Some practice is needed to give the test. Many props, all inexpensive and readily available, are needed. Age norms for each of the tasks are included. Parts of the Vallett are often used in devised tests.

Vane Kindergarten Test (1968)

The Vane Kindergarten Test covers perceptual-motor, and vocabulary development, and has a Draw-a-Man subtest. Part of the test is administered in small groups and part individually by the school psychologist. It is for children age four to six and takes about thirty minutes to give. The score is given as an IQ. Minimal training is required.

Teacher Observation Instruments

Published and unpublished instruments are included in this category. Observation is generally informal and subjective, as behavior is difficult to put in precise categories. Observation instruments usually have a rating scale. Some common types of rating scales are ranking lists, checklists, descriptive rating scales, numerical rating scales, and graphic rating scales. The ranking list is used when comparisons among children in a group are made according to some trait; each child is placed in order from first to last as he relates to his peers on some criterion variable. A checklist consists of a number of statements or descriptions which are checked if they apply to the child being rated. A descriptive scale is one in which several key words or phrases are presented to the rater. The numerical and graphic rating scales are those in which an individual is given a score for different items without reference to any group. On the numerical rating scale, a rater checks which of several item descriptions best characterizes the child being rated. In the graphic rating scale, the items to be evaluated are placed on a horizontal line continuum; the judges place a mark anywhere on the line between the two extremes. Observations may be process- or product-oriented. They may focus only on behavior, for example, "Is the child fidgety, with nervous mannerisms?" Or they may ask the observer to see how a child functions with a particular task and what is the nature of the product, for example: "Can the child print his first name from memory?"

Observations are usually done over a period of time as opposed to the one-time situation of a test. There is some question as to how the data of the two types of instruments compare. It has been the author's experience that the results of the screening tests done during the school year correlated well with teacher observation.

Teacher Observation Instruments, published and unpublished, are summarized in Table IX and areas of development measured are indicated. The published instruments are described

TABLE IX

Teacher Observation Instruments

Name of Instrument	Areas of Measurement				
	Physical	Perceptual-Motor	Cognitive	Speech & Language	Social Emotional
*California Preschool Social Competence Scale					X
*Child-Early Identification Screening Inventory	X	X		X	X
*Preschool Attainment Record	X	X	X	X	X
*Rhode Island Pupil Identification Scale		X	X		X
*Verbal Language Dev. Scale				X	
Alaska Learning Disabilities Ranking Scale		X	X	X	X
Behavior Checklist (Hawaii)	X	X	X	X	X
Maryland Systematic Observation Instrument	X	X	X	X	X

*Published

first. The publishers are listed in the appendix.
Some training is necessary for all instruments in order for there to be common agreement in interpreting what is to be observed.

Published Teacher Observation Instruments

California Preschool Social Competency Scale (1969)

The California Preschool Social Competency Scale is a rating scale designed to measure the adequacy of interpersonal behavior and the degree of assumption of social responsibility in children of age two to five. The behaviors included are situational in nature and were selected in terms of common cultural expectations to represent basic competencies to be developed in the process of socialization. Each item contains four descriptive statements, posed in behavioral terms, representing varying degrees of competency. The CPSCS contains thirty items designed to be rated by a classroom teacher. The nature of the items requires the rater to have had considerable opportunity to observe the child in a variety of situations. The checklist requires ten to twenty minutes to complete.

CHILD: Early Identification Screening Inventory (1974)

The Early Identification Screening Inventory is part of the CHILD (Childhood Identification of Learning Disabilities) program designed for early identification, diagnosis, and treatment of children with learning disabilities in kindergarten to third grade. The inventory has one hundred items and screens six areas of studied behavior: visual-motor, visual, speech and hearing, physical and behavior, psycho-motor, and psychological.

Preschool Attainment Record (1966)

The Preschool Attainment Record combines an assessment of physical, social, and intellectual functions in a global appraisal of children from birth to seven years of age. The Record includes eight categories of developmental behavior: ambulation, manipulation, rapport, communication, responsibility, information, ideation, and creativity. For each category, there is one item for each six-month span. Mean age for expected performance of each behavior is provided. Total scores may be converted to attainment ages or attainment quotients. It takes about twenty minutes to complete the record.

Rhode Island Pupil Identification Scale (1973)

This scale is used to help the classroom teacher identify

children with learning problems. It has been standardized on children from kindergarten to grade two. It consists of a two-part checklist; Part I refers to behavior which can normally be observed in the classroom, and Part II deals with behavior which is most readily observable through written work. Observations are scored on a scale of 1 to 5 ranging from whether a behavior exists "never" to "always."

Verbal Language Development Scale (1959)

The Verbal Language Development Scale is an extension of the communication portion of the Vineland Social Maturity Scale. The information is compiled in an interview with the parent and is used for children from one month of age to fifteen years. It has the advantage of tapping the child's behavior in familiar settings. There are many items for the younger ages (talks, imitates sounds, uses names of familiar objects) and fewer but more complex descriptions for the older years. Half credit is allowed for behaviors that are in an emergent state. The scale consists of a total of fifty items: six on listening, thirty-one on speaking, five on reading, and eight on writing.

Unpublished Observation Instruments

Observation instruments have been used as part of pilot screening programs. The states of Alaska, Hawaii, and Maryland have developed their own forms to be filled out by the classroom teacher as the first step in the screening program. The Alaska checklist focuses on achievement and the Hawaii tests on behavior. The Maryland instrument combines both.

The Alaska Learning Disabilities Ranking Scale (1973)

This checklist was created as the initial screening for kindergarten children who might have learning disabilities. It was part

Alaska Learning Disabilities Ranking
Scale (Individual Checklist)*

Sample Questions   YES   NO

1. Can this child count by rote to ten?

2. Can this child say the alphabet by
    rote?

3. When compared with his/her class-
    mates, can this child listen atten-
    tively and follow oral directions
    without frequent repetitions or
    failure to complete them?

4. When shown a picture of a single,
    common object (e.g. an animal,
    building, utensil, etc.) and is
    asked to name it and use it in a
    complete sentence, can he do so
    as well as the majority of his
    classmates?

5. When shown a story picture (e.g.
    a picture from a basal reader) can
    the child make a story of at least
    three sentences to describe it?

6. Can this child match any eight
    randomly selected pairs of lower
    case letters of the alphabet? (e.g.
    b, d, g, p, q, m, n, w and w, q, n,
    b, m, g, d, p)

7. Does this child demonstrate the
    ability to imitate letter sounds
    when requested to do so by the
    teacher?

8. Does this child know two of the three
    following facts: first and last name.
    address and telephone number?

9. When shown the eight basic colors
    (red, yellow, blue, green, orange,
    purple, black, brown), can the child
    identify at least seven of them?

10. Can this child present from memory
    the nursery rhymes, songs and
    stories learned in class as well
    as the majority of his classmates?

*Courtesy of Roger Clyne, Anchorage Borough School
District.

Figure 4.

of a federally funded Title VIG project. The primary focus of the checklist is on specific behaviors or achievements. When the checklists for all the children are completed, the classroom teacher ranks the children in order of severity, beginning with the most severe case first. There are thirty questions in the checklist. Part of the checklist is shown in Figure 4. The number of "no" questions is divided by thirty. The higher the percentage, the more likely it is that the child will experience problems in first grade and should be considered for special intervention.

Behavioral Checklist (State of Hawaii, 1973)

This checklist was devised by the Children's Health Services Division of the State of Hawaii as a first step of a preschool screening project. It was used in the preschools, nurseries, and day care centers. This checklist focuses on behavior with no involvement with specific tasks (see Figure 5).

Dr. Iwakami (1975) reported that the teachers had a training session to learn to use the checklist and to establish a common interpretation to many questions. Follow-through is done with children who:

1. have clusters (three or more) of items checked within any one sector, except those that are confined to the social-emotional area. Children who may have emotional problems are first discussed with the teacher and parents to decide whether screening would be useful or whether a direct referral for mental health services would be more appropriate.
2. have several (five or more) items checked although they are scattered and do not seem to convey a coherent picture of the problem.
3. are deemed by the teacher to need more screening, regardless of the number or type of items checked. This includes children who have only one or two items checked, but who are considered below average in overall functioning.
4. do not seem to present any real or identifiable problems, but who are an enigma to the teachers.

Children's Health Services Division
Department of Health, State of Hawaii

Name _____ Birth Date _____

Behavioral Checklist*

Please circle all the items which describe this
child's behavior.

Speech-Hearing-Language
1. does not speak English or is bilingual
2. speech is scanty, excessively non-verbal
3. speaks in isolated words or sentence frag-
   ments, but not in complete sentences
4. baby talk; often unintelligible
5. many errors of articulation
6. stutters or blocks on words
7. can't follow a set of directions given orally when other children can
8. only hears, understands, or remembers certain parts of verbal direction - usually
   the last part, but sometimes the first
9. gives foolish or inappropriate answers to
   questions; tells incoherent stories
10. misbehaves, wiggles or disrupts the class
    when language is introduced - such as story
    time, or listening to verbal material
11. slow progress shown in growth of vocabulary,
    or ability to express himself

Academic-Intellectual
12. very poor listening ability; seems not to pay
    attention at all
13. attention shifts rapidly; easily distracted
14. listens but does not understand; requires
    constant reinstruction or simplification
15. seems not to remember anything; forgets
    instructions as well as rote lesson materials
16. little or no utilization of feedback; con-
    tinues to use ineffective methods after ex-
    perience or example of better methods; cannot
    be swayed
17. poor persistence, usually gives up quickly

Physical-Motor
18. does not have ordinary endurance; tires very
    easily
19. very frail physically
20. usually clumsy, stumbling, or jerky in body
    coordination
21. does poorly in manual tasks
22. tempo very slow, deliberate or dawdling
23. high-strung, tense
24. fidgety with nervous mannerisms
25. hyperactive, motions always quick

*Used with the permission of the State of Hawaii De-
partment of Health.

Figure 5.

Social-Emotional
26. keeps to himself; overly shy or withdrawn
27. a complete follower; seems not to have any
     ideas of his own
28. children actively avoid or attack him
29. a very uncooperative child
30. poor relations with adults: complains, can-
     not accept or give affection; aggressive;
     seeks excessive attention or in inappropriate
     ways such as crying, causing trouble, etc.
31. usually antagonistic, fearful, or irritated
32. adjusts poorly to anxiety, disappointment, or
     strain; becomes aggressive; cries long or
     loudly; requires excessive reassurances; seem
     to have feelings hurt much too easily; unduly
     moody
33. poor self-concept; lacks self-confidence

In terms of overall functioning, this child seems to
be: (Circle one)

     (1) Above average   (2) Average   (3) Below average

The Maryland Systematic Teacher Observation Instrument (1974)

This instrument covers five basic areas of development: psycho-motor, sensory/perception, language, cognition, and affect/motivation. Figure 6 has some sample items. The screening is done approximately eight weeks after school has begun. Each question is coded into one of the five basic areas of development. There are thirty-six questions. If a student scores below a cut-off score for the whole test or in a specific area he is referred for further assessment (see Chapter 7 for further description of the Maryland program.)

Parent Surveys

Parent surveys are designed to gather information relating to the child's development from those persons who should know the child best, i.e. his parents. The participation of parents in evaluating their own children's readiness can relieve school personnel of the resentment or resistance with which parents sometimes

Maryland Systematic Teacher Observation Instrument*

Items	Always	Often	Sometimes	Seldom	Never
1. says "huh" or "what" after he has been told something or asked a question	.___	..___	...___	....___	.....___
2. finishes task late	.___	..___	...___	....___	.....___
3. can tell about a picture while looking at it	.....___	....___	...___	..___	.___
4. names and locates at least five parts of his body	.....___	....___	...___	..___	.___
5. knocks over things when reaching for them	.___	..___	...___	....___	.....___
6. fumbles for words, uses a wrong word, or says he forgot what he was trying to say	.___	..___	...___	....___	.....___
7. cringes or pulls away when approached by others	.___	..___	...___	....___	.....___
8. can recognize own name in print	.....___	....___	...___	..___	.___
9. stays with the activity at hand	.....___	....___	...___	..___	.___
10. can tell about a recent school activity (i.e. field trip)	.....___	....___	...___	..___	.___
11. follows directions	.....___	....___	...___	..___	.___
12. can repeat sentences such as "I like to play outside" in correct order	.....___	....___	...___	..___	.___
13. drowsy, sleepy, or sleeps	.___	..___	...___	....___	.....___
14. names common objects such as chair, desk, table	.....___	....___	...___	..___	.___
15. fights, shouts, or shakes his fist as a preferred means of solving problems	.___	..___	...___	....___	.....___

*Used with the permission of the Maryland State Department of Education.

Figure 6.

respond to judgments by the teacher or guidance worker. The active involvement of parents while their children are still of preschool age also enlists them on the side of the teacher and prepares them for future cooperation. Table X summarizes the published parent surveys which are described.

TABLE X

Published Parent Surveys

Name of Survey	Physical	Perceptual-Motor	Cognitive	Speech & Language	Social Emotional
Areas of Assessment					
Child Behavior Rating Scale					X
Early Detection Inventory	X	X	X	X	X
Preprimary Profile					X
School Readiness Checklist			X	X	
School Readiness Survey		X	X	X	X

Child Behavior Rating Scale (1962)

This scale has been developed for the objective assessment of personality adjustments of children in kindergarten through the third grade. The items are six-point rating scales on the behaviors, attitudes, attributes, or status of the examinee or his parents. CBRS provides measures in the significant adjustment areas of self, home, social, school, and physical adjustment and a global score indicating total adjustment. The scale is self-administering and is completed by a person who has observed or knows directly the behavior of the child to be rated. The scale takes about five to ten minutes to rate.

Early Detection Inventory (1967)

The Early Detection Inventory measures general school readiness in preschool children. Areas of assessment are: social-emotional behavior responses, readiness tasks (verbal self-awareness, concept development, awareness of left/right, awareness of body image), motor performance, vision, hearing, dental health, speech, medical history, and family and social history. Both the child and one of his parents are needed to complete the instrument. Administration time depends on the number of personnel assigned to the testing session. At least the following are needed: an experienced educational tester, a vision examiner, a hearing examiner, a dentist, and a speech therapist. Several readily available props are needed.

Preprimary Profile Introduction to My Child (1966)

This profile provides organized information about the nature and interests of children as they enter school for the first time — in prekindergarten, kindergarten, or first grade. The instrument contains rating scales in the following areas: self-care, classroom management (the social behavior of the child), skill development, language development, and previous experience. The instrument, which is basically self-administering, is completed by a parent or an adult who lives in the same household as the child. It may be filled out in about fifteen minutes.

School Readiness Checklist — Ready or Not (1963)

This is a checklist of developmental skill levels covering growth and age, general activity related to growth, practical skills, remembering, understanding, general knowledge, and attitudes and interests. It is for children age four to six and takes fifteen to thirty minutes to complete.

School Readiness Survey (1967)

The School Readiness Survey is designed to help the parent understand the capacities and developmental needs of his child, aged four to six; the items require the child to choose an appropriate picture, figure, work, or symbol, or to answer orally. Subscores are: number concepts, discrimination of form, color naming, symbol matching, speaking vocabulary, listening vocabulary, and general information. The total score and each subscore are related to likelihood of readiness.

Information-Gathering Questionnaires (unpublished)

There is information which can be collected as part of a screening program that would help to understand the child's needs better. This includes background history and parent expectations. While everything that happened to the child prior to the moment he is screened is part of his background history, there is certain information that is more relevant than other.

Wilborn (1974) compared the background history of 100 learning disabled students with the background histories of 200 students who demonstrated satisfactory academic performance. All students involved in the study were comparable in terms of socioeconomics and ethnic factors. The items studied included such things as perinatal and developmental stages, prematurity, prolonged labor, low birth weight, late or abnormal creeping, prolonged tip-toe walking, and ambidexterity after seven years of age. The results of the study showed that approximately 80 percent of the children with known learning difficulties had at least one perinatal and/or developmental abnormality.

All school districts take certain basic medical and family information when a child enters. Background history questions need careful thought. To ask a lot of personal questions that have no relevance to educational planning or to collect data without intent to use it is unprofessional. Parents always have the right to refuse to give personal information, and it is important that they be informed of this right. Public schools have little time and personnel to do research; however, information collected in background history forms could provide data to study nutrition, development, sibling order, parent's learning problems, and so forth in relation to the child's ability to learn effectively.

Each school or institution can develop forms which suit its program. Figure 7 is the form used at the laboratory school.

In some published screening instruments, information-gathering forms are included.*

- K-Q Questionnaire — Parent Questionnaire
- School-Community Program in Early Child Development, Evanston, Ill. Child Behavior Profile, pp. 13-16
- Preschool Screening System — Parent Questionnaire — medical history and developmental profile, pp. 47-52
- DIAL — Parent Questionnaire, pp. 78-87

Information on parent and child expectations of what will happen to the child and what he will learn in school are not usually included in screening programs. At the laboratory school there is increased interest in that question, though as yet no formal research study has been done. Expectations are very important because success can be defined as meeting expectations. When there is not a match between the parent and the school's expectations for the child, the child is confused and caught in the middle. A question about expectations is included in the screening program (see Figure 7). The primary teachers also include a question relating to expectations in their preschool questionnaire. Generally there is a match. Two examples of a mismatch will help show the importance of the question, "What do you expect your child to learn in school this year?"

Of two children entering first grade, one had been part of a kindergarten diagnostic assessment. Rita was a well-behaved child of average intelligence who functioned adequately in school except in activities relating to the auditory channel. She scored low on the Wepman Test of Auditory Discrimination and on the Illinois Test of Psycholinguistic Ability (ITPA) subtests of auditory reception, auditory memory, auditory closure, and sound blending. Her parents' expectations were very precise; they

---

*See appendix for publishers and addresses.

VANDENBERG LEARNING CENTER
State University College
New Paltz, NY 12561

Kindergarten Developmental Screening

MEDICAL EVALUATION AND HISTORY

Date_____

Person Interviewed_____

Name of child:_____Birthdate:_____

School:_____Sex: M___ F___ C.A._____

Telephone #_____Name of person interviewed:_____

Relationship:_____Nursery school: Yes___No___

Name & address:_____

Number of years attended:____Length & no. of sessions
                                per week:_____

FAMILY HISTORY

Father:_____Age range: 20-30___30-40___over 40_____

Occupation:_____Highest level of education attained:_____

Mother:_____Age range: 20-30___30-40___over 40_____

Occupation:_____Highest level of education attained:_____

Marital status: Married___Separated___Widowed___

                Divorced___Other___

Guardian (if other than both parents):_____

Who is responsible for child if parent(s) work outside of
    home?_____

Other adults living at home:_____Relationship:_____

Language(s) spoken at home:_____

Brothers and/or sisters of child:

		Any Speech, Hearing, Reading or Other Educational Difficulties
Full Name	*Age*	
_____	___	_____
_____	___	_____
_____	___	_____
_____	___	_____
_____	___	_____

Figure 7.

Are any children in your home adopted or foster children?

Yes _____   No _____

If yes, please name: _____

Do they or your other children know they are adopted?

Yes _____   No _____

Do any medical conditions run in the family including close relatives?

1) Convulsions_____   7) High blood pressure_____
2) Asthma_____   8) Strokes_____
3) Diabetes_____   9) Heart attacks_____
4) TB_____   10) Cancer_____
5) Congenital defects____   11) Anemia_____
6) Mental retardation,   12) Other_____
   etc._____

Prenatal and Natal Information

Was there any unusual problems during pregnancy? Yes__No__.

If yes, approximately what month?_____. Nature of the

problem: (eg. hepatitis, german measles, kidney complica-

tions)_____

_____

Normal delivery_____   Premature_____
Caesarian_____   Baby's birth weight_____
Breech_____   Was baby in an incubator_____
Forceps_____   Was oxygen administered_____

Medical History

Severe or unusual illness: Yes__ No__ If yes, age:_____

Illness:_____

Any behavior change:_____

Severe fall or injury: Yes___ No___ If yes, age:_____

Injury:_____

Unconscious_____How long?____Convulsions:_____

Has your child had any evidence of hearing problems?

Yes___No_____ If yes, type:_____ Treatment_____

Has your child had any evidence of vision problems?

Yes___No_____ If yes, type:_____ Treatment_____

Is your child allergic? Yes___ No___ If yes, what is child

allergic to?_____

Has your child had any convulsions? Yes___ No___ If yes,

age:___ After high fever?_____Without fever?_____

Frequency:_____

At what approximate age did child start using words mean-

ingfully?_____

Was there anything unusual about speech or language?

Yes___ No___ If yes, explain:_____

_____

Has your child ever been hospitalized for an illness or

surgery? Yes___ No___ Nature of illness or operation:____

_____

At approximately what age did child walk?_____ Does your

child have many accidents?_____ Does your child take vita-

mins? Yes___ No___ Does your child crave sweets? Yes_____

No_____ Does your child consume a lot of sweets?_____

Any special eating habits or problems?_____

Does your child eat breakfast on school days?_____

What is his/her typical bed time hour?_____Any diffi-

culty with bed time?_____ Usual amount of sleep daily?__

Does the child have opportunities to play with other chil-

dren?_____

Any further information which is felt to be helpful in

knowing your child may be added here:_____

_____

_____

_____

Social - Emotional

How does your child like to spend his/her time?_____

_____

_____

Does your child have any fears? Yes___ No___ If yes,

explain:_____

_____

Do you read to your child? Yes___ No___ Types of stories,

etc._____

How much time does your child spend watching T.V.?_____

_____hours.

What type of show does your child enjoy?_____

What do you expect your child to get out of school?_____

_____

_____

What do you expect the school to do for your child?_____

_____

_____

Are there any questions you would like to discuss with

the school psychologist?

wanted Rita to learn to read with a phonetic-based method. After conferencing with the parents, who were both college graduates, we found that they both had had initial difficulty in learning to read and never mastered phonics; therefore that is what they wanted for their child. We were able to explain Rita's sensory makeup, which was probably similar to their own and helped them to understand that Rita would learn to read (as she did) but phonics was not the method of choice.

Tom was new to the school and was described by his teachers as a child who reacts in a hostile manner to limits and is physically forceful to his peers. He didn't willingly want to do activities other than those of his own choosing (chooses blocks, checkers, Candy Land® games). He has a short attention span and a low frustration level.

Following is the verbatim account of his mother's response to the question "What are *your* expectations for your child in first grade this year?" "I expect that Tom will *know* his alphabet and his numbers and that he will be able to recognize them. I also want him to be able to read and write on his own. Now, he copies sentences out of books to practice writing but he does not understand the separation of words in sentences. Tom and I were disappointed with kindergarten because Tom was ready to learn to read and write and he wanted to do so. This was because he had been going to nursery schools since he was three years old and expected to work when he entered school rather than play, which is what he did."

"I am interested in the method you use to teach the kids to read. If you are using the books that contain stories that add words with each new story, they are in my opinion only good to a point. My experience with children and this type of book is that they read the picture rather than the words and from here they begin to memorize. This summer I began working with Tom on phonetic sounds of words which I felt to be the superior method to teach reading and with the little work I gave him he is able to hear the sounds of letters in words."

Figure 8 is Tom's picture of a person drawn at the beginning of the school year. The picture is representative of Tom's test results and expresses anger, frustration, and immaturity in a bright child.

Where there is a mismatch between the parent, who expects her child to be in a formal reading program, and the school, who expects a child at Tom's stage of development to be in a more physically oriented, less formal reading readiness program, the child is caught in the middle. It was important for Tom, for the school and the parents to work through their differences in expectations.

Physical Examinations

Vision and hearing examinations are included in many screening programs. In the thirty screening programs mentioned in Table VII, thirteen included vision and hearing screenings, one solely for vision and one for hearing. Other physical examinations may be recommended as part of the diagnostic process.

Vision Screening

Vision screening usually identifies many children who need to

Figure 8. Figure drawing. Tom, age 5 yrs. 11 mos.

be referred for eye examinations.

In the University City School District, (Missouri, 1969) screening, 10 percent of 320 children were noted as having visual defects. In the Arlington, N. Y. screening, 46 of 600 tested were referred for eye examinations and another 131 were to be observed closely throughout the school year (*Mid-Hudson Channel*, 1972). A report from Colorado Springs indicates that 34 percent of 265 children tested had faulty vision (Colorado, 1968).

The type of vision screening will differ according to the expertise of the examiner. The American Optometric Association has a Checklist for Possible Visual Abnormality which can be used for screening by the parent, teacher or school nurse (see Figure 9).

In the Arlington, New York school district the local optometrists all take turns being involved in the screening. The nurse/teacher may use the Snellen Chart, the Keystone Telebinocular, or other instruments which she feels are appropriate.

Hearing Screening

The following are seen as high risk factors causing a hearing problem. Children who have these conditions in their background history should be more closely scrutinized.

A. Prenatal
   1. rubella
   2. Rh incompatability
   3. hepatitis
   4. medicine and drugs
   5. prolonged labor
   6. other complications
B. Familial history of hearing loss
C. Postnatal
   1. prolonged unconsciousness
   2. prolonged fevers
   3. head trauma
   4. allergic conditions
   5. chronic head cold with congestion
   6. earache with or without drainage
   7. conditions requiring prolonged antibiotic treatment
   8. mumps (can result in unilateral deafness)
   9. cerebral palsy, cleft palate, or other physical anomolies.

Checklist for Possible Visual Abnormality*
The ABC's of Vision Difficulty

This list can be used to indicate to the parents, the
school nurse, or the practitioner, the need for a vision
examination. One check ( ) should be for signs or symptoms occurring occasionally, and two checks ( ) for
those occurring frequently.

A's - Appearance of the eyes:
   Eyes crossed - turning in or out - at any time. ___ ___
   Reddened eyes.   ___ ___
   Watering eyes.   ___ ___
   Encrusted eyelids.   ___ ___
   Frequent styes.   ___ ___

B's - Behavior Indications of Possible Vision
     Difficulty:
   Body rigidity while looking at distance
     objects.   ___ ___
   Thrusting head forward or backward while
     looking at distant objects.
   Avoiding close work.   ___ ___
   Short attention span.   ___ ___
   Daydreaming.   ___ ___
   Turning of head so as to use one eye only. ___ ___
   Tilting head to one side.   ___ ___
   Placing head close to book or desk when read-
     ing or writing.
   Frowning or scowling while reading or writing. ___ ___
   Excessive blinking.   ___ ___
   Tending to rub eyes.   ___ ___
   Closing or covering one eye.   ___ ___
   Dislike for tasks requiring sustained
     visual concentration.   ___ ___
   Nervousness, irritability, or restlessness
     after maintaining visual concentration. ___ ___
   Unusual fatigue after completing a vision
     task.   ___ ___
   Losing place while reading.   ___ ___
   Using finger place while reading.   ___ ___
   Saying the words aloud or lip reading. ___ ___
   Moving head rather than eyes while reading. ___ ___
   Difficulty in remembering what is read. ___ ___
   Persistent reversals after the second grade. ___ ___
   Confusion of similar words.   ___ ___
   Poor eye-hand coordination.   ___ ___
   Unusual awkwardness.   ___ ___

C's - Complaints Associated With Using the Eyes:
   Headaches.
   Nausea or dizziness.   ___ ___
   Burning or itching of eyes.   ___ ___
   Blurring of vision at any time.   ___ ___

*Reprinted with permission of the American Optometric As-
sociation.

Figure 9.

Hearing is screened by the nurse/teacher or some equally competent trained person. The audiometer is used to measure hearing acuity, the sharpness, clearness, or distinctness with which one is able to hear a sound. The child should be able to respond to the frequencies of 500, 1,000, 2,000, and 4,000 at an intensity of 25 db.

At the Evanston, Illinois (Holliday, 1975) preschool screening clinic the following procedure is used to measure hearing acuity, i.e. the sharpness, clearness, or distinctness with which one is able to hear a sound. The child is conditioned to respond to a sound. The child is taught to "play the game" by responding to audiometric tones by raising his hand, by dropping blocks or clothes pins into a basket, putting pegs into a peg board, or any toy or game which will hold the interest of the preschool child. The tester demonstrates the test and then teaches the child to respond through practice until he has the idea.

Some children will not or cannot respond to an audiometer testing. In the Missouri State Department of Education "Guidelines for an Early Childhood Screening Program" (1973), the following is suggested as procedural guidelines for hearing screening:

Identification Environment

a. The room should be reasonably quiet and should contain toys and objects which will draw and occupy the child's attention.
b. Two people should be involved with the child: one whose role is that of playing with the child, and another who, while out of the field of vision of the child, will employ various sound sources.

Stimuli

a. It is important not only to be able to note how a child responds, but also to note whether such responses occur with stimuli incorporating various frequencies, i.e. pitch components. Toy noisemakers, including toy drums, bells, crickets, whistles, flutes, pop guns (not cap pistols), kazoos, etc., are excellent for this purpose. Also, it is important to use speech as a stimulus. It must be remembered that testing with such gross utensils offers no calibration of intensity

and inferences must not be made regarding that parameter.
b. It would be recommended that persons involved with this program first practice on normal youngsters in order to familiarize themselves with the sounds of the toys and the way in which the children respond.

Devised Tests

Many screening programs use devised screening instruments. The majority of published screening instruments, particularly those published before 1970, do not meet many of the ten criteria for such an instrument. Multidimensional instruments most useful for screening have initially been devised for use with a particular school population or from a funded program of which screening has been a part. The process of validating an instrument and developing norms is long and tedious. Many districts and/or projects have developed useful instruments which they keep within their program and are continually improving to meet their needs but are willing to share upon written request.

DIAL, K-Q Questionnaire Preschool Learning System, and The Yellow Brick Road are examples of instruments which emerged from screening programs and have now been published. The Evanston School Community program in early childhood development published their screening instruments in their report booklet which can be purchased.

The Vallett Developmental Survey of Basic Learning Abilities (1966) and Handbook in Diagnostic Teaching (Mann and Suiter 1974, Chap. 4) describe categories of behavior with specific tasks to assess them. They are often used when devising instruments for local use.

While many of the devised instruments also fall short in meeting the ten criteria, the examination of many instruments helps a planning committee to devise their own or to select what is most appropriate to meet their particular needs.

ZEIS (Research edition, 1975)

Stemming from the frustration of finding a suitable screening instrument which meets the ten criteria for a suitable screening instrument, the author has devised an instrument. The ZEIS has evolved over a period of eight years and work with it is continuing. It was initially developed to meet the needs of a small urban school district but subsequently has been used with a diverse population.

The ZEIS is a short individually administered instrument which is designed to identify early kindergarten and prekindergarten children who may have special learning needs. It screens out children who need further diagnosis to determine if they are potential high risk learners, or are so able that they could benefit from enriched learning experiences.

The screening consists of twelve questions relating to language, cognitive development, auditory and visual memory, gross motor, visual motor development, body image, directionality, and laterality. The questions are divided into three parts: verbal, pencil and paper tasks, and non-verbal performance. The ZEIS is scored on the basis of 100 points. The questions cover a developmental range of three to seven years with emphasis on four- to five-year-old development. There is a checklist for recording relevant observable behaviors, i.e. independence-

Screening Program

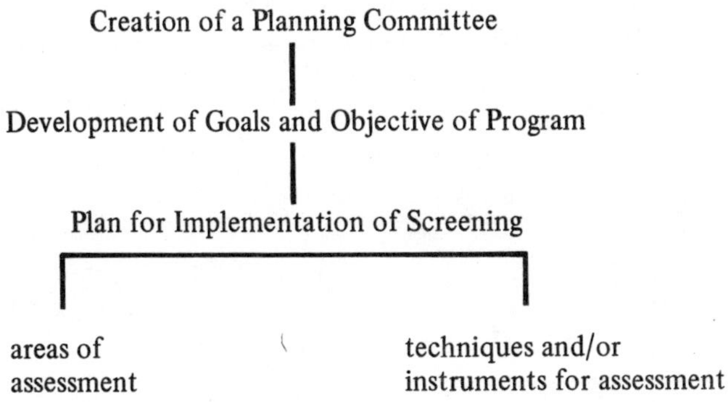

Creation of a Planning Committee

|

Development of Goals and Objective of Program

|

Plan for Implementation of Screening

| areas of assessment | techniques and/or instruments for assessment |

Figure 10.

dependence, speech. A checklist of Koppitz emotional indicators is also included to be used by the school psychologist to evaluate the figure drawing question. While normative data has been developed, local norms are encouraged. No individual question is intended to be a measure of competence in an ability, but to present part of an overall indication of the child's development.

The screening may be administered by teachers, paraprofessionals, and other educational personnel after one training session. A training film has been made which shows a complete administration. In addition to its use for individual screening, the ZEIS gives an overview of the entering kindergarten population. The ZEIS, directions for administering and scoring, and normative and other technical data are in Appendix D.

Figure 10 outlines the steps in the screening program which have been described so far.

Chapter Five

PLANNING TO IMPLEMENT
THE SCREENING

To implement the screening, a plan for procedure needs to be developed. This plan includes time and place of screening; how and when to notify parents; the amount and type of parent involvement before, during, and after the screening; the routines for the child, parent, and staff on the day of screening; and the training and supervision of involved personnel. Cost is a factor that may influence some of the decisions relating to procedure.

What Age to Screen

The age at which the school should assume responsibility for its students is a controversial question.

Most existing school screening programs involve kindergarten

TABLE XI

Grades and Grade Combinations in Which
Screening Was Done

Grade & Grade Combinations	No. of School Districts
Kindergarten only	83
Prekindergarten and kinder-garten	31
Prekindergarten only	28
Kindergarten and Grade 1	18
Grade 1 only	11
Prekindergarten, kinder-garten and Grade 1	6
	177

Report to New York State legislature, 1975.

85

and prekindergarten children. A few screen three-year-olds. In New York State, in a survey of 736 school districts, 177 had some early educational screening program. Table XI shows the grades in which the screening took place.

The small number of school-related screening programs for three-year-olds usually are for both three- and four-year-olds with accent on the four-year-old. Screening of three-year-olds is mostly by referral or at the request of the parent or preschool teacher. Perhaps the question of what age a school should screen can best be determined by the feasibility of following the screening with a reasonable and continuous program.

Most school screening programs concentrate on the child about to enter or already in kindergarten. These children range in age from four to five-and-a-half, depending on the time of year of the screening and the schools cut-off birth date for kindergarten entry. At this age children are accessible to the school. The prekindergarteners may be contacted through the registration process or through prekindergarten programs. The kindergarten children are in school and are readily available for screening. The rationale for screening before school entry is that the staff can know the child's educational need before entry and do appropriate planning. When there is need for diagnosis and remediation outside of the school, the process can be started. If special placement in or out of school is necessary, this can be done before the child's entry.

The advantage of screening early in the kindergarten year is that the child is there and is comfortable in the environment and usually familiar with the adults who do the screening. There is also opportunity to observe the child over a period of time in learning situations.

Educators and parents who generally have not been involved with screening programs have expressed concern that the preschool experience may be anxiety producing for the child. The author has observed many types of screening and rarely has found this to be the case. Generally the child who is very anxious either reflects a very anxious parent, or is a child whose coping style is to meet any new situation with great trepidation. Both of these behaviors are important to know about. In the author's first experience with screening, of the 147 children involved, only two children cried and had difficulty separating from their parents.

Kindergarten teachers can compare this with their experience on the first day of school. Comments from children have been "what fun," "I did school work today," "I went to school today like my sister (or brother)," "Can I take this home (drawings, etc.)?" "Can I come back soon"?

Screening at the end of the kindergarten year or early in first grade is usually related to reading readiness and is most often used for placement rather than as a first step for total educational planning for the child.

Personnel Choice for Screening

Who will do the screening will be determined by factors such as:

1. availability of various personnel,
2. time of year,
3. how much knowledge and training is necessary to administer, score, and interpret the assessment instrument considered,
4. school policies and community attitudes toward use of volunteers,
5. interest in screening by classroom teachers and specialists,
6. budget,
7. union contracts.

It is possible to use a whole range of personnel including volunteers, who may be parents, students, or other members of the community, and specialists hired for the occasion.

When a team approach is used for the screening, then those with less training can be supervised by or work with those who are more knowledgeable or more experienced. It is important that, in so far as possible, the kindergarten teacher be involved because she is the one who will be most intimately involved with the child and may have most experience with five-year-olds. If one of the goals of the screening is some modification of the regular classroom curriculum, then the screening needs a maximum involvement of regular class personnel.

The use of volunteers has both positive and negative aspects. Volunteers are usually willing and available. Using them is one way of educating members of the community about the program as well as keeping costs minimal. On the other hand, volunteers may not be as reliable as paid personnel and should be used only when the tasks assigned are specific and can be assessed objectively. In interacting with young children, there is a tendency for inexperienced personnel to misinterpret certain behaviors and be too lenient or too strict in assessing the child.

Specialists bring expertise to the screening; in most instances, therefore, the specialists are best used for training and supervision of other personnel rather than in actual assessment, unless the instrument or technique selected requires specific expertise. For example, a nurse/teacher would be essential in operating the audiometer in a hearing screening. In school systems where there are never enough specialists to meet the needs of the whole school, it is costly in time, money, and morale to have a screening program which utilizes only specialists.

In Wappingers Falls, New York, there are two screening teams (1,000 children screened) composed of a school psychologist as the leader, a speech therapist, school nurse/teacher, a physical education teacher, and two kindergarten teachers.

In Peotone, Illinois (a large school district) the screening team consists of a director, psychologists, social worker, speech therapists, learning disability teacher, teacher aides, clerical help, regular classroom teachers, adult volunteers, and high school students.

In Plattsburgh, New York (211 children screened) the screening is done by the classroom teacher in addition to the gym teacher, and nurse/teacher, and the speech therapist. In Fallsburg, New York (74 children screened) the kindergarten teachers do the entire screening. In Greenwood Lake, New York (67 children screened) the screening is done by two special education teachers, one reading specialist, one resource person, and the school nurse. In Highland, New York (126 children screened), the screening is done by the school psychologist and reading teacher.

Time and Place for Screening

When three-year-olds are screened, it is either at a clinic which may be held within a school or at an outside agency, or as part of the preschool program such as day care, Head Start, or public or private nurseries. In Evanston, Illinois, three-year-olds are seen at their preschool clinic, but the primary target is the child entering kindergarten the following fall. In addition to screening at its learning center, the Evanston clinic team does screening at preschool center sites throughout the community, such as at Head Start and at various day care centers. Periodic Saturday screenings are held for the convenience of working mothers (Holliday, 1975).

Some three-year-olds are screened through a survey. The Division of Special Education in the state of Vermont, in conjunction with the University of Vermont, is planning a survey of preschoolers with a questionnaire to screen for educational handicap. The focus is on children entering school, but information will be collected about three-year-olds too (Vermont, 1975).

Prekindergarteners can be screened in the spring or summer before school entry. Screening may be done on the registration day or by special appointment. If school is in session and regular school staff is used, the personnel involved need to be released from their usual duties. This may be accomplished by cancelling kindergarten classes on screening days, reducing the length of one or more kindergarten sessions, or having the screening after school hours. In all the programs surveyed, only one school district screened after school and on Saturday. This practice was discontinued after one year. In some school districts where the kindergarten teachers screen, aides, specialists, or substitutes take over the class. During the summer, regular school staff and/or specialists may be hired especially to screen. Although this is a more relaxed procedure and the staff can concentrate their full attention on the screening, its drawbacks are that it is more costly and children may be away on vacation. Summer screenings are usually done in the morning when it is cooler, with the staff working with the assessment results in the afternoon. In Wappingers Falls, New York, the children are screened over a six-week period during the summer. The staff works from 7:30 A.M. to 2:30 P.M. and screens by appointment from 8 A.M. to 12 noon, Monday through Thursday. In the afternoon, the data is collated and evaluated. Friday is used for parent conferences.

The screening may be held in the child's home school or in one or more centrally located schools in larger districts. A single class-

Letter to Parents Informing them of Screening Program*

WAPPINGERS CENTRAL SCHOOL DISTRICT

Dear Parents,

This letter is being sent to the parents who have a child eligible for kindergarten beginning September 19____ Its purpose is to briefly describe the Kindergarten Initial Needs Development Program (KIND) so that parent and child will be better able to anticipate some aspects of the first year of school. The KIND program was implemented as of July 1, 1973, for all the kindergarten registered children who reside in the school district.

The KIND Program is an educational plan developed by teachers and administrators in the Wappingers Central School District for kindergarten children. It enables each child to progress at a rate which may better fit his or her developmental and intellectual growth patterns within realistic perimeters of a public school. A child's growth pattern is sequential in nature, but sometimes the rate is uneven. Awareness of *where* each child is in relation to this developmental growth and skills pattern is extremely important particularly at the outset of school.

In conjunction with the KIND program, each prospective entrant will have the advantage of a preschool screening. This preschool screening, which takes place during July and August, is an integral part of the whole KIND program. This assessment function will include screening in the areas of conceptual, linguistic, and psycho-motor development, as well as in various medical aspects. The preschool screening will also assist in the identification of various strengths and weaknesses in the modes of learning of the entering children. This screening will assist the teaching staff to develop a more complete image of the whole child, to build upon areas of strengths, to remediate areas of weaknesses, and thusly to enrich each child's learning environment. In this way each child will have a greater opportunity to meet success at the onset of the school experience.

In order to facilitate the planning for your child's participation in the screening, you will be notified by mail regarding an appointment. This notification will take place approximately 6 weeks after the completion of the April 22-23 kindergarten registration. The screening will be held in a designated elementary school, not necessarily the one he/she will attend in September. It appears at this time that the professional team which will meet with each child will consist of a school nurse/teacher, speech therapist, early childhood teachers and a physical education teacher. The child will spend approximately fifteen minutes with each staff member while the parent will meet with the developmental learning specialist and the school nurse. During this time, you will have an opportunity to share the medical history and your observations and feelings regarding the development of your child. No one knows your child better than yourself. Also, you and your child will have an opportunity to visit a kindergarten classroom and a school bus the day of the screening.

Individual parent conferences will be held on the Friday of the week of the child's screening. The screening results will be shared and explained to each parent at that time and it is not necessary for the child to be present.

Interest has been indicated by many parents regarding the growth and development of

---

*Reprinted with permission of school district.

Figure 11.

children. Three discussion groups on the topic "What Are Five-Year-Olds Like?" have been planned and scheduled for your convenience. It is hoped and suggested that interested parents will find *one* of these discussion groups that is convenient to attend. Dr. Dorothy Hayes, Professor in Education at the State University of New Paltz, will be the speaker. These meetings are scheduled as follows:

Topic: "What Are Fives Like?" (Please attend *one* of these meetings)

Wednesday, March 12, 1975 — Oak Grove School at 9:30 AM
Wednesday, April 16, 1975 — Fishkill School at 9:30 AM
Thursday, April 24, 1975 — Myers Corners School at 7:45 PM

If home and school have a basic understanding on how children grow and learn, how can it be used to formulate early childhood programs? This will be the topic of another program offered to parents. Dr. Lois Nichols, Professor in Education, at the State University of New Paltz will be the speaker. This meeting will be held just on the one date listed and all parents are invited.

Topic: "How Early Childhood Programs Are Formulated"

Thursday, May 9, 1975 — Myers Corners School at 7:45 PM

Between April 21st and May 22nd, the following elementary schools will be holding KIND informational meetings for parents of registered Kindergarten children. These meetings will explain the why and the how of preschool screening in the Wappingers Central School District.

Schedule:

Evans	April 21, 1975	10:00 AM
Gayhead	April 24, 1975	9:30 AM
Brinckerhoff	April 28, 1975	9:45 AM
Fishkill	April 29, 1975	10:00 AM
Myers Corners	April 30, 1975	9:30 AM
Vassar Road	May 1, 1975	9:30 AM
Kinry Road	May 6, 1975	1:30 PM
Oak Grove	May 7, 1975	10:00 AM
Sheafe Road	May 8, 1975	9:15 AM
Fishkill Plains	May 22, 1975	9:30 AM

Your cooperation with school is always needed and appreciated both by your child and the professional staff. If you know of a neighbor with an entering child who did not receive this letter, would you be so kind to share this?

Sincerely,

Richard J. Stapleton
Director of Elementary
Education

room, a group of classrooms, or special rooms may be used depending on the nature of the program. When children enter the district after the screening has been held or miss the regularly planned sessions, one day or part of a day may be set aside early in the term to screen them.

Kindergarten children may be screened in class, but it is more desirable to take individuals or small groups of children to a special location.

Parent Notification of Screening

Parents are usually notified by mail about prekindergarten screening. The letter may give a specific appointment time or request parents to contact someone for an appointment.

In Arlington, New York, the superintendent of schools sent out an initial letter which was followed up by an appointment letter from the building principal. This letter was reenforced by newspaper and radio releases prepared by the coordinator of the screening program. In Wappingers Falls, New York, the director of elementary education sent a letter in February to parents of children identified in the school census as being ready for kindergarten the following fall (see Figure 11). This was followed by an appointment letter in June.

In the "Early Intervention for Children and Parents" Title III project in Union County Intermediate Education District, La-Grande, Oregon, a letter was sent directly to the child (see Figure 12).

The letter to the parents may be preceded or followed by announcements in the media and/or parents meetings called by the school or the parents organization.

In Horseheads, New York, each school in the district had a parents' meeting. The Center Street Elementary School sent the letter shown in Figure 13 before its meeting.

An outline of the prekindergarten parents' night held at the Ridge Road School in Horseheads is in Figure 14.

The state of Missouri guidelines (Missouri, 1973) for screening programs says that community groups and agencies including pediatricians, physicians, hospitals, well baby and mental health

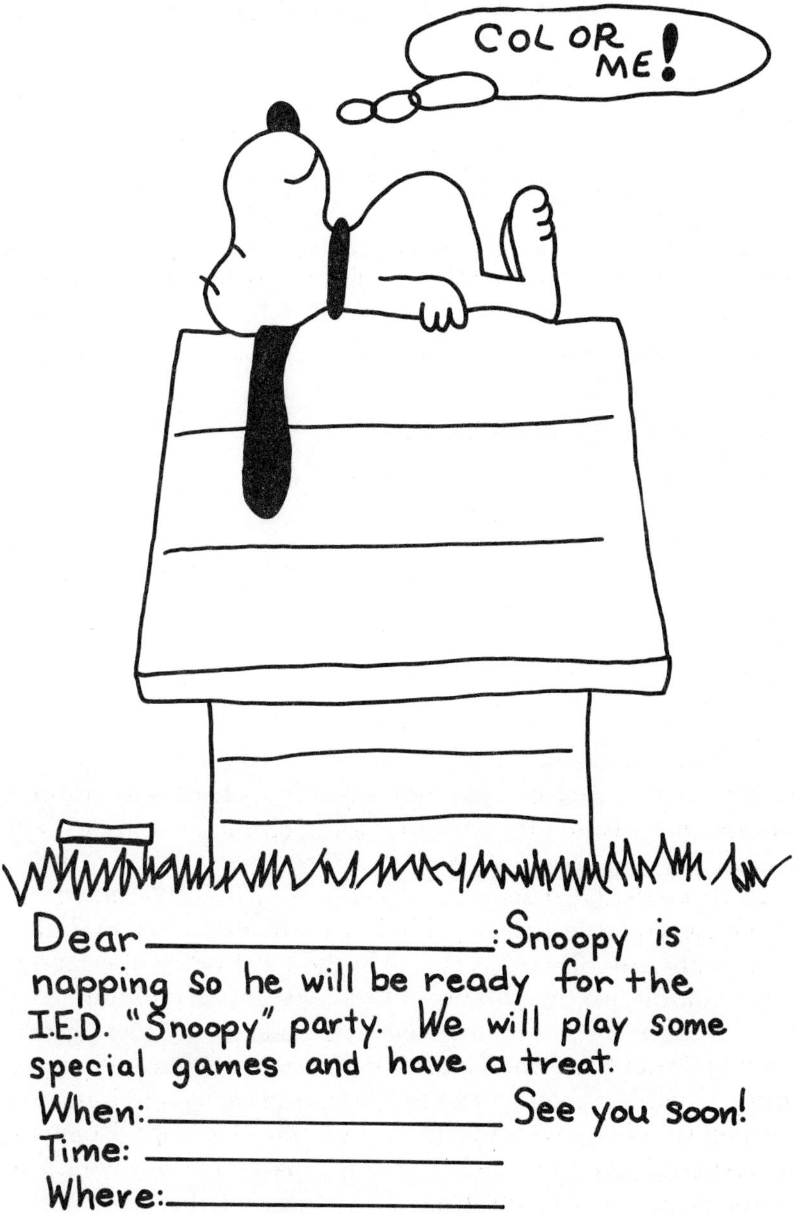

Dear ____________________: Snoopy is napping so he will be ready for the I.E.D. "Snoopy" party. We will play some special games and have a treat.

When: ____________________ See you soon!

Time: ____________________

Where: ____________________

Figure 12. Letter to child. Used in Title III project "Early Intervention for Children and Parents," Union County Intermediate Education District, LaGrande, Oregon.

CENTER STREET ELEMENTARY SCHOOL*
Horseheads, New York

May 31, 1973

Dear Parents and Guardians:

You are invited to attend a pre-kindergarten meeting at Center Street Elementary School Auditeria on June 5, 1973 at 7:30 PM.

A film on "Early Recognition of Learning Disabilities" will be presented. You will also have the opportunity to meet some of our staff and get acquainted with our kindergarten program.

Information will be available to help you to get your child off to a good start in the Fall of 1973.

We sincerely hope that all parents will attend.

Sincerely,

Eugene M. McLain
Principal

EM:hk

———————

*Reprinted with permission of the school district.

Figure 13.

clinics should be informed of the screening. Head Start and other public and private programs providing child care and early education also may be notified.

In Brookfield, Missouri School district has a prekindergarten clinic for children entering kindergarten the following fall. In March an announcement is put in the local newspaper and on radio stations asking parents of prekindergarten children to call the school and leave their names and addresses. Other agencies such as Head Start and County Welfare are contacted for assistance. A letter is then sent to the parents of each child informing them of the objectives and date of the clinic. They are also invited to a parents' meeting which is held approximately one week prior to the clinic. At this meeting, the purpose of the clinic and all pertinent information is discussed. The parents are asked to fill out the standard enrollment forms at this time. All staff members are there to answer questions and talk with parents.

*Prekindergarten Parents' Night**

P E P Program
(Progress in Early Primary)

Ridge Road Elementary School
Horseheads Central Schools
Horseheads, New York

Parents arrive; name tags are acquired.
Introduction — Mr. Norman W. MacLaury, Principal
A. Introduce speakers,
   Mrs. Rosa Lee H. Johnson, School Psychologist
   Mr. Larry Kennedy, Reading Specialist
B. Purpose of the meeting: to explain our innovative practice involving early primary, particularly kindergarten.
C. What is Screening?   Purpose?   Procedure?   Results?
   (Mrs. Rosa Lee H. Johnson)
   1. Hand-out of *Individual Profile Sheet* on each child so they can be followed by parents as information is discussed.
   2. Developmental sheets given out.
   3. Review of tests given in Prekindergarten Screening Program.
   4. Review of kindergarten program.
   5. Role of the school psychologist in the school; particularly concerning early primary children.
D. The Reading Program
   1. The role of the reading specialist
   2. Participation in Prekindergarten Screening Program
   3. How children are selected for program
E. Question Period
   1. General questions
   2. Refreshments served
   3. Specific questions concerning individual child

---

*(Johnson, 1974). Reprinted with permission of the school district.

Figure 14.

Another letter is sent to the parents just prior to the clinic again informing them of the date and other pertinent information. A bus schedule is included at that time.

Parent Involvement — Day of Screening

Parent involvement ranges from staying with the child to active participation in a planned program. Often the parents are asked to complete background history or other types of forms. These forms may have been sent out prior to the screening day and are brought in completed. In some schools, the completion of background history or developmental observations is done with the nurse/teacher, school psychologist, or school social worker. This provides the opportunity for either party to raise questions and discuss matters of concern.

In Peotone, Illinois, the parents receive a questionnaire in the mail which they bring to the screening. On that day, they are asked to fill out control cards and record their child's name and birth date on a name tag which is affixed to the child. The child is then taken to the kindergarten room for play. Toys and games are provided and juice and cookies are served before the screening begins. The parents have an orientation meeting and then coffee is served. The presentation consists of a detailed explanation of the prekindergarten program and reasons for it.

In some schools planned programs are given; in others, staff members are introduced and question and answer sessions follow. In other schools, the parents' socialize and have opportunity to get acquainted. Younger siblings are generally welcome and stay with the parent. Very few programs give parents results or similar feedback on the day of the screening.

Method of Administration

The instrument or technique chosen determines the method of administration. Some published and devised tests lend themselves to be administered in stations. This method has members of a team of examiners at individual stations. The child then moves in turn from examiner to examiner. The DIAL (Mardell, 1975) suggests a team of one coordinator and four "operators" for a twenty- to thirty-minute procedure. In this way it is suggested that six to eight children can be screened in an hour. The Yellow Brick Road (Kallstrom, 1975) is designed to follow the "Wizard of Oz" theme. The child receives admission tickets to the Land of Oz and follows the Yellow Brick Road to four testing stations. The ZEIS may be administered either by one person or by three at three stations.

The use of stations seems to expedite the screening process; at each station there are the necessary materials for that one part, and the examiner may be a specialist or someone specifically trained for that task. Also, the several people interviewing the child will have an opportunity to share impressions of the child's functioning.

There are disadvantages involved in the use of stations: the young child is forced to interact with a large number of new faces and situations; it is more difficult to observe variations in the child's behavior as they try different tasks; and sometimes the child may have to wait between stations and may become restless and anxious. When volunteers are used, a team approach might be more effective if it is coordinated by a professional. Separate records may be kept at each station to be coordinated later, or they may be sent along with the child. Arlington, New York gives the child a check sheet which he carries along from place to place (see Figure 15). The author has not been able to find any research which compares the two methods. Other facets of the program may determine which would be a better choice.

Preschool screening requires the child to come with a parent or other adult. Arrangements have to be made for both parent and child. The first decision is whether the parent will be in the room when the child is to be screened. In some programs it is felt that it is helpful for the parent to observe the child's performance, and arrangements are made for the parent to be in the room. They feel that this procedure is educational, and it is easier to discuss the child afterward. Others feel that separation from the parents is part of the school entry process. It is felt that the presence of parents influences the child's behavior because it is sometimes difficult to prevent the parent from interacting with the child. The time during which the child is being screened provides an excellent opportunity for staff-parent and/or parent-parent interaction.

In the Preschool Screening System, Hainsworth (1974) suggests that the examiner greet the child warmly and do everything possible to make the child feel happy and comfortable. "It should be explained to the child that Mommy (or whoever is bringing the child) will be waiting outside the test room door reading while he

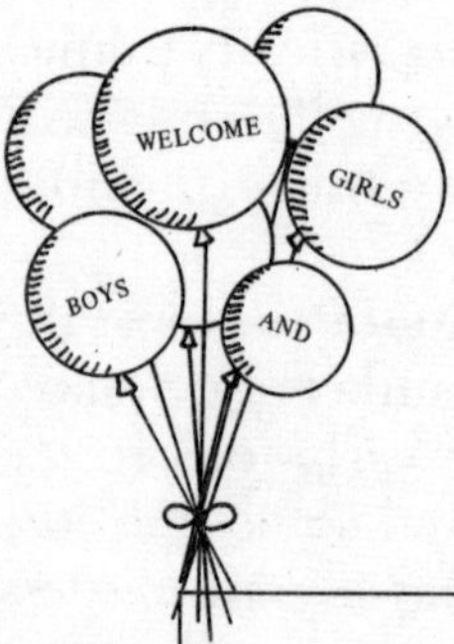

NAME _____

SCHOOL _____

GYM	
SCHOOL ROOM	
HEARING	
SPEECH	
VISION I	
VISION II	
SURPRISE	

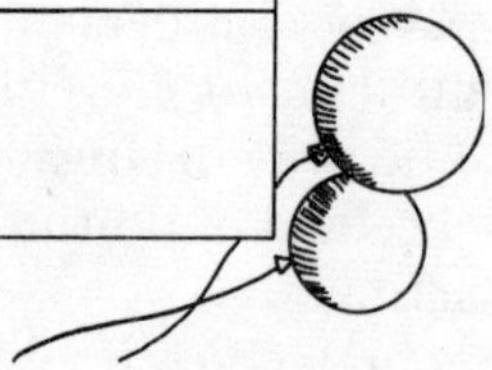

Figure 15.

or she comes in and plays some fun games." Hainsworth says that if necessary, the examiner could tell the child she has a surprise for him, i.e. lollipop, as soon as she has finished. If the child has extreme difficulty separating from the parent, he suggests that she enter the room with the child and if necessary remain during the testing period.

In the DIAL screening, Mardell (1975) has the parents remain in the screening room in a predesignated parent area throughout the screening procedure to avoid separation anxiety. The child is introduced to a play area where he may relax and acclimate himself to the new setting, await his turn, and interact with other children.

In the Wappingers Falls KIND program children participate in a get acquainted session held in a kindergarten room staffed by a kindergarten teacher. After a short period of time they leave the room and go to the different stations set up in five classrooms along a corridor. The parents remain in the kindergarten room to fill out forms and discuss the program.

In Peotone, Illinois as many as twenty children are screened during a one-and-a-half-hour session. Children are tested in individual screening stations, each test taking five to ten minutes. Between tests the children are allowed to play in a kindergarten room. While the children are screened, the parents are in a different room being given extensive orientation concerning the program and are served coffee. In Beacon, New York, the children are seen by one examiner while the parents fill out forms and chat with each other. Waiting children play together in a kindergarten room.

In many programs a reward is given to the child at the end. This may be a piece of candy or a snack, a school-related item such as a pencil or a notebook, or the opportunity to take home something the child may have made while waiting to be seen. Many programs have the child wear a name tag with the first and last name and the child's date of birth. This also may be something for the child to take home. It is the author's perception from experience that the interaction is rewarding in itself and no tangible reward is necessary.

To further identify the child for later discussion, particularly when a large number of children are seen, a videotape or a Polaroid picture of each child may be taken and appropriately identified.

If a child fusses and does not wish to be screened, either another appointment should be made for the child to be seen or an appointment with the parents be made to determine if more information is necessary before interacting with the child again. The results of screening an unwilling child should be considered as not valid. Some children, for a variety of reasons, may just have a bad day; others may need more time and help to adjust to a school-related situation.

Training and Supervision for Screening

For a screening to be effective, specific training of personnel is vital. Screening is a short procedure and everyone needs to work from the same set of instructions. Training sessions may be through workshops or meetings with instruction supported by use of manuals when available. In training to administer the DIAL, for instance, it was found that there was a need for visual devices. An inservice packet was developed which included a twenty-eight-minute color video tape of testing procedures. In addition, slide tape presentations were developed and used. The DIAL team consists of five adults with at least two professionals, one of whom is always a language therapist. Except for these two, it was found that a paraprofessional staff is as effective as professionals as long as they can pass written and performance tests by a score of 80 percent. It was found that team substitutions were necessary for day-to-day operation. Preliminary training usually included a few extra staff persons to fill in for absentees.

In Project First Step, Warwick, Rhode Island, a group of volunteers were trained to do the testing through the use of videotape. This training developed leaders who in turn could train new volunteers. The volunteers, after testing, go on and do other things for the early recognition and intervention program including classroom observations, teaching small groups, making materials, contacting parents, and even running some parent groups.

In Oconomowoc, Wisconsin, screening is done over the summer with a devised instrument. Volunteers are used and are recruited from the Red Cross, Junior Women's Club, Jaycettes, and students from the junior and senior high school. An inservice program to instruct volunteers starts in the latter part of June and continues to mid July. It is conducted by the pupil personnel staff. A screening team has nine members, one staff member from the pupil personnel team, two paid aides including the two who screen vision and hearing, and four volunteers. The vision and screening aides are trained separately. The professional staff member is responsible for the total operation of the program and for giving a presentation to parents while children are being screened. Each paid aide is responsible for the supervision of a team of two volunteers. Volunteers are sent a reminder postcard a week before the scheduled screening and receive a telephone call the day before.

The Miriam School in St. Louis, Missouri uses volunteers and school personnel. They have an initial training session of a minimum of two and a half hours to discuss the goals of the program and to examine the test manuals. There is a demonstration by the trainer of how to give the test, as well as a period of ten days in which the trainees use to practice giving the test to young children outside of the school environment, i.e. neighbors, friends, relatives. A second session is held for the purposes of item by item examination of the tests, discussion, and answering questions raised by the trainees. The trainees are tested by the trainer for administration and scoring of the instruments.

Cost

Costs of screening programs vary greatly. School districts have implemented programs with the only cost being the price of the assessment instruments. The screening was done on school time with school personnel who were made available by reordering priorities and rearranging schedules. Other programs have large budgets and special personnel. These programs are generally funded through federal and state grants. In most instances, it is too soon to tell whether these programs will be continued when the funding is not forthcoming.

It is very difficult to give valid cost figures. One figure informally suggested by a federal agency, without any supportive data, was that the screening would cost about $4.00 a child. One school district budgeted $100,000 for a summer screening program in which almost 1,000 children were seen (KIND, 1973). Another school district screened almost 1,000 children in October of their kindergarten year with no cost to the district. Teachers volunteered their time for the evening training sessions and there was no parent involvement (Newburgh, New York, 1975).

Items which influence the cost of a screening are:

1. type of personnel used
2. availability of personnel
3. use of staff or specifically hired personnel
4. time of year of screening
5. equipment and materials used
6. type of parent program and notification

These items do not include the follow-through program which must be considered before any budget is complete. Too often, the major portion of time and funds is spent in extensive diagnosis and evaluation so that neither time nor money is left to modify educational programs in light of the findings. How relevant a screening program is to the total school program may influence what funds are available for its budget. Despite a high priority, many school systems have such tight budgets that screening programs can only be implemented by rearranging existing resources. Innovative educators are often told that it is a great idea, but could be implemented only as long as it costs no money, and many have gone ahead.

The state of North Carolina developed a vignette "Bobbie Goes to Screening" (Landsberger, 1975) which was prepared as a means of describing to the general public the philosophy and procedures of their screening program. It is reproduced here with their permission.

BOBBIE GOES TO SCREENING

It was not only Bobbie, but Bobbie and his mother who set off down the road to go to Screening. The day had come for the

Screenmobile to get to their part of the county. Bobbie had heard about it for a long time and seen it on a TV show for kids the day before. He'd heard enough to know that it was for him because he was now — ahem! — four years old, and this was for All Fours. There were going to be some fun things there — but it *was* somewhere he had never gone before and — to be honest — he was a little scared of it all. So it was not surprising that on their walk to the little church where they were headed, Bobbie ran ahead of his mother, then turned and ran way back behind her, then ran up ahead — eager, scared, eager, scared — that was Bobbie!

His mother was feeling sort of the same way. She was glad they were going to do something helpful for young children, and she thought it was going to be helpful all right. The first grade teacher in their school was someone they all trusted, and she had asked the people around there to bring in their four year olds. There was a poster about the Screening in the doctor's office and that, too, had reassured her. The lady who had come to see her about coming had assured her that no one had to feel that they *had* to come. But as nearly as she could tell, Ms. Parent (that was the name of Bobbie's mother; oddly enough) felt she should go and take Bobbie and she had signed her name accordingly and been given this appointment. Now that they were on the way, she felt a little hesitant because, like Bobbie, she had never gone to this before. She began to feel quite relieved when she remembered her neighbor would be arriving there with Mary Jo at almost the same time.

When they turned a corner and reached the edge of the church grounds, they could see the Screenmobile parked right by the playground area. There was some equipment which must have come in the van. A big climber and some little sawhorses and boards were set up, and one or two tricycles were sitting there. Bobbie ran ahead to get on the green tricycle, and a young man came out of the Screenmobile to say hello to him and to welcome his mother.

It was his mother they wanted to talk to first, and did so just inside the door while Bobbie tried out the novelties in the play area. She sat where she could see him, and he could see her. Bobbie showed off all the goodies to Mary Jo, from the house next to his, when she arrived a few minutes later. The young man whose name was Dan — Dan Outdoors in fact — remained on the playground and joined in with the four-year-olds to show them how to get started at tossing bean bags at a target painted on the side of the van itself.

Ms. Parent had brought in the paper where Bobbie's physical examination was recorded. This included the testing of his vision and hearing and some of Bobbie's "history" so far, like when he began to walk and when he had had chicken pox and the like. It was a woman from the same county who talked with her now, a Ms. Grownup. There were several questions about what Bobbie liked to play with, whom he played with, and several about his talking.

It was when they got to Bobbie's talking that Ms. Parent felt a little nervous, but at the same time, relieved. Bobbie began to talk more or less at the same time other children do, but it was very hard to understand him, then and now, even hard for her at times. He seemed to want to avoid talking too, especially away from home, and this made him seem shy. Actually, Ms. Parent felt he wasn't really so shy. She and her husband didn't really know whether this trouble Bobbie had with talking was serious or not. Once Ms. Parent began on the topic of Bobbie's speech and their feelings about it, she went on for quite a long time.

Ms. Grownup responded by saying that she would pass along this question about Bobbie's talking to the young woman who would be giving the Denver Development Screening Test to Bobbie in a few moments. Ms. Grownup was sure they had some ways to inquire about this and that they would perhaps decide it would be good to get her to bring Bobbie back for an extra visit. She commented that many children did come back for one or two or even more extra visits. Ms. Grownup said, too, that she thought Ms. Parent would enjoy watching Bobbie and listening to his answers on the Denver to get a picture of how he seemed to be coming along in all kinds of development. She added that Dan would be observing Bobbie in his outdoor play and might express some opinion about Bobbie's speech to add to the other information.

The two of them went to another room to meet Ms. Child who was to go through the Denver items with Bobbie. Ms. Parent went out to get Bobbie to come in to eat a cookie and to see what there was to play with in Ms. Child's room.

It was apparent that Bobbie loved to put a pencil in his hand. He drew a person really impressively, as well as making almost perfect copies of the circle and even the square. Of course when he came to the language items, the going did indeed become difficult, and Ms. Child had trouble attempting to determine what he was saying in order to write it down. She certainly did not want to ask him to repeat too much and maybe have him stop trying to talk, but it was almost impossible to catch the words and know what he was saying he would do "when he was cold," "when he was hungry," "when he was tired." She noted that his hearing seemed sharp, because she dropped her voice to give directions: "Put the block *on* the table," "... *behind* the chair," and Bobbie responded correctly immediately. He went on to have a great time with the balancing, hopping, and ball-playing items.

Ms. Child went in to check with Ms. Chief about whether they were actually finished. Ms. Chief agreed with Ms. Child that it probably would be good to wait until another day to pursue more language testing, and that Bobbie could go back to the playground with Dan and some other children for a few minutes while they talked to Ms. Parent.

Ms. Chief joined in the conference between Ms. Grownup and Ms. Parent at this point. In fact, Ms. Chief went over the record of Bobbie's physical exam and the Denver test as well as the notes Dan had brought in to her about Bobbie's playground activities before he had come in for the Denver testing. It was very reassuring to Ms. Parent, not only to see how healthy Bobbie seemed to be, but to see how very well Bobbie's fine and gross motor development were progressing, and that his comprehension seemed to be so good. He had a grasp of the meaning of different prepositions, and his quick responses to analogies indicated a child who already had learned a great deal about the world around him, and had acquired many of the understandings basic to communication with others. Furthermore, he had played together with great joy on the playground with the other child, though he had spoken almost not at all. He smiled, he beckoned to the other youngster and to Dan, he pointed to one thing and another — but he spoke hardly a word.

It was clear to all that here was a boy who was going to need further examination and probably some help from a speech therapist. Ms. Parent wanted to come back the following day with her husband to talk to them about what they felt was best to do. Ms. Chief wrote down the alternatives which they had arrived at: (1) to return to the Screening Team for more thorough examination, and meanwhile the Parents as well as Ms. Chief would begin looking for a speech therapist who was well recommended for four-year-old boys, or (2) to go directly to the Developmental Evaluation Center (DEC) located in Countyseat, 30 miles away, for their more thorough evaluation and recommendations. Ms. Chief said she would consult with her Regional Supervisor to ask for her recommendations, in view of how long a wait there would be before Bobbie could visit the DEC. She also would inquire all she could about where they might find the probably-needed therapist.

Ms. Chief handed Ms. Parent a small pad of paper and asked her to write down words she noticed Bobbie say clearly during his ordinary home activities. This not only would furnish some additional information but would give Ms. Parent something constructive to do relative to what might be a source of some anxiety. Ms. Chief also made it clear that both Bobbie's father and mother would be receiving some guidance as to how they could be of the most help to him.

They made the appointment for Ms. Parent to come the next day with Mr. Parent who could be home from work by 5:15. Bobbie would of course come, too, because he obviously had had a great time there.

Ms. Parent took home some pamphlets on "How Four Year Olds Play" which looked interesting, and a leaflet which explained whom to contact in their county if they were uncertain or unhappy with the Screening Team's treatment. She made a note to call to say, on the contrary, how much better she felt that her concerns were now out in the open, and that someone was going to help Bobbie talk better.

Going home, too, Bobbie ran ahead and then ran back behind his mother. Now he was eager to get home, but eager to go back to the Screenmobile, too! He asked his mother over and over to tell him when they were going to go back to Screening.

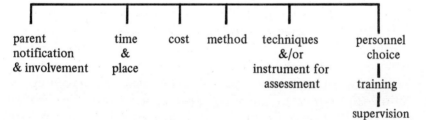

Screening Program

Creation of a Planning Committee

Development of Goals and Objective of Program

Plan for Implementation of Screening

| parent notification & involvement | time & place | cost | method | techniques &/or instrument for assessment | personnel choice |

training

supervision

Figure 16.

Chapter Six

FOLLOW-THROUGH AFTER SCREENING

AFTER the potential high risk child has been identified, the challenge is to be able to help this child in such a way that his risk of failure is reduced. There are three components to the follow-through process: the child, the parents, and the school.

The Child

How does a school determine which children should participate in a follow-through program? The decision will be influenced by the relationship of the goals and objectives of the screening program to the total school program, the size and nature of the population, and the money and resources available to implement the program. Is the screening program to be a short-term remedially oriented project or is it the start of "personalized learning"? The larger the school district, the more precisely the criteria for follow-through need to be outlined. A rule of thumb which a school district might use to establish the percentage of follow-through participants is the percentage of already enrolled students all through the grades who have been of special concern. If that percentage is more than 15 to 20 percent, then perhaps the total educational program, rather than the children, needs to be assessed.

There may be a group of children who do not fit the designated criteria for potential high risk but about whom the screening team feel a degree of uncertainty. For example, if the lowest 10 percent are designated potential high risk, this may be the next lowest 5 to 10 percent. These children may be placed in a "watch and wait" category. Their classroom functioning will be observed, and after a period of time in school a determination may be made as to whether they need to be diagnosed.

Children may not do well during the screening for many reasons. From the screening results, no assumption can be made as to why the child performed as he did, but only that he seemed less competent than other children in his age range. Depending on the nature of the assessment and the clinical knowledge of the assessor, questions may be raised which can initially guide the direction of the diagnosis. These questions cannot be regarded as answers, nor acted upon prescriptively without more information. For example, a child may do poorly on a copy forms task. The author has observed programs where the child is then checked off as needing help in this area and is inundated with activities designed to improve ability to copy forms. What do we know about this child? One thing: he did poorly on the copy form task. Have we asked: Did he attend the question and understand it? Was he hungry, tired, distracted? Did he have difficulty seeing the form? Was his perception distorted? What strengths did he demonstrate? Is he so totally immature that his performance is consistent with his total development? Short isolated performance cannot be assumed to have validity. The screening has identified the children that we need to know more about. The next step, diagnosis, provides the information about the child necessary to confirm or reject the hypotheses that the child seems to be a high risk learner. If the risk is confirmed, then more knowledge about the child and how he learns is needed to plan a personalized educational program.

The goal for the child's program is most important. Too often, the expectation is that some program or technique of short duration is going to take a child at the end of the continuum of special needs and convert him to one who can be successful without any extended extra help. What can one realistically expect as a goal for a child whose special needs are identified early? It must depend on the child and the program possibilities.

Wunderlich (1970) describes three categories of children who experience early learning difficulties:

1. "slow bloomers" — children with uneven or irregular maturation (these children eventually catch up),
2. the persistently immature who consistently remain behind in the maturation process,
3. the perceptually handicapped, brain injured, environmentally deprived, etc. children who have a variable outcome

depending on the quality and quantity of environmental encounters.

A child may be included in more than one group. Children vary in their ability to learn but they are alike in their need to experience success, to be accepted, and to feel reasonably good about themselves.

These elements, therefore, must be embodied in any program which is developed even though these programs vary greatly. Follow-through programs tend to be short-term, ranging from a few weeks to a year, and tend to be more group-oriented than personalized. They often depend on the commercially packaged curriculum. Screening programs for preschoolers seem to have more flexibility. There do not seem to be published longitudinal studies of how these identified children have fared subsequently. The knowledge of how to make a difference through education programming is in its infancy. It is the author's firm belief that any follow-through program has to be flexible, diverse, long-range, and have goals and objectives to assess its progress. To this end, Zeitlin and Nichols (1975) have developed a model for personalized learning which describes a process that can be used in all learning environments. It focuses on the child within the context of the expectations that impinge upon him. It outlines the steps to develop and implement learning experiences within the constraints of the school system of which he is a part. The process is often difficult and time-consuming, but in initial field testing the results have been most encouraging.

The Personalized Learning Model

The model for personalized learning is shown in Figure 17. It is an interaction model based on field theory. The essence of field theory states "whether or not a certain type of behavior occurs depends not on the presence or absence of one fact or a number of facts viewed in isolation, but in the constellation of the whole." (Lewin, 1951). The theory recognizes the interrelationship of psychological and sociological factors. Each child functions within his own constantly changing field. Change in one part of the field results in change of the entire field. Each student's field is

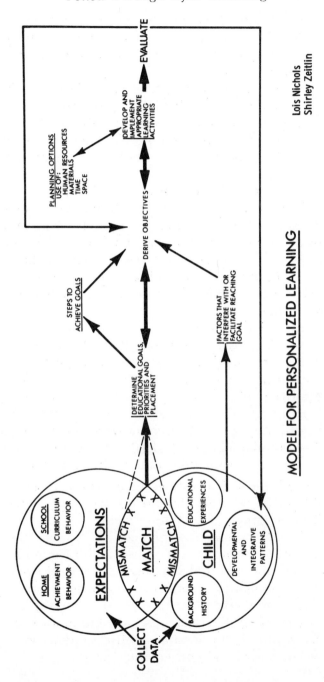

MODEL FOR PERSONALIZED LEARNING

Lois Nichols
Shirley Zeitlin

Figure 17.

determined by his total life experiences and is influenced by the field of those with whom he interacts. This influence and interaction creates a group field which has properties similar to the individual field.

The first step in the process of personalized learning is to identify those parts of the child's field that most influence the educational process, collect information or data about them, and then interpret the data in relation to how it matches and mismatches the expectations of the home and school which are imposed upon him.

The expectations which seem most to influence the child's success in school are the expectations of the home for achievement and appropriate behavior, and the school's expectation for achievement of its curriculum and for appropriate behavior. When these expectations are not clearly defined, the child may be caught in the bind of different and possibly conflicting expectations. A problem also exists when the school and home expectations do not match.

To identify, collect, and interpret data is the definition used in this book for diagnosis (see Chapter 2). The three areas of the child's field that seem to influence his learning potential most are background history, educational experiences, and developmental and integrative patterns.

The American Academy of Pediatrics (1973), in a statement on Early Identification of preschool children who may have learning disabilities, says that children judged to be at risk on screening should have formal evaluations in the following areas:

1. medical, neurologic, and emotional health and needs of the child, including a complete history of the pregnancy, birth, and development prior to assessment;
2. visual and auditory development, including acuity, discrimination, memory, sequencing, and integration;
3. language and speech development, including comprehension, grammatical construction, articulatory ability, rhythm, and voice;
4. ability to integrate visual, auditory, and motor systems;
5. general information level or intellectual development (assessed on verbal and nonverbal tasks);

6. environment for learning, including an understanding of the family's attitudes, priorities, and learning proficiencies.

These six areas may readily fit into the three previously mentioned.

To implement the personalized learning model, data is collected and interpreted. Goals and objectives are derived with appropriate strategies for implementation.

Background History

While everything in the child's life history contributes to his development, certain unique factors are particularly relevant for particular children.

Information on background history is collected through questionnaires, interviews, and examination of existing records and reports. The process may have been started as part of the screening.

Following are areas of information which may be factors in understanding a child's present functioning. Until the information is collected one cannot tell if it may have relevance in understanding the nature of a particular child's educational need.

1. atypical prenatal, natal, or postnatal experience,
2. adopted or foster child?
3. number and age of siblings, number of people residing in home,
4. ethnic and cultural background,
5. parents' age, education, and occupation,
6. family history of disease or learning problems,
7. language spoken in home,
8. quality of family relationships,
9. developmental landmarks,
10. health background, hospitalizations, accidents, high fevers, seizures, or other traumatic experiences,
11. significant factors in the child's physical environment.
12. whether parents are aware of the problem; if so, need age problem was identified and parents' description of the problem.

Identify Educational Experiences

The identified child may have had no, or very limited, formal educational or school experiences but may have had many opportunities to experience himself as a learner. If the learning experiences have been successful, they will have increased motivation to learn, built knowledge and skills, and reinforced the child's concept of himself as a successful learner; of course, unsatisfactory experiences do just the opposite.

If the child has had a preschool experience, information is collected from school records. Interviews and questionnaires also provide information about informal learning experiences.

Developmental and Integrative Patterns

The five areas of development for which information is collected are physical, perceptual-motor, speech and language, cognition, and social-emotional. These areas of development are not independent of each other. The integration of these five factors enables the child to process information, and affects the child's total functioning (Denhoff, 1971). Uneven or atypical development in any of the five areas, or the lack of integration among them, is a major cause of learning problems. The two previous categories relate to the child's past and to the environment with which he is interacting. Information in this category is collected through direct interaction with the child. The ideal situation is to have the services of a multidisciplinary team, each contributing their expertise to the understanding of the child. This ideal team includes the following disciplines: education, psychology, medicine (neurology, pediatrics, psychiatry, endocrinology, audiology), speech and language pathology, social service, and nutrition. Very few schools or communities have the time, money, or personnel for an ideal situation. When no specialists are available, the classroom teacher has to use whatever formal and informal diagnostic tools she has in her repetoire or has access to in various publications.

There are many published assessment instruments which can

be used to collect detailed information about the five areas of information and integrative patterns. These instruments generally require training to administer and interpret; some require certification in a specific specialty. For example, the individual IQ tests such as the Stanford-Binet or WPPSI (Wechsler Preschool and Primary Scale of Intelligence) are administered by a psychologist. Each specialist generally has particular diagnostic tools which he prefers to use.

School personnel who may be involved in diagnosis include the school psychologist, social worker, school physician, language and speech therapist, reading, learning disability specialist, nurse/teacher, physical education teacher, resource room, and classroom teachers. A sampling of published tests which are commonly used by school personnel for diagnosis of prekindergarten and kindergarten children are described in Appendix E.

Some children, because of their particular problems, are not testable by standardized instruments. These children may have severe speech or language problems, or severe physical or behavior difficulties. The clinician may use standardized assessment instruments but must describe the scores as not valid because of stated reasons. This is especially important for individual IQ tests. Information for prescriptive purposes can be collected by using parts of tests which are appropriate for a particular child.

Although this is a tremendous task, there are many things the classroom teacher can do to diagnose a child's need whether specialists are or are not available. The master teacher may have many diagnostic skills which are used intuitively and are based on knowledge and experience with many children. There is an increasing number of packaged programs and books which are commercially available to help the teacher. A concern is that they may be used indiscriminately and mechanistically with concentration on the package rather than the child. Used thoughtfully they can help to raise questions about a child's educational needs and to provide ideas and activities to meet these needs. If diagnosis and prescription could be perceived as one hyphenated word, diagnosis-prescription, it would reenforce the continuity of the process. How a child functions in his learning program is diagnostic data for ongoing educational planning.

In addition to package diagnostic prescriptive programs there are many guidelines and theoretical frameworks which the teacher can use when observing the child. The use of an outline or guidelines help the observer to focus on specific areas of behavior. A sampling of diagnostic tools for the teacher which also have prescriptive recommendations or programs is described in Appendix E.

Diagnosis of atypical physical development, dysfunction, and disease are the province of the medical profession. The school can refer the parents to a clinic or practitioner. The nurse or social worker can help the parents find the resource and provide other assistance where needed for the family.

Each community has resources outside the school which can be utilized for diagnosis. Many communities have directories of these resources.

The collection of information concerning parent's expectations for their child was discussed in Chapter Four. School expectations can be determined through observation and analysis of the educational program and how it is implemented and supported by teachers and administration.

The data collected about the child is interpreted by identifying how it does or does not match the expectations of the school. If the expectations of the school are to match the curriculum to the child, regardless of the child's development, there are no mismatches. If the expectations of the school are that children have age-appropriate readiness for kindergarten, then the child who is very immature or handicapped in a particular area has specific mismatches in terms of being able to succeed with the prescribed curriculum. In the design of a screening program outlined in Chapter Two, personalized learning is in the area of mismatches on the assumption that where there are matches, no special planning is needed for the child. When an entire class is involved in a personalized learning program, the matches and mismatches provide many common areas of instruction for all children.

In a screening program, educational goals are set for the child which will move him closer to matching the curricular and/or behavioral expectations of the school. As an example, an

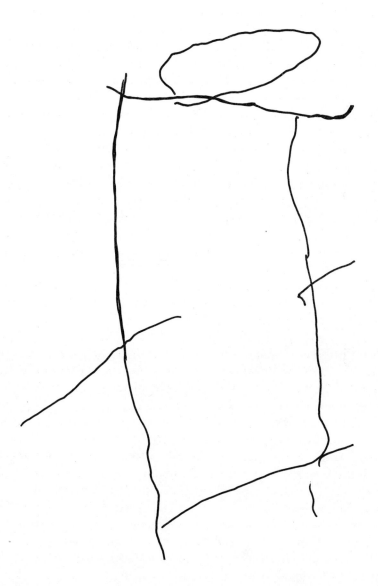

Figure 18. Figure drawing. Jack, age 4 yrs. 7 mos.

oversimplified set of data about Jack will be used. In an initial screening, Jack was found to be in the lowest 10 percent of the incoming class; he scored 41 on the ZEIS (see Figure 18 for his very immature figure drawing). The kindergarten program he is entering is quite flexible; activities are child-centered and directed toward experiencing motor, cognitive, and social learning that will move the child toward learning to read, developing a concept of numbers, and being a responsible group member. Jack has a very short attention span, and his expressive language is limited, often with confused syntax. His visual-motor development is also very immature. The goals set for Jack are: to increase the quantity and quality of expressive language, to improve visual-motor functioning, and to increase attention span. Initially, these goals are seen as equal in priority. These goals, along with typical classroom goals that he might be able to meet, are shared with the parents. Expectations are modified so that Jack will be assessed as successful if he accomplishes the objectives that move him toward these goals.

This example underscores the idea that to implement the goals developed for a child, he is placed in the most appropriate learning environment available.

There are theoretically many options for placement for school-age children with special needs, but in reality it rarely works out that way. Figure 19 describes a hierarchy of placement ideally available. Some schools have used screening as a tool for keeping children who "are not ready" from entering school without providing any alternatives. In a few instances of chronologically young and immature children who just need more time this may be appropriate, but they are the exceptions rather than the rule. With the concept of mainstreaming gaining increasing support, effort is made to have children who are at all able to cope to be in a typical classroom at least part of the time. They may attend a resource room part of the day or go out of the classroom for periods of time for tutoring or other special programs.

The next step in the process of personalized learning is to derive objectives from the goals. Two aspects are considered: the steps to achieve the goal, and the factors within the child's development and experience which facilitate or interfere with reaching the goal.

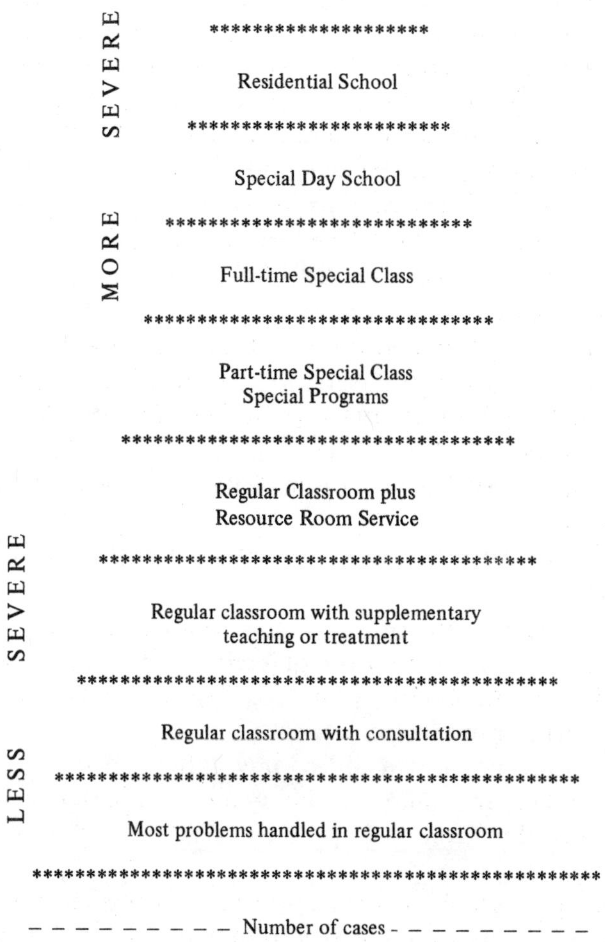

```
    E                 *********************
    R
    E                   Residential School
    V
    E                ***********************
    S

                      Special Day School

    E              ****************************
    R
    O                 Full-time Special Class
    M
                  ********************************

                      Part-time Special Class
                         Special Programs

              ***********************************

                      Regular Classroom plus
                      Resource Room Service

    E       *****************************************
    R
    E         Regular classroom with supplementary
    V                    teaching or treatment
    E
    S     ********************************************

                Regular classroom with consultation
    S
    S   ***********************************************
    E
    L       Most problems handled in regular classroom

      ***************************************************

      – – – – – – – – Number of cases – – – – – – – –
```

Figure 19. Hierarchy of placements for children with special needs. Adapted from M. C. Reynolds (1962).

For example, to achieve Jack's first goal, to increase quantity and quality of expressive language, some of the steps are to develop a larger vocabulary, to talk more, to use proper word order, and to develop a sense of English grammer. Some of the things that interfere with achieving this goal are a limited vocabulary, a preferred motoric mode of responding, poor auditory memory,

difficulty with auditory discrimination, limited language models
at home, and a late start in talking. Some of the things that may
facilitate Jack's reaching the goal are good intelligence, active
curiosity, high motivation, a cheerful manner, a special interest
in animals, and a desire to interact with other children and adults.

From the analysis of the task and the knowledge of the child's
strengths and weaknesses, objectives are derived. Initial objectives
to help Jack achieve the goal — to increase quantity and quality
of expressive language — might be:

- to speak in whole sentences;
- to increase ability to use words to make needs known;
- to increase the number of words known to describe objects;
- to increase the amount of spontaneous talking he does in the
  classroom;
- to improve short-term auditory memory for three-part verbal
  instructions;
- to learn to discriminate between common sounds in the environment.

The next step in the process is to develop appropriate learning
experiences to implement the objectives. The experiences developed will depend on what planning options can be utilized in the
child's learning environment.

These options or variables may differ greatly in different
schools and environments and may tend to change over a period
of time. An educational plan is only as useful as its potential to be
implemented.

The implementation of a specific learning experience for a
child in a kindergarten classroom may require planning for appropriate time, space, materials, and an available helping person,
or may depend on the awareness of the staff of the type of experience a particular child needs and their ability to capitalize on
spontaneous situations. For example, to implement one of Jack's
objectives, to increase ability to use words, to make needs known,
a ten-minute small group activity can be planned, two times a
week, where role playing is used in the housekeeping corner to
talk about different activities that are being carried out. The
helping person can facilitate the talking by asking appropriate
questions and occasionally modeling appropriate responses.

The same objectives can also be implemented by the teacher, when interacting with Jack, by not responding to his nonverbal expressions of needs and when necessary helping him to phrase his statements and occasionally supplying a needed word.

Within each school and classroom there are variables that can be managed that allow for a degree of flexibility in a program. Key variables that have the potential to be managed are time, materials, human resources, and space.

Time

Time is unmanageable; it moves inexorably and children are in school for a set number of hours and days in the week. There are many ways to manage the time available, but all of them require preplanning and making decisions on:

- amount of time spent on one activity each day;
- number of days spent on an activity;
- amount of time spent on each aspect of an activity;
- amount of time spent in a particular placement or grade;
- time of day planned for an activity.

Materials

How many teachers have thrown up their hands in despair and exclaimed "Oh what I could do to help Johnny if only I had such and such material"? Classroom materials can often be created very inexpensively from "junk" or readily available material to be used to help meet a specific objective. For example, everyone is familiar with the 1001 uses of an empty egg carton. Many funded screening programs have created guides for materials and activities developed in their programs. An example is "The Project First Step Information Processing Curriculum" (Title VIG, B, 1974) developed by the Hainsworths as a result of their program in the Warwick, Rhode Island schools. This curriculum includes six volumes of resource materials. Common toys and games, generally perceived as "play" material can often be utilized to help achieve specific objectives.

Human Resources

Human resources include the whole range from highly trained specialists, to volunteers, to other children in the class. It is an unmanageable variable when specialists are not available in a community or school policy does not support the use of volunteers or teacher aides. Elementary, junior, and senior high students have all been used as helpers in the classroom. Even in kindergarten, peer teaching is possible; a child who has mastered a skill can help a child who has not. Experiences can be planned for individuals, small groups and the entire class. It is not always necessary for an adult to be directly involved.

Whatever resource people are used, it is important that they have a positive attitude toward the child and be willing to accept him as he is.

Space

Use of space is initially determined by the place or places available. In these places, space can be utilized in many ways. For example, is the room filled by desks in a row or by a variety of learning centers? Can the child who is highly distractable find a place to work? Is there space for activities which require lots of movement? Can a corridor or outdoor area be used? Is the classroom extended by trips into the community? Space can be rearranged as often as desired.

In most school situations, the four variables of space, time, materials, and human resources have some potential for being managed in a way to facilitate more personalized programming. The flexibility, teaching style, and administrative support given to the classroom teacher will influence her ability to manage these and other resources.

To complete the personalized learning process, the learning experiences are evaluated in two ways: how well they have achieved the stated objectives, and what impact they have had on the total functioning of the child. If the objectives are not met, new experiences may be planned, or after several tries the objectives may be reexamined to determine if they are really the most appropriate initial steps to reach the goal.

If the objectives are met, then the impact on the child is examined. If the goals are still appropriate, new objectives to move the child closer to the goal are set. Evaluation takes place as often as the classroom teacher feels it is necessary.

Development of follow-through programs for the child is a slow tedious process, both in terms of helping the child and in developing a satisfactory program within a school. The prognosis and the amount of time needed to help a child succeed varies. Statistically based research does not always measure the value of a program. For some children, to grow an inch is much harder than for other children to grow a foot. In the case study of Eddy described in Chapter Two, progress has been slow and is measured by how adequately he meets the immediate objectives set.

Examples of Follow-Through Programs

The utilization of the personalized learning model as a process is a goal for follow-through programs. Knowledge and experience are gained through sharing the successes and failures of the developing screening programs throughout the country. The following are some examples of follow-through in existing screening programs.

In a Greenwich, Connecticut screening program, diagnosis was done in a five-week diagnostic summer program (Humes, 1975). Of the 697 children screened in the spring of the kindergarten year, sixty were identified as potential high risk. These children were invited to attend one of two 2-hour daily programs. During that time, the children participated in appropriate diagnostic procedures and activities in each school under the direction of a team of four specialists: a learning disability teacher, a physical education teacher, a school psychologist, and a speech and language therapist. Basically, through the services of each of the four specialists a concerted effort was made to identify specific strengths and weaknesses in order to establish effective diagnostic and prescriptive teaching procedures. During the first few weeks, each team member contributed specific diagnostic information based upon observations and administration of instruments measuring fine and gross motor skills, vision, visual and auditory perception, language, and cognition. As more information was obtained, greater attention was given to the specific area or areas of deficits by including the child in those programs which would be most beneficial. Most often, children were seen individually or in small groups. All children, however, were assembled as a group at various times, for example for language-oriented opening and closing activities, snack time, and occasional playground time.

During the five-week period, two parent interviews were conducted by the psychologist. At the end of the program, a report was sent to the pupil's home school. It included the diagnosis and recommendations for an educational program in first grade.

In Anchorage, Alaska (Title VIG, ESEA, 1973), those children identified in kindergarten through screening programs as being high risk were placed in "modified primary classes" which had a maximum of fifteen children. Each teacher of a modified primary class, with the assistance of the specialist in psychological evaluation and the project director, was responsible for making an individual educational diagnosis of every child in the class and for developing, with the assistance of the learning disabilities specialist, an educational prescription which is consistent with the diagnosis and the curriculum outline. The individual teachers in the classes were responsible for analyzing the results of the screening process for each child and for using further formal and informal diagnostic procedure.

Peotone, Illinois (Title III, ESEA, 1971) had three placement options as follow-through of their prekindergarten screening. Children identified as having severe learning problems were given a thorough diagnostic evaluation consisting of a psychological battery, a social history, and a classroom observation. These children were placed one-half day in a learning disability classroom and one-half day in a regular kindergarten classroom. Each learning disability kindergarten was staffed by a learning disability teacher and a teacher assistant. Each class was limited to a maximum of fifteen children. Remediation was provided in six general areas: speech, language, audition, vision, fine and gross motor development, and emotional-social development.

Children whose screening test scores indicated that they possessed learning deficiencies yet who did not qualify for the learning disability kindergarten, were scheduled for special instruction in the regular classroom. A professional diagnostic team consisting of a speech therapist, a social worker, a psychologist, and a staff of learning disability consultants provided special educational services to children enrolled in regular kindergarten classes.

Consultant services were available to teachers for all children in the regular kindergarten classes throughout the school year. These services included inservice workshops, demonstrations of teaching materials and techniques, assistance in establishing parents' volunteer programs, and consultation in instructional planning.

In Warwick, Rhode Island, Project First Step had a flexible program of placement ranging from a fortified kindergarten program to what they call a developmental kindergarten for children who have moderately severe information processing deficits or behavioral organization difficulties. This class had fewer children and more individualized programming than the regular kindergarten (Denhoff, 1971). The most severe learning problems were placed in a demonstration class for diagnostic teaching. The child moved from one placement to another as his needs changed.

To help the identified preschool child, special programs have been created. In Appleton, Wisconsin, approximately 1,000 children were screened in the spring prior to kindergarten entrance (Title VIB, ESEA, 1971). Children who seemed to have special needs were enrolled in Title I summer school classes. In the fall, forty-seven children were enrolled in a preacademic oral communication program. Most of these children attended only this half day class. Some children attended kindergarten in addition and thus were in school all day.

The Ferguson-Florissant School District in Missouri, (Title III, Sec. 306 ESEA, 1974-1975) conducted a Saturday School for all four-year-olds in their district. The program had four parts: diagnosis, a morning or afternoon session, school on Saturday, home teaching visits for children with special problems, and parent follow-up. Children identified through screening as having handicapping conditions were mainstreamed within the program. Those children requiring individual attention for a portion of the day were worked with by high school or college student volunteers, under the supervision of the classroom teacher. Children with extremely severe problems or handicaps usually needed the full attention of an adult. Specialists or instructional aides provided the one-to-one relationship. Saturday School teachers conveyed pertinent information about each student to the kindergarten teacher who received him. Special services continued for former Saturday School students with hearing problems. Elementary guidance counselors followed up on those children who needed further service.

In Chesterland, Ohio at the West Geauga Local Schools, follow-through activities of the screening program are conducted in a separate classroom by trained mother volunteers at each school. The skills are both on a group and individual child basis and utilize a wide range of purchased and self-constructed instructional materials. The plan established for each child is of a prescriptive nature which is evaluated on a daily basis by the volunteers after bi-weekly goals are established by the classroom teacher, mother coordinators, and mother volunteers. A daily log is kept for each child by the volunteers. This provides a record of the task, and level of performance of the child on each of the tasks. Interim evaluations are also completed by the mother volunteers at the mid-year and end of the year. The elementary counselors and psychologist work closely with the volunteers to help with those children presenting severe learning or behavioral adjustments.

Des Plaines, Illinois did a research to determine what would be a most effective way to follow through their screening (Bradley, 1975). This small stable suburban community near Chicago has a multiethnic school population ranging from lower to middle upper class. The screened population (1971-72) was divided into two groups; 435 children in experimental group A and 406 children in experimental group B. The population of 804 children screened the year before (1970-71) served as the control group.

In the control group no test results were given to the kindergarten teacher. In the experimental group, after the pretest was administered, the kindergarten teachers were given the results of the screening test. A learning profile on each child was compiled in the areas of visual-perception, gross motor, and auditory perception. The results were evaluated and interpreted by a team of specialists which included the kindergarten teacher, the speech therapist, and the learning disability teacher. The child's specific deficits were discussed and learning styles studied. A coordinated resumé of the pertinent information of each child's strengths, weaknesses, and maturation level was compared with the district's developmental norms (statistics gathered over a five-year period of administration of the Des Plaines Kindergarten Screening Test).

The design of experimental group A was similar to that of the control group. The difference was that the teachers were given the pretest results, a profile on each child, and an evaluation and interpretation of the results.

Experimental group B had the same design as experimental group A except that one extra dimension was added. The children in this group were divided into four groups according to the common deficiencies that needed remediation. After every two-week period, each pupil's progress was evaluated. If the behavioral objective was reached in the given skill, he was moved to another area in which he needed improvement. This team approach started in November and ended in May.

During the two remediation periods the specialists concentrated on teaching deficient skills rather than depending on the child to learn the skills incidentally from the regular kindergarten program. The extra planning time used in developing specific objectives as well as selecting and preparing teaching activities did not seem to show the benefits in furthering or broadening each child's potentials. The data revealed that there was no significant difference between experimental group A and B. The prescriptive remediation and the extra time allotted for working with groups of children did not indicate any appreciable gain over the regular kindergarten program. The results reenforce the need for a personalized integrated approach to follow-through programs rather than a group approach. It is necessary to diagnose the individual child at every step of the way if he is to be moved on a continuum to achieve the goals set for him.

The Parents

Involvement with parents is the second component of the follow-through program. Parents were notified of the screening, and there may have been some prescreening meetings and/or parent involvement on the day of the screening. When the screening is completed, notification of the results to parents of all children involved generates good feeling between the school and the community. Notification of results should not be in terms of specific scores or results but rather a generalized statement such as "Your child performed successfully in all areas of the screening." Schools may provide the opportunity for parents to discuss their child's results even though no concern has been expressed. A letter to the parents may include a general statement such as "If you would like details concerning your child's direct performance, please feel free to contact us" or the letter may direct them to call the appropriate resource person such as the school psychologist or elementary school guidance counselor for an appointment to talk about their child. In Evanston, Illinois a letter is sent to all parents of children screened inviting them to call if they would like the results (see Figure 20). Some parents seek this reassurance or look for help with other child-related problems.

Dear _____

The staff of District No. 65, Program in Early Childhood Development appreciates your allowing your child _____ to participate in the screening program and would now like the opportunity to share the results with you.

Please contact me at (telephone number) at your earliest convenience. If I am not in, please leave your name, number and the most convenient time to return your call.

Thank you for your cooperation.

Sincerely,

Figure 20. Letter to parents. Evanston, Illinois (1974).

When the screening raises a question, parents need to be advised about the next steps. If a referral outside the school is to be made, such as for vision or hearing, it is important to tell the parents that a child's questionable results are just that and that there may or may not be a problem. The visit to the specialist will determine the answer. Diagnostic procedures in school should also be explained to parents. A disservice is done when an air of mystery surrounds school behavior. It creates unnecessary anxiety and ill will. It is just as inappropriate to use scare tactics and make unwarranted statements like: "Your child is emotionally disturbed," "a slow learner," "immature," etc. A description of behavior and the implication for learning is more appropriate. When a special need has been identified, in so far as possible, there is an obligation to the parent to communicate the information personally.

Many pilot programs, screening as well as others, relating to educating young children, involve the parents through informational meetings, individual and group counseling, training the parents to work with the child at home, and involvement in the school program.

In Wellesley, Massachusetts (1969-70) the psychologist had individual conferences with preschool parents. When the children entered kindergarten, the psychologists formed a Mother's Discussion Group which met regularly for over a period of six weeks. Parent discussion groups are important in enlisting the cooperation and involvement of parents in developing a good start for every child in the school.

If a child has a problem, counseling is directed toward helping parents understand the nature of the child's problem and the implications for the child in school and at home. If a parent understands the impact of an atypical child on the functioning of a family he may develop his insight and hopefully decrease his sense of guilt. This in turn will help the child.

In the Ferguson-Florissant School District in Missouri, a theme of their preschool screening program is "Parents as Partners" (Ferguson-Florissant, 1974). The Saturday School described earlier in the chapter uses parents helpers in the classroom program. Parents are expected to assist at least once very two months. Parents continue the learning experiences of the Saturday School with skill-developing, fun games, and activities at home through the week. A weekly home activity guide provides ideas for things to do at home that relate to the skills being emphasized at school. Following is an example of an activity taken from their guide:

> Show your child an apple (orange or lemon, etc.). Ask: "What do you think is inside the apple?" Cut the apple in half and show him the seeds. "What would happen if we planted the seeds?" Show a picture of an apple tree. (You may want to plant the orange or lemon seeds. Citrus seeds usually sprout indoors). Then, place on the table: apple seeds, a picture of an apple tree, an apple, and a picture or a product made from apples (pie, juice, etc.). Ask: *"Which comes first? What next?"* Let him place the items in proper sequence as you discuss them.

Home teaching visits of thirty to forty-five minutes are regularly scheduled by the teacher to work with an individual child in the program or a few neighboring children and their parents. The home teacher helps the parents to set appropriate expectations for the child's learning behavior. Evaluation results indicate that their program of parent involvement has resulted in an increased understanding of parents as evidenced in their attitude toward the child. Parents were found to be more accepting of their children; aware of their children's needs, using positive motivation and reinforcement techniques; and were more competent in their interaction with the children. Approximately 75 percent of the parents fulfilled at least their miminum commitment to the Saturday School and approximately 80 percent were found to be using learning activities with their children in the home.

The Rockwood School District in Portland, Oregon also has a program called "Parents as Partners" (Title III ESEA, 1973) where parents are used as aides, clerical helpers and as listeners to individual children in the prescriptive education which is part of their screening program. Children are assessed in September and October and then there is post evaluation counseling for parents regarding the findings. There are also weekly parent meetings in the early evening. Baby or childsitting service is available. Topics discussed include child development, coping, understanding the child, and normal and abnormal behavior. The evaluation of the parents' participation included the statement that "to parents who participated, the school is no longer a threatening agency;" it had become an extension of family life. The parent's participation continued through first grade. A research study was done which compared the reading achievement of matched pairs of students whose parents took an active participatory role and those who did not. The percentile rankings from the total reading section of the Metropolitan Achievement Test were used for the analysis of differences which existed between groups. The children whose parents participated had significantly higher scores (at .01 level of significance).

The Parent Education Readiness Program (PREP) developed in 1973, was used in Detroit, Michigan to identify four-year-old children with a high risk of school failure and planned a program of intervention by training the child's mother to teach him at home and enrich the home environment. In the fall, all children who were four by December 1 were screened. Forty-eight children were selected based on indication of potential learning problems and parental willingness to serve. Preference was given when the child was the oldest in the family. Preparatory workshops for the parents were held. Four groups of twelve four-year-olds met once each week for two and one-half hours in demonstration groups, while their parents observed the techniques. One teacher worked with the children while another worked with the parents. Assignments were given to parents to follow daily routines at home which were geared to the individual needs. The assignments included visual-perceptual exercises, auditory discrimination, language training, local field trips, etc. Both parents attended a series of evening group parent sessions with a school social worker to discuss child management techniques, aptitudes and other relevant topics. Research and evaluation data indicated that highly significant gains were made by the participants in comparison to a matched group of nonparticipants.

Many screening programs include education of all parents such as the one in Oconomowoc, Wisconsin, (see Chapter 7) where there are regularly scheduled meetings and parents are informed through leaflets and other printed material distributed before or during school registration or at the time of screening.

Home training programs for young children with identified learning disabilities, language lags, and mild mental retardation have been encouraged by schools and agencies. Generally, specific activities or ways of interacting are taught to the parent who then tries it at home with the child. The following is an example of activities suggested to parents, for interacting with a child who has a problem with language development (Lowenthal, 1974-75).

> The child should be encouraged to ask for things, rather than just pointing to them; for example, before giving him a cookie, have him try to say the word. Experiences and real objects will help a child comprehend his world and increase his vocabulary. The grocery store is a good place to point out names of cans of food, fruits, vegetables, meats, etc. A "pretend store" can be set up at home with empty food packages. The child can be encouraged to name these and classify them as to whether they are fruits, vegetables, etc. A picnic game can be a good device to strengthen short-term auditory memory and verbal expression. The parent says, "I'm going on a picnic, and I'm bringing peaches." The child then repeats this and adds a food of his own, and so on back and forth between them.

Not every family situation lends itself to the home program approach. Neifert (1973) describes four types of families where it may not work. The first family situation is when the mother feels that something is wrong with the child but receives little or no support for her views from the father. A second type of family in which home programs often fail is the family in which a power struggle exists between mother and child. The third type is the multiple problem family. This type of family has so many other problems that the potential for success of a home program is questionable from the start. The fourth type of family is one with a large number of children. The mother usually cannot find time to implement a home program because of the demands of her normal function in every day family life.

Parent Organizations such as Association for the Help of Retarded Children and Association for Children with Learning Disabilities augment school programs of parent education and involvement with their own counseling and educational programs. Ideally, there is a mutuality to the school and organization effort. The parent is an important member of the educational team for all children. For children with special needs, parent involvement is essential. To overlook the parent is often to make the child a pawn of the anxieties and expectations of the school and home.

The School

The third component of the follow through is the use of the information from the screening to assess and improve the existing educational program for all children.

Analysis of the Group Data

An item analysis of the screening data shows strengths and weaknesses of the total class in particular areas. The screening provides information on the range of abilities in the total group. Two years of testing on the ZEIS in a small urban school district is graphed in Figure 21. The shape of the curve is typical of the school districts that comprise the ZEIS normative study (see Appendix D). There is a bell-shaped curve with a "tail." The "tail" generally comprises the potentially highest risk population. The curve will peak and skew at different points for different populations. Specific instruments may facilitate the observation of relationships between relevant characteristics. For example, do most children who have language problems also have discrimination problems? What percentage of the population functions significantly different in one sensory channel over the others? This information can influence the type of learning experiences developed for the class.

Examination of Existing Programs

Programs need to meet the needs of the learners, not vice versa. The group results can be used to see if there is a match between what is being taught and what the present population is ready to learn. The screening committee may be used or a new committee can be formed to examine the screening results and compare them to the plans for the kindergarten year. It is important to remember, when evolving any plan, that children cannot be helped

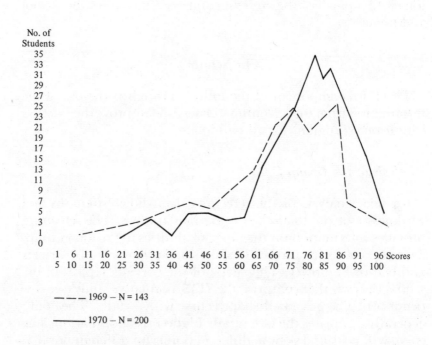

Figure 21. 1969 and 1970 kindergarten screening of a small urban school district using the ZEIS.

individually or collectively in a kindergarten which is not child-centered. In many schools there is little communication between grade-level teachers, and a diversity of programs and philosophies may coexist. Screening programs often facilitate a sharing and the development of some common goals and also a more cohesive group of teachers and, hopefully, administrators.

The increased awareness of the teacher to various aspects of a child's behavior helps her to observe each child more carefully and recognize commonalities and differences. The observation of the child and examination of the curriculum help the teacher to structure the environment more effectively to achieve the desired learning.

Many of the pilot programs described in this book were the result of initial experiences with screening. Most of these projects have been supported by federal funds and many have become models for other schools to duplicate. In one school district which had an extensive screening program, the screening committee with specific information to support their requests came up with two major recommendations which were accepted by the Board of Education:

1. the necessity for a greater variety of suitable teaching materials to better meet the wide range of individual differences, and
2. the hiring of two developmental learning specialists to work with the teachers to implement personalized learning programs.

How to keep records and report to parents in ways that reflect the child's growth and strengths and weaknesses was a problem that was identified in many screening programs.

Inservice

Classroom teachers generally have minimal formal education in helping children with special needs. Screening programs often identify valid areas of learning in which these children need to grow, either in the classroom or in other devised programs. Inservice courses can be arranged to help the staff develop the necessary skills. One day or several session workshops using the school specialists or specialists in the area are helpful. Arrangements can often be made with local colleges for credit courses taught in the school district.

Teachers must be encouraged and supported to try new teaching and learning methods and techniques. When several teachers in a school are sharing the learning experience, they become resources for each other.

Evaluation

Evaluation is the assessment of the ways in which objectives for the program were met. Through evaluation procedures, programs can be continuously examined and improved, and when necessary the objectives revised or changed. Tools for evaluation are questionnaires given to parents and/or teachers, informal

Wappingers Central School District

Preschool Screening Parent Questionnaire
November, 1973

1. How did you gain your initial knowledge of the
    KIND Program?

    a) Informational meeting (ex. PTA, etc.)_____
    b) Newspaper releases_____
    c) Letter indicating the appointment time for
        the Summer Screening_____
    d) Other_____

2. Is this your first child to attend kindergarten
    in the Wappingers Central School District?
                                    YES_____ NO_____

3. Did your child enjoy the experience at the pre-
    school screening? (Based upon the child's re-
    action at that time)   YES_____ NO_____
    COMMENT:_____
    _____
    _____

4. Did the visit to school, the school bus experi-
    ence, etc., help your child feel more secure
    and/or comfortable in coming to school?
                                    YES_____ NO_____
    COMMENT:_____
    _____
    _____

5. Do you feel that the parent conference held on
    Friday during the Summer gave you helpful in-
    formation regarding your child?
                                    YES_____ NO_____
    COMMENT:_____
    _____
    _____

6. During the parent conference this summer, were
    you made aware of a possible strength or weak-
    ness in an area such as Speech, Vision, Hearing,
    Enrichment, etc.?
                                    YES_____ NO_____
    COMMENT:_____
    _____
    _____

7. If you were made aware of any follow-up mea-
    sures to be done early in the school year, are
    you now aware that it is being done?
                                    YES_____ NO_____
    COMMENT:_____
    _____
    _____

8. Since school has begun, have you been made aware
    of any area where a strength or weakness may
    exist which was *not* identified in the preschool
    screening?

Figure 22.

                                                    YES_____ NO_____
IF YES, PLEASE COMMENT:_____

_____
_____

9. What additions or changes would you recommend
    to be included in the preschool screening?

    a) With regard to your child_____

    _____

    b) With regard to the parent_____

    _____

10. How do you think we could best inform the
    parents of the KIND Program in the *future*?
    a) Informational meeting (ex. PTA, etc.)_____
    b) Newspaper releases_____
    c) Letter indicating the appointment time for
        the summer screening_____
    d) Other_____

11. What additional suggestions and/or comments can
    you offer to strengthen the preschool screening
    program? General comments regarding any area
    of KIND thus far: (preschool screening - which
    includes the parent conferences, grade level
    meetings, November parent conferences, etc.)___

    _____
    _____
    _____
    _____
    _____

                              Name:_____
                                    (optional)

discussions and observations, and pre- and post test results. In Wappingers Falls, New York (KIND, 1973) both parent and teacher questionnaires were used for feedback (see Figures 22 and 23). The initial screening was held during the summer, and 1,028 questionnaires were distributed in November at the first parent conference for the kindergarten children. Four hundred and fifty-eight (45%) were returned; of this number, 399 (87%) wrote in one or more comments or suggestions. Generally parents expressed satisfaction with the program, as did the teachers.

As screening programs are relatively new, and there is little longitudinal research to support one set of choices over another, each school must evaluate its own program and make decisions about any redesign needed. It is through the cumulative experiences of several years of trial, analysis, and redesign, where appropriate, that effective programs develop.

WAPPINGERS CENTRAL SCHOOL DISTRICT
PRESCHOOL SCREENING KINDERGARTEN TEACHER QUESIONNAIRE
November 1973

NAME_____ SCHOOL _____

1. What area(s) of the Preschool Screening have been *most* beneficial in your planning for each child? Please explain:

2. What area(s) of the Preschool Screening have been *less* beneficial in your planning for each child? Please explain:

3. What area(s) of the Preschool Screening could be of more benefit to you in your planning? (include either *new* areas or areas which should be tested in more depth) Please explain:

4. Do you feel that the Preschool Screening and the contact made with the home during the Summer assisted you with the November conference(s) you have just completed?

YES_____ NO_____

Please explain:

Figure 23.

KINDERGARTEN SCREENING PROGRAM

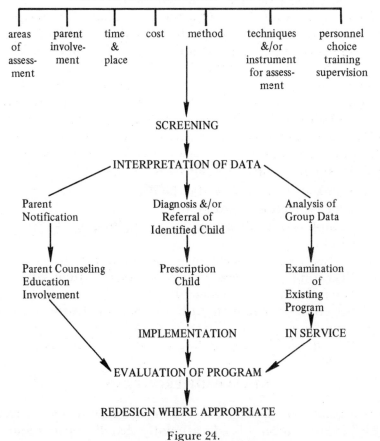

Figure 24.

Chapter Seven

PREKINDERGARTEN AND
KINDERGARTEN SCREENING PROGRAMS

$\mathbf{T}$HERE is no ideal kindergarten screening program. Pilot programs throughout the country are developing a body of knowledge and experience which can be used to develop increasingly effective programs. The projects described in this chapter were chosen because each has an emphasis or characteristic that merits consideration for program development. The descriptions of all the programs but one are from literature, and from letters and discussions with the program directors. The author is directly involved with the program at New Paltz.

The programs described range from screening and diagnosis to comprehensive parent involvement and preschool programs. They are all based on the assumption that the earlier and better you know the potential high risk child and his family, the greater the child's potential for successful learning experiences. In this chapter, the following programs will be described:

1. Statewide Program — Maryland.
2. State Guidelines — Missouri.
3. Comprehensive Preschool Screening Program — Evanston, Illinois.
4. Early Parent Involvement — Oconomowoc, Wisconsin.
5. Year-long prekindergarten program of parent education and screening — Ransomville, N. Y.
6. Screening Program in an Urban School District — Grove City, Ohio.
7. Personalized Learning Program — New Paltz, N. Y.

STATEWIDE PROGRAMS

Some states are passing laws requiring screening programs for early identification of educationally handicapped children.

140

Other states are establishing guidelines which encourage school districts to set up screening programs. Maryland has a law requiring screening and a state-wide program to implement it. Missouri has a law that guarantees every child the right to an education that is appropriate to his developmental needs. To assist the schools in identifying the needs of children at an early age, the Missouri Department of Education developed guidelines for each child.

Maryland

Section 98C, added to Article 77 of the Annotated Code of Maryland by House Bill 234, mandates evaluation for the purpose of identifying learning disabilities and the development and implementation of appropriate educational programs by January, 1975. The law states:

> 98C. Programs to evaluate students entering primary grades; education programs for disabled students.
>
> (a) The State Board of Education shall cause to be developed and implemented a program to be administered by the boards of education of the several counties and of Baltimore City whereby each student entering his first year in any primary grade in any public school is evaluated for the purpose of identifying learning disabilities, regardless of etiology.
>
> (b) The State Board of Education shall provide guidance and coordinate the development and implementation of education programs based upon the needs of disabled students in the public schools in Baltimore City and the several counties of Maryland. (1973, ch. 519)

To implement this program the Maryland State Department of Education (1975) has established a model plan and guidelines. The basic plan includes procedures for conducting early screening of all students, administering continuous assessment of students, and developing instructional strategies based on the screening and/or assessment findings. The screening uses the expertise of the classroom teacher and draws on information from parents. This first phase has six components. A parent interview/ checklist which is used starts out by advising the parents of their rights, that they have the right not to respond to anything which they feel may invade their privacy. The questions cover five areas: family, general information, environmental information, health information, and developmental information. It is recommended that this be completed at kindergarten registration or early in the school year. Approximately eight weeks after the child has entered school, the teacher completes the Maryland Systematic Teacher Observation (see Chapter 4 — checklists). The instrument contains thirty-six items within the five basic areas of development: psychomotor, sensory/perception, language, cognition, affect/motivation. When the need for further observation is indicated by the first two instruments, a third instrument called "The Intense Observation of Behaviors" is used. This form lists additional classroom behaviors (symptoms), appropriate teaching strategies and accompanying instructional strategies in the five basic areas (see Figure 25 for sample page). The fourth component is the use of published instruments of tests selected by local central office staffs for further diagnosis. The fifth component is prior data records from vision and hearing tests which are on file in the school. The screening program is coordinated by the principal who organizes an educational management team.

The second phase of the screening program is the educational assessment. This phase provides for the approximately 15 percent of students who are expected to need individualized services.

In-depth diagnosis is provided by appropriate specialist(s) who may be school-based or system-based. They will recommend and administer appropriate tests. It is then required that an Educational Management Plan be written and implemented by the specialists and a school team. This plan is developed in a team conference of involved personnel. The curriculum should be comprehensive in nature and include the five basic developmental areas.

The educational management team may decide that some children should bypass Phase II and move directly to the third phase of the program which is "to provide comprehensive and in-depth services (assessment and/or educational) unavailable in local education agencies but accessible through interagency and community services"(Maryland, 1975). To accomplish this, the local

Sample Page of Instructional Strategies in Maryland Screening Program

Other Classroom Behavior Characteristics for the Teacher to Observe	Classroom and Teaching Strategies that Teachers Should Use with Children	Kinds of Materials
Visual	The teacher will:	
Child holds materials too close to eyes or too far away	1. check classroom lighting 2. ensure the child is seated so as to see materials 3. ensure materials are clearly reproduced and print is of adequate size for a child this age 4. ensure instructional materials are posted at the child's eye level	
Child consistently squints eyes	5. recommend for further screening of vision (Phase II)	
Visual-Motor		
Child has difficulty in stringing beads	1. ensure the child has adequate vision 2. check for refinement of small muscles 3. provide experiences with clay, fingerpaint, paints and brush, scissors, paste, and other manipulative materials	manipulative materials, art materials, scissors
Child has difficulty in manipulating puzzles or similar materials	1. ensure the child has adequate vision 2. check for refinement of small muscles 3. provide experiences with clay, fingerpaint, paints and brush, scissors, paste, and other manipulative materials	manipulative materials, art materials, scissors
	4. have the child pick up or sort out objects; e.g., buttons, nails, screws	nails, buttons, screws

Figure 25.

principal and other appropriate specialists meet with the parents to discuss a student's referral to the appropriate agencies. The principal implements the referral process, which is defined by the local school system.

The plan calls for annual review in each school system by a committee appointed by the superintendent and includes a representative of the Maryland State Department of Education. The plan includes preservice and inservice training of school personnel, with preservice activities including orientation sessions for the total school staff and parents concerning the plans, objectives, and dynamics of the screening program. In-service work includes in-depth training of the staff for delineation of roles and building of competencies. Special emphasis is given to the role of the classroom teacher.

Missouri

In August, 1973, law HB 474 was passed which guarantees each child the right to an education that is appropriate to his educational needs. A screening program is seen as one way of assisting the schools in identifying the needs of children at an early age. In 1973, the Missouri State Department of Education published "Guidelines for an Early Childhood Screening Program." The purpose of early screening of children ages three through five as described in the guidelines is "to identify suspected physical, behavioral, and educational problems that may interfere with their ability to achieve success in school. A screening program, which should be offered to all children, is also intended to gain better understanding of the diversity and variability of their developmental levels."

Screening is defined as the use of relatively simple devices which are valid and reliable in terms of determining relative normalcy, and is administered on initial contact with the population. Intervention initiated on the basis of the test results should lead to "a significantly different effect than if deferred to the time when the problem would be normally identified."

The goals of the screening are: to develop public awareness for the need for early identification, to assist parents and teachers to become more knowledgeable of the variability in early childhood development, and to plan educational programs of a developmental nature for children so identified to be carried out at home, at school, and in the community.

The guidelines suggest procedures for organizing early screening programs. Schools or community agencies can implement the program; a cooperative arrangement should exist between the two. Broad procedures for implimentation of the programs are included. National and state resources are listed, such as mental health, speech and hearing associations, associations for retarded, blind, crippled children, etc. These listed agencies have directories which list services and, when appropriate, licensed or available practitioners.

Suggested screening instruments, as well as procedural outlines for vision and hearing screening are listed and described. Parent involvement is seen as an important component of all programs.

The following four programs are described as possible models for program development:

The Kansas City Model is carried out by the Southeastern Jackson County Mental Health Association. In this program, volunteers are trained to administer the Denver Developmental Screening Test (Frankenberg and Dodds, 1967). This model is seen as an outreach model and appropriate to communities having fewer professional resources available.

The St. Louis Model is an agency-based model, having the availability of many professional resources. It is carried out by the St. Louis Department of Health, Mental Health Division, through their Child Health Clinics. As part of each three to five-year-old's health examination, the Denver Developmental Screening Test is administered. Following the administration of the test, the results are shared with the parent either by the psychologist or social worker. Depending on the needs indicated, the parents are counseled in ways in which they can close the gaps in their child's development, or they are referred to an appropriate community resource. It is the agency's intent to make the results available to the child's school upon entry.

The Miriam School Model is based on a pilot program initiated in 1972 which utilizes local school personnel and trained volunteers for screening. The parents are invited to a prescreening orientation meeting. All results of the screening are reported to the parents as well as to the school. When the results are reported to the parents, suggestions for further evaluation, educational planning, and other types of referrals are appropriately made.

The Brookfield Model is a screening program implemented by a school district serving a small town and surrounding rural area. In the spring before kindergarten entrance, a prekindergarten clinic is held at the school. The staff for the clinic is the elementary school principal, two kindergarten teachers, elementary counselor, speech therapist, school nurse, and kindergarten teacher aide. The broad areas evaluated by a devised instrument at the screening are: cognitive development and skills, motor skills, language and speech development, social-emotional development, and attention to task and work habits. After the screening, the staff has a conference on each child and then letters are sent to parents of all children. Parents of children who seemed to have a special need are invited to a conference where the findings and recommendations are explained. A six-week summer program is one alternative used for helping the identified children with special needs.

By 1974, 50 percent of the schools in Missouri had initiated screening programs. In response to the needs expressed by the schools for a comprehensive assessment measure to be used at kindergarten entrance, the Early Childhood Education Section of the Missouri Department of Elementary and Secondary Education has developed the Missouri Kindergarten Individual Development Survey (KIDS) (Mallory, 1975). This instrument is designed to be given by the kindergarten teacher or other examiners in approximately thirty minutes, in either spring or early fall. The test surveys development in number concepts, language, verbal concepts, paper and pencil skills, auditory-visual skills, and gross motor skills. The Missouri KIDS is prepared for machine scoring, with the results for each child and the class returned to the teacher. A parent questionnaire is included to obtain additional relevant information. This questionnaire is optional, to be used at the discretion of each school district. KIDS will be included in the statewide testing program in September, 1976.

Evanston, Illinois

Evanston has a school-community preschool clinical program which includes screening, diagnosis, intervention programs, and interaction with the school that the child enters.

Background

The project was started in 1971 through funding by Title III, Sec. 306 ESEA. Illinois public law 323 which required school districts to provide education for handicapped preschool children became effective July 1, 1972. This focused on the need to find procedures to identify this population and develop programs for them. The Evanston community does have a variety of resources but all areas of need were not being met. The program attempts to bridge the gap between already-existing resources in the school and community and the needed services for preschoolers.

Program

The goal of the Evanston program is "to identify the relative strengths and weaknesses of the individual child and to prescribe instructional programs that will build on the strengths and supplement the weaknesses (and), minimize the likelihood of youngsters being labeled (Holliday, 1974). The objectives of the project are:

• to screen on a multidisciplinary basis virtually all preschool children three to five years old prior to kindergarten entry,

• to identify through diagnostic evaluation children for whom failure or problems in kindergarten are probable for necessary treatment and/or referral,

• to identify the talents and resources of handicapped children in the district,

• through diagnostic evaluations, to initiate intervention programs to meet individually identified needs (physical, social, cognitive, language and emotional) prior to kindergarten entry,

• to facilitate the coordination of efforts of a range of community agencies directed toward the amelioration or prevention of personal and social problems,

• to provide the administration and kindergarten teachers

with information about the entering kindergarten children,
- to provide kindergarten teachers with the background necessary to understand and take into account individual differences among their pupils.

One aspect of the program is to create a better fit between the child entering school and the school itself. This means bringing about changes in the schools to better meet the needs and strengths of all children in the community as they enter the school system.

To implement the objectives, screening is done in the following specific areas: gross motor/perceptual development, fine motor/perceptual development, cognitive or learning development, speech and language development, social-emotional development, and vision and hearing acuity. Diagnostic evaluation is done for children showing weaknesses in those developmental areas. When appropriate, the staff provides intervention in the form of individual or group therapy, recommendations to parents and teachers, and/or referral to Evanston agencies for additional services. Information and recommendations relative to a child's strengths and weaknesses are made available to the kindergarten teacher when the child enters school. In-service seminars and practicum are provided for preschool, Head Start and kindergarten teachers and paraprofessionals. These seminars provide information about the child's growth and development within a multidisciplinary framework. They assist the teachers in identifying, describing, and analyzing ethnic, racial, cultural, and organizational obstacles within the school, which prevent compatability between the child and the school. In the inservice course, a specific project is developed in the school which is designed to eliminate incompatability or improve compatability between the child, the school, and the community. At these seminars a learning program is planned which is designed to assist in the development of the preschool or kindergarten child's potential abilities.

The program functions as a coordinating and liaison vehicle through which community agencies, already working at providing special services for children of preschool age, can maximize their efforts through formal cooperation with the school district. Referrals are made to and accepted from such agencies. A Community Advisory Council facilitates this effort. Figure 26 illustrates the processes involved in the program.

The center staff consists of a program director, program coordinator, curriculum developer, program evaluator, psychologist, nurse, learning development specialist and educational therapist, speech and language clinician, and professionals-in-training.

The screening for the entire school district is done at the center and is voluntary. Parents arrange for an appointment and bring their child. The primary target population each year includes all children entering kindergarten the following fall. A secondary target population includes the remaining children, three to five years old, whose parents or preschool teacher requests the screening because of a concern about the child's development.

The program operates within the following schedule: Mondays, Tuesdays, and Wednesdays are used for intervention at the project Learning Center and/or at Preschool Center sites throughout the community, such as Head Start and daycare centers. Therapy ends at 2:30 on Wednesday to allow for team therapy planning and staff meetings. All day Thursday and Friday until noon are designated as screening times plus an occasional Saturday for the convenience of working parents. After the Friday morning screening, time is allotted for staffing children who were screened and for diagnostic planning. Friday afternoons are used for diagnostic evaluation of children exhibiting weaknesses on the screening.

Screening is done at six stations. Appointments are scheduled for six children within an hour. Each child is involved for approximately forty minutes. The staff devised their own screening instrument which they call the Screening Instrument for Evaluating Developmental Skills (SIEDS). It is based upon existing developmental norms in the areas of speech and language, fine motor, gross motor, and cognitive development plus tasks that would evaluate the child's perceptual skills. The parent is urged to bring the child to the screening so that parent-child interaction can be observed, and the parent is asked to complete a social-emotional evaluation. When the child is reluctant to participate, the parent may accompany the child through the screening

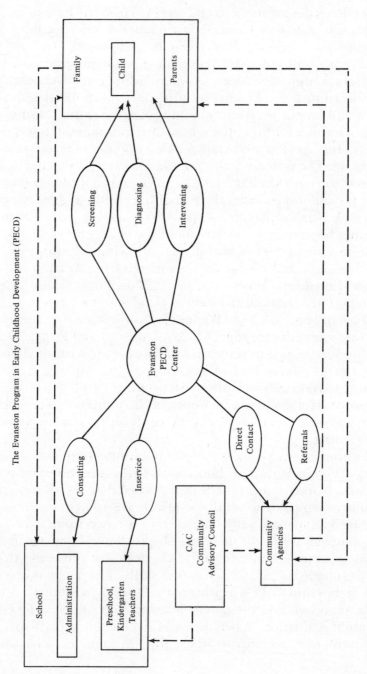

The Evanston Program in Early Childhood Development (PECD)

Figure 26.

(Holliday 1974)

stations. At the staff meeting after the screening the status of the child is determined. Three categories are used: pass, follow-up, or watch and wait. Those children designated as "Pass" have performed satisfactorily in all of the screening areas, and no concerns have been expressed by the parents or staff; the parents are notified of this by letter. No additional contact is made with these children or their families. At any time, the detailed screening results may be obtained by the parent, or by the preschool teacher with the parents' consent. The following September, the child's screening results, presented in terms of relative strengths, are disseminated to the child's kindergarten teacher.

The "Follow-up" category is for children who need to be contacted following the initial screening. They may have demonstrated weakness in one or more of the screened areas or a specific concern has been expressed by the parents or staff.

The "Wait and Watch" is for those children who either demonstrated a minor weakness, had difficulty completing the task, or for reasons such as immaturity or illness had to terminate the screening. In the last two categories, an appropriate staff member is chosen to contact the parent and suggest the next steps. That staff member is then responsible for coordinating that child's follow-through program. Formal and informal diagnostic procedures are used for follow-up. In formal diagnosis appropriate specialists will see the child for diagnostic testing. Testing is not always possible because of the inappropriateness of a test for a particular child or because the child is unable to cope with the test. In these cases informal diagnosis is made during the initial therapy sessions. The staff presents activities, starting at that level where the child has success, and proceeds with tasks which become increasingly difficult, until it can be determined where the child is functioning.

The intervention program consists of three alternatives depending upon the child and the nature and severity of the weaknesses shown in the screening. In instances where they are relatively mild, no formal diagnosis is made but recommendations are made to parents and teachers. These recommendations are in the form of activity packets devised by the staff in the areas of gross motor, fine motor, cognition, and language. These children would be recontacted in four to six months and a reassessment made.

If a child's needs, as outlined by the diagnostic evaluation, cannot be met by the staff and can be better served by a community agency, then the child is referred accordingly. Community resources are primarily used for long-term therapy, for medical evaluation, or for consultation.

The third intervention is enrollment in a therapy program. Children enrolled in individual or small group therapy usually have more severe problems and need a concentrated and structured program. Treatment may be recommended for any one or combination of the screening areas: speech, cognition, fine motor, gross motor, and social-emotional. Again, one staff member is responsible for a particular child, but if the child has weaknesses in more than one area, he may see other staff members during therapy, or one teacher can provide all therapy while getting consultation from another professional on the staff. Prior to the therapy session, a lesson plan is prepared for each child; it includes objectives for the day, activities selected to accomplish these objectives, and comments corresponding to the activities. Three afternoons a week there are multidisciplinary group therapy sessions where the room is divided into three areas: speech and language, fine motor, and gross motor. Ten children who have difficulty in more than one area participate in these sessions. The children are divided into smaller groups and spend about fifteen minutes in each area working with staff members.

During these group sessions, the nurse conducts a parent involvement group. The parents also observe the children in the therapy session so that they can be actively involved in the child's program and give feedback on the child's progress. When a child is enrolled in therapy, ongoing evaluation is conducted. Rescreening is attempted at six-month intervals wherever possible.

Kindergarten teachers directly receive information on their children who were screened by the program. An appointment is made during the spring to arrange for a meeting the first week in September between each kindergarten teacher and a program staff member. During this meeting the teacher receives a computer print-out of relative strengths on each child in her room who participated in the screening. The teacher also receives a narrative written profile on those children who receive some type of follow-up. This report includes a summary of the implemented intervention progress noted and staff recommendations. Certain social-emotional cases are sent directly to the district's chief social worker. Vision and hearing screening results are forwarded to the individual school nurse. The speech and language information is given directly to the school district's speech clinicians.

The program in early childhood screening is a comprehensive preschool screening program which focuses on identifying relative strengths and weaknesses. It involves the parent, child, and school in helping the child to achieve success in school.

Oconomowac, Wisconsin

The Oconomowac program involves parents from the time of the birth of the child and provides resources for education and support through the preschool year. The parents have an active role in the screening and follow-through program.

Background

Oconomowac, Wisconsin is a village-like, lake community nearly midway between Madison and Milwaukee. It has a population of about 20,000, with seven elementary schools with 2700 students K-6 and a teaching staff (K-6) of 129. In August 1973, Chapter 89 of the Laws of Wisconsin was passed. This law guarantees the right to public education for all children with exceptional educational needs and includes a provision for screening of each child when he first enrolls in a public school district.

Even prior to this law the schools sought to identify children with special educational needs and to establish a relationship with the parent and the child from birth through an integrated effort with the local hospital and community agencies. In 1970, the school district published a forty-page booklet entitled "Getting to Know You," subtitled, "Your Child between the Ages of 0 to 3 years." The writing of this booklet was a joint effort of the school, the local hospital, the Department of Health, and the

Visiting Nurse Association. The book describes developmental activities and child-rearing information for each age range and includes such things as sleeping and eating habits, signs and symptoms of illness, developmental milestones and age-appropriate toys (with suggestions of how to make these). This book is distributed in the maternity ward of the local hospital and to other individual parents as needed, based upon contacts by the pupil service staff members.

The second fifty-three page booklet developed is entitled "Helping Children Through Their Tricycle Years" (1970) and is given to parents as they bring their children to the preschool screening program.

The school district has conducted a prekindergarten screening program since the summer of 1967. Their present program was developed from a continuing evaluation of their cumulative experience.

Program

The Screening program has two parts:
1. Project HAPPE (Home Aid for Parents in Pre-School Education), a Title III ESEA project;
2. Early Childhood Screening Program for three and four year olds, a Title VIB ESEA project.

The goal of Project HAPPE is to develop a comprehensive program in parent education related to the health and management of preschool children. To accomplish this goal they have implemented or are in the process of developing the following programs:

DIAL Harmony is a phone aid for parents of preschool children. Harmony is a library of taped consultations dealing with common concerns about raising preschoolers. Each tape is a three-to five-minute recorded message prepared and reviewed by professionals in the field. The topics include medical, dental, nutritional and general concerns, safety, developing skills, and several tapes under the headings of "Parents are Important Too," "Working Together," "Anticipating Important Events," and "Building Emotional Strengths." There is an advertised phone number which is available seven days a week, twenty-four hours a

day. A pamphlet describes each tape and gives an access number.
The parent selects the tape he wants to hear, calls the telephone
number, and asks for the tape by number.

Partners in Growth is a series of audio-visual programs dealing
with issues concerning the health and development of preschool
children. Each program is ten to fifteen minutes long and has
been designed to provide information and practical suggestions
for those working closely with preschool children, including parents, teachers, and babysitters. Titles of some of the programs are:

- **Time to Talk** — language development, birth to three years
- **Grow Baby Grow** — newborn care and stimulation
- **Mirror, Mirror** — developing self-image and self-confidence,
     birth to five years
- **Just For Fun** — importance of play three through five years

Programs are now being developed which will screen to identify and intervene in health and developmental problems that
could affect learning for ages eighteen months through four
years. A hospital program is planned to work in cooperation with
hospital personnel to conduct maternity ward discussion groups.
A program of community parent discussion groups will also be
established related to the general goals of the project.

The Early Screening Program is for children aged three to five.
The goals of this program are:

1. identification of handicapped youngsters,
2. involvement of parents in the educational process,
3. parent education,
4. plans for early intervention and remediation.

Screening is seen not as a program, but as a step prior to programs. "Screening can be considered as a way of identifying individual needs so that the needs can be matched with the program
that will best meet those needs" (Oconomwoc, 1974). To initiate
the screening, mailing lists are compiled from the school census,
and a letter is sent to the parents giving the time blocks for different attendance areas and requesting the parents to call for an
appointment.

The parent is seen as a prime evaluator of his own child. The
parents are asked to complete four questionnaires relating to

health and general development, developmental status, hearing, and social-emotional development. Included in the screening procedure is a parent-child interview with the nurse. Some of the questionnaires are completed at home, others during the interview. The developmental status questionnaire is completed by the parents at home prior to the screening (see Figure 27). This instrument has the additional purpose of allowing the child to have some initiation to the screening procedures prior to arriving at the screening site. The children are screened at six stations for gross motor behavior, language assessment, receptive discrimination (perception) vision, hearing, and general development. The parents are encouraged to accompany the child if they so desire, or if the child wants the parent with him. The parents are asked to sit behind the child but in such a position that they may observe the procedures. The assessment instruments used for the screening are the Cooperative Preschool Inventory (Caldwell, 1970), a devised language assessment and gross motor evaluation, the Developmental Test of Visual-Motor Integration (Berry 1967) the Verbal Auditory Screening for Children (VASC), and the Keystone Visual Survey Test.

The parent-child interview is held after the child finishes the assessment.

The interview provides an opportunity to clarify any negative indicators and to observe the child's interaction with his parents. It is also an opportunity to discuss any concerns that the parent may have regarding the child's development and to discuss services for preschool children offered by the district and the community.

At the completion of the screening, the parents are informed that as soon as the results are evaluated they will be notified of any problem areas. Parents of children who show no problems are sent an appropriate letter, while parents of children who indicate possible problems are contacted for further assessment. Parent evaluation cards are mailed to the parent along with the results letter (see Figure 28).

This program is used to identify children who are eligible for special assistance under Chapter 89, and children who are eligible for other early intervention programs. Those who are suspected of

```
                    Oconomowoc Public Schools
                    Early Childhood Screening
                         Home Screening

Name_____ Age Yr.____ Mo._____
```

Please have your child try the following activities.
He may not be able to perform all the activities.
The directions may be read twice but additional help
should be avoided.

Please bring the complete form with you to the screening.

Read these directions to your child and record his
response:

		Correct	Incorrect	No Response
1.	Point to your neck.	—	—	—
2.	Close your eyes.	—	—	—
3.	Put the toy car under the box.	—	—	—
4.	What does a doctor do?	—	—	—
5.	Show me which way a ball will fall.	—	—	—
6.	How many feet do you have?	—	—	—
7.	Which is bigger; a man or a boy?	—	—	—
8.	What color is grass?	—	—	—
9.	Count to 5.	—	—	—
10.	On the back of this page, have the child draw a picture of himself. (May also be a picture of mother or father.)			

Figure 27.

Assessment Form Completed by Parents

Oconomowoc Public Schools
Early Childhood Screening

1) How long were you at the
   screening site?   __ 50 min. __ 60 min.

2) How did your child react
   to the length of the   __ bored   __ tired
   screening?   __ happy

3) Upon arrival home, did
   your child talk about
   screening as a happy
   experience?   __ yes   __ no

4) Would you recommend
   continuing the screen-
   ing in the future?   __ yes   __ no

5) What is your overall
   impression of the
   screening   Negative   Positive
   (circle one)   1 2 3 4 5 6 7 8 9

COMMENTS:

Figure 28.

having a problem are referred to a multidisciplinary team for further assessment. The preschool consultant and the speech clinician, when language is involved, meet with the parents either in the office or make a home visit to plan activities and a summer program at home for parents and children. The parents of children eligible for specially funded programs are so advised.

In the Oconomowoc Project parents are perceived as prime educators of the child, and partners in the school educational team.

Ransomville, New York

The Ransomville program is a year-long preschool parent education and child readiness program which includes a screening.

Background

Ransomville is a small rural community in northwestern New York state. It is part of the Wilson Central School District which incorporates segments of five towns and has a school population of 2,200. There are two elementary schools, one of which is the Stevenson School which has the described program. It has 425 children with two half-day kindergartens taught by the same teacher.

Ransomville has no nursery schools or regular preschool programs. Homes tend to be far apart and young children often have no available playmates other than siblings. The majority of the parents are blue collar workers. Approximately 25 percent of the school children receive free lunches or other partially subsidized meals. In 1970 a parent education and child readiness program was established to acquaint both parent and child with the school personnel, to share expectations, and to provide opportunities for some prekindergarten experiences. At the same time, a volunteer mother program was established. A checklist form was used to match parents interests and availability to the school's needs. Parents were used for such diverse purposes as helping in the classroom, clinical duties, and baby sitting for parents' meeting. The screening program was added in 1973.

Program

There is a year-long bi-weekly program for parents and children who will enter school the following September. At each meeting there is a program where the parents meet with various school personnel and are provided with information "on ways that they can better prepare and ready their child for school the following year." (Mallast, 1975) While the parents are in session, the children are in a different room and have a program of readiness activities. Parents with babies are encouraged to use the provided baby sitting service which is supervised by volunteer mothers. Car pools are encouraged by sending a map and names and addresses of all families involved. Each meeting is forty-five to fifty minutes long (see Figure 29 for schedule of meetings).

Stevenson Elementary School
Preschool Program 1974-1975

DATE		PARENTS	ROOM	CHILDREN	ROOM	BABYSITTING
Sept.	12	Orientation & Bldg. Tour - Principal & Supt.	Portable	Librarian	Library	Room 114
	26	Health Services	Portable	Phys. Ed. Dept.	Gym	Library
Oct.	10	Psychologist	Portable	Art Dept.	114	Library
	24	Speech Therapist	Portable	Librarian	Library	Room 114
Nov.	7	Food Services	Portable	Reading Dept.	Library	Room 114
	21	Librarian	Library	Music Dept.	Portable	Room 114
Dec.	5	Art	114	Phys. Ed. Dept.	Gym	Library
	19	Reading Dept.	Portable	Art Dept.	114	Library
Jan.	9	Psychologist	Portable	Reading Dept.	Library	Room 114
	23	Physical Ed.	Portable	Art Dept.	114	Library
Feb.	6	Kdg. Testing Program	Cafeteria	Music Dept.	Portable	Library
	20	Music Dept.	Portable	Phys. Ed. Dept.	Gym	Library
Mar.	6	Speech Therapist	Portable	Librarian	Library	Room 114
	20	Bus Safety	Cafeteria	Principal & Bus Driver	Cafeteria	Library
*Apr.	10	Bus Safety	Portable	Reading Dept.	Library	Room 114
	24	Film: "Learning Disabilities - Early Recognition"	Cafeteria	Art Dept.	114	Library
May	8	Psychologist	Portable	Phys. Ed. Dept.	Gym	Library
	22	Kdg. Teacher	124	Music Dept.	Portable	Library
June	5	Program Evaluation - Principal	Portable	Librarian	Library	Room 114

NOTE: On April 10th, children will have the experience of riding the school bus to school. They *will not* be taken home after the preschool session is completed. It is the parents' responsibility to see to it that their child is taken home.

Figure 29.

The preschool readiness program involves resource and supportive personnel from the district. Insofar as possible, those staff members are scheduled to have the regular meeting time open so that they can participate in the program as needed. Parent volunteers also assist as teacher aides at all readiness sessions.

Starting in January through April, six children are scheduled at each meeting at fifteen-minute intervals to be screened. Screening is done at four stations: (1) hearing and vision, (2) drawing, (3) motor coordination, (4) general knowledge using the School Readiness Survey (Jordan and Massey, 1969). The parents complete questionnaires about family and social history and the behavior and development of their child.

After each child has been screened, the school psychologist looks over the results and identifies children who may have special needs. The principal meets with each parent for a twenty to twenty-five minute conference and discusses the results. He, when appropriate, may make recommendations for referral for vision and hearing or suggest activities for the parents to do with the child at home in a problem area.

At each parent meeting the speaker distributes mimeographed handouts relating to the topics under discussion. At the end of the year parents have a complete preschool handbook. The handbook includes suggested readiness activities, books parents might like to read to their children, good health habits, suggestions for language development, motor activities, etc. A parent evaluation form for the whole program is distributed at the June meeting and used as one tool to reassess the program each year. The results of the screening are given to the kindergarten teacher in June so that she may familiarize herself with the children and plan the program for the following year. She particularly observes the children about whom concern has been expressed, and, when necessary, calls upon the resources of the child study team which includes the nurse/teacher, resource room teacher, speech therapist, and the school psychologist.

The total program helps children to become oriented and accustomed to the school and its personnel. The parents begin to see the school as a resource; they learn about the school program and start to develop relationships with the staff and other parents of incoming children. Through the screening and the readiness program the staff becomes aware of the strengths and weaknesses of each child before they enter school. The small size of the school and community and the ongoing involvement of the elementary school principal facilitate a very personalized approach to screening and parent-child involvement.

Grove City, Ohio

Southwestern City Schools in Grove City, Ohio have a screening program in seven elementary schools where the population is described as predominantly economically disadvantaged. The screening is done twice by devised checklists, once before the child enters kindergarten, and again before entry into first grade. Screening is followed by diagnosis and educational programming.

Background

The school district is the tenth largest in Ohio with a school population of 17,500. There are seventeen elementary schools. The district covers an area of 130 miles and includes urban, suburban, and rural areas. The socioeconomic levels range from very high to very low.

From 1964-67 the school district did a study on the prevention of learning disabilities in the district. One outcome was to focus on early identification and remediation or effective treatment. In 1967-68, an Experimental Kindergarten Readiness program was devised. By use of a devised checklist, the entire kindergarten population was screened. The thirty children with the highest number of errors were selected and administered a battery of diagnostic tests. Of this group, fifteen were selected who had characteristics most similar to learning disabilities children and had an IQ over 90. These fifteen children became the experimental group and were placed in a separate class with a teacher and aide. They were supported by consultants and special programs and materials. A control group received no special attention. At the end of the year the experimental group had a mean score in reading achievement of 2.04 (S.D. 48) and the control group of 1.56 (S.D. 67). The arithmetic achievement score for the experimental group was 2.39 (S.D. 21) and the control group 1.49 (S.D. 56) (Cennamo, 1969).

In 1968-69 a Title I reading program was implemented. Its objectives were to improve the perceptual ability and reading level of the students, to improve their school and social adjustment, and to enlist the aid of parents in solving problems of their children. The program had two thrusts: It was preventive for children in first grade and remedial for children in grades two through six. In the preventive program 139 children were identified through a devised checklist as performing poorly in those areas which underlie basic abilities of reading (Title I summary report, 1968-69). Over a period of seven months of instruction, the first grade group averaged twelve months growth. Ongoing work in the area provided the background for the present program.

Program

In 1973-74, a Title I ESEA program was devised for identification and follow-through for kindergarten and first grade children who may have learning disabilities in the seven elementary schools of the district with the largest number of children from economically disadvantaged homes. The staff devised a sixteen-question checklist which drew from the Stanford Binet Test and the Vallett Development Survey of Basic Learning Abilities (see Figure 30). The staff regards these items as things the average kindergarten child can do successfully. An error score of six is usual for selecting the program population. Validation of the instrument was a survey of the classroom teachers involved. They were asked if the children selected for the program were the same ones they found to have problems in the classroom. The percentage of agreement was over 95 percent. The score is adjusted upward or downward depending on the number of children that can be handled in a particular building. All children entering kindergarten are given this instrument in the fall of the kindergarten year. At the same time, the child's ability to identify letters, consonant sounds, and words, and his vision and hearing, are checked. If any problem in vision, hearing, or speech is detected or suspected, a referral is made immediately to the nurse or speech therapist.

A second devised checklist is administered to all the kindergarten children at the end of the school year. It is an extension of the initial kindergarten checklist, and the items are regarded as things the average first grade child can do successfully. The use of the second checklist assesses growth and enables the school to pick up on those children who may have slipped through the first screening (Rudder, 1974-75).

The children identified by the checklist receive a diagnostic battery of tests. The area of greatest difficulty that has been identified are in language development and visual and auditory perception. When appropriate, some of the identified children may be placed in a special class.

Children who are identified as having a special need stay in regular classes but are given extra help through the reading and

```
Teacher Checklist for        Name_____
Kindergarten Readiness
                             Date Tested_____
Southwestern City Schools
Grove City, Ohio             Birthdate_____

                             Handedness  R    L    M
```

1. Jumps with both feet 5 times,
    maintaining balance.   Yes__ No__
2. Hops on left foot 5 times and
    stops, maintaining balance.   Yes__ No__
3. Hops on right foot 5 times and
    stops, maintaining balance.   Yes__ No__
4. Can skip around teacher (or 4
    steps forward).   Yes__ No__
5. Follows 3 commands in order:
    Place pencil on table.
    Close the door.
    Hand the paper to me.   Yes__ No__
6. Ties a knot around finger   Yes__ No__
7. Cuts a strip of paper into 2
    pieces   Yes__ No__
8. Can copy a circle from model   Yes__ No__
9. Copies a square from model   Yes__ No__
10. Paper folding task (triangle
    from Binet).   Yes__ No__
11. Copies simple pegboard design
    (a square).   Yes__ No__
12. Vocabulary test:
    a) What is a ball? b) A hat?
    c) A stove? d) An orange?
    e) An envelope?   Yes__ No__
13. Repeats verbatim:
    "Jack likes to feed little
    puppies in the barn."   Yes__ No__
14. Repeats digits: (two trials)
    641   352   Yes__ No__
15. Repeats digits: (two trials)
    9-6-8-1   5726   Yes__ No__
16. Draw a picture of a person for me.   Yes__ No__

Teacher should total error score here._____

Figure 30.

learning centers. Parents are encouraged to take an active part in their child's treatment program. The teacher and assistant visit each child's home to explain the program to the parents. The parents are invited to visit the learning and reading centers in order to see the materials and equipment the child uses, and to gain a deeper understanding of his child's needs. When there are severe home problems the staff provides supportive services. For those children who qualify there is a summer program at the end of the kindergarten year.

The center staff work with the children four days a week. The fifth day is used for planning, coordinating with classroom teachers, and for inservice education. Workshops are organized so that teachers and assistants may prepare materials needed in working with the children.

Both parents and staff regularly evaluate the child's progress and the program.

New Paltz, New York

The laboratory school at the State University College at New Paltz is working toward personalizing learning for all children. When individual developmental patterns and learning styles are identified, educational programs are designed and implemented which reach curricular goals in a variety of ways. The program is matched to the child's needs within the framework of a classroom.

Background

New Paltz is a college community with a population of 10,000 in the Mid-Hudson region of New York state, 75 miles north of New York City. The laboratory school, called the van den Berg Learning Center (VLC) is part of the State University College and is a department within the Faculty of Education. There are approximately 400 children from nursery school to eighth grade with the equivalent of two classes at every grade level. Except for a federally funded preschool migrant program, the children are chosen by lottery and range in ability, as measured by standardized tests from the first to 99th percentile.

In 1971, the school started working toward the long-range goal of personalizing learning for all children. The first master plan established alternative environments for learning (see Figure 31) and pilot projects in a rather shotgun approach to acquire some experience with which to move toward this goal.

The first step was to design and implement a screening program. The ZEIS was developed (see Appendix D) and field-tested

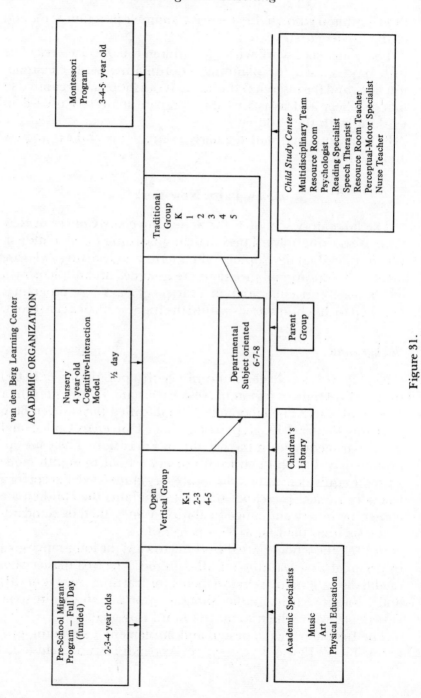

Figure 31.

as an appropriate instrument for screening. For follow-through, a process for personalized learning had to be developed which would systematize the complexity of meeting individual needs within a school system and become a basis for record keeping. The model for personalized learning is the result of that thrust (see Chapter 4).

The first step toward personalizing learning is to clarify curricular expectations and then to collect data about a child's present status as a learner. The educational program is derived from this information. This raises many questions. What is the most meaningful information to collect to describe the child as a learner? How do you collect it? What do you do with it, and finally how do you assess each stage for effectiveness?

In 1971, a three-phase pilot project was designed:

• Phase I was the diagnostic evaluation of the entire kindergarten class (1971-72).

• Phase II was the translation of the developed diagnostic profile into an educational prescription for the same children in first grade (1972-73).

• Phase III was the refinement of the use of the personalized learning process and the longitudinal study of these children over a five-year period to determine if they were successful as learners, i.e. that they made continuing progress and enjoyed going to school. The diagnostic battery will be reexamined to determine which tests, if any, have value for determining curricular choices and defining problems evidenced in the learning process (1976-77).

In Phase I, the following tests were used:
1. an audiometer test,
2. a Keystone Visual Survey test,
3. a perceptual Eye Examination,
4. a Sensory Awareness Survey for four- and five-year-olds devised by the physical education teacher,
5. The Oseretsky test (1946) to identify general motor disability areas and whether there is retardation or acceleration in the motor level,
6. The Bender Motor Gestalt test (1946) scored by the Koppitz system (1964),
7. The Draw-A-Person test scoring based on scales devel-

oped by Goodenough and Harris (1963), Koppitz (1968) emotional indicators were scored,

8. The Wepman Test of Auditory Discrimination (1958),
9. The Frostig Developmental Test of Visual Perception (1963),
10. The Illinois Test of Psycholinguistic Ability (ITPA) Kirk, (1968).

Thirty-two children who completed the battery remained in the program. All tests but three were administered by college students trained and supervised by the child study team. The three tests relating to vision and hearing were given by the nurse/teacher and an optometrist. Each child was tested individually, in short sessions, over a period of four months.

The results were recorded on an individual profile sheet, analyzed by the child study team, and discussed with the parents.

As a result of the testing, seven children were referred for further eye examinations, two for hearing, and one for neurological examination.

Each test, except for the Oseretsky, showed a wide range of development. On the Oseretzky all of the children but one scored above their chronological age.

The mean and range of the results varied for each test and for each child. For example, the Bender Gestalt test results showed 22 percent of the children below age expectation and 19 percent above. The Draw-A-Person, used as a measure of cognitive maturity, showed 47 percent of the children to be below average expectation for the age range and only 9 percent above.

In May 1972, 70 percent of the children were chronologically six years old or younger, 25 percent had a psycholinguistic language age (PLA), as measured by the ITPA of six or younger. Twenty-two percent of the students had a PLA between seven and eight years.

This group, chronologically young, ranged widely in development. Individual profiles reflected uneven development with identifiable strengths, weaknesses, and learning styles. The strongest impression gained from examining the individual profiles was the overlapping commonalities and the uniqueness of each child's profile.

It was clear to the child study team that too much testing had been done for the amount of information gained. Initial assessment of the battery was negative for several instruments. The ITPA requires too much training and time to administer. The total results are useful for children with special needs but do not seem to be valuable enough for typical children to warrant the amount of the specialist's and child's time invested. Particular subtests may be more relevant in identifying a child's particular learning style and developmental pattern. The Oseretsky did not seem to give enough relevant data to warrant its inclusion in future batteries. The use of the Frostig is also questionable in comparing the usefulness of the results with the amount of time spent in administration. The results reinforced what we already knew: that young children vary greatly in their own development, and within a given group of kindergarten children there is a wide diversity of abilities. For some children there was evidence that one learning channel was more adequately developed than another.

Phase II of the program was initiated in the fall of 1972. The development of a classroom which utilized individual prescriptions was very complex and required a certain amount of trial-and-error learning on the part of the teachers and their helpers. The pilot classroom consisted of eighteen first graders who were part of an open space vertically grouped classroom of thirty-five first and second grade students. Two teachers assumed responsibility for instructing the children and supervising the college students who were to gain experience in working with children at different levels of competency. Personalized learning was planned in three areas: math, language arts, and development of positive attitudes toward school. Because of the pilot nature of the first year of the program, there was only a loose design for evaluation. Metropolitan Readiness tests were given as a pretest and California Achievement tests were given as a posttest.

Parents were asked to complete a questionnaire which included their expectations for their child in the first grade. The diagnostic team met with the classroom teacher and used the personalized learning model to develop the appropriate learning experiences. Consideration was given to developmental level, preferred learning style, and unique strengths or weaknesses. The objectives were compared to parent's expectations, and when there were gross differences, further conferences were held with the parents.

An attitude survey was administered to the children in the pilot class. Despite a search of the literature, an effective instrument which measured attitude toward school in first graders could not be found. The Child Study Center team created such an instrument. This instrument as yet has not been statistically evaluated and can only be said to have face validity. The results of the survey were that 53 percent of the total responses expressed positive attitudes toward school, 28 percent expressed no special feelings, and 19 percent expressed negative attitudes.

A questionnaire was used to request a parental evaluation of the child's attitude toward school at the end of the first grade. On the whole, the responses were quite positive.

Record keeping was complex and centered on each child's folder. It included diagnostic material and a record of the prescriptions. Anecdotal records, observations, records of work completed, samples of the child's work, sociogram survey of class feelings, a social-emotional checklist, and records of parent conferences were kept in the folder.

Objectives were continuously evaluated by the staff and were changed as necessary. Group evaluations were made in math and reading. The children remained in the same classroom through third grade and at the time this book was written all the children but two were in fourth grade. One boy was in a fifth grade class and one girl was in third grade. Eight of the children had at one time been part of the resource room program, with four still going. At the end of the third grade, reading scores on the Gates McGinitie ranged from 2.1 grade equivalent to 6.9+ or the top of the test scale. In math the PEP (Pupil Evaluation Program) test scores ranged from the 25th to the 90th percentile. It was premature and difficult to assess on a comparative basis what benefits accrued, if any, from the personalized learning approach. The children varied as much in achievement as they did in their initial diagnosis. Initial observations indicated that the children with problems in the basic skills had instruction at their level and had many other satisfying learning experiences. Those children who started with many strengths were capitalizing on them. There are children like Peter who initially showed some of the characteristics associated with high risk children such as very poor perceptual motor functioning, who were able to capitalize on strengths such as sound-blending and be extremely successful. Others like Arthur who has a family history of delayed reading because of language-related problems have plodded ahead. Arthur had many language development experiences and enough successes to feel good about himself, although he is reading well below grade level. Karen, who was a late starter in the reading process, despite no obvious mismatches took until fourth grade to develop competencies in her basic skills and now is progressing rapidly. Most of the time, all of the children seem happy in school and feel good about themselves. Information from parent conferences support these observations.

In 1974-75, a new battery for baseline assessment of kindergarten children was devised which taps a wider range of abilities. Each part, except for vision and hearing, is administered by a college student with a minimum of training. It is a goal to reduce, if possible, the number of tests in the battery and still get the most relevant baseline data for program development and record keeping. The teachers are now more experienced and proficient with personalizing learning. Longitudinal studies of these children will also be made.

The battery includes the ZEIS which is given to the children in the spring of the nursery year. In the fall of the kindergarten year all children are screened by the nurse/teacher for visual skills in the area of simultaneous vision, lateral imbalance, vertical imbalance, near and far point fusion, binocularity, and stereopsis. The Keystone Telebinocular is the instrument used. In addition to evaluating visual skills, responses to the test questions provide information about language development, eye-hand coordination, and spatial relationships. At the same time, hearing is checked by use of an audiometer. Any defects detected during the evaluation are brought to the attention of the parents for appropriate follow-up. The nurse/teacher also has each parent fill out a background history form (see Chapter 4).

Over a period of three months in the spring, the college students, after a training period, administer the following tests:

1. Piaget tasks of conservation; number, substance, quantity and length
2. the Bender Motor Gestalt Test scored by the Koppitz system
3. the Token test
4. Auditory Association Subtest of the ITPA
5. Sound-Blending subtest of the ITPA
6. Perceptual Motor Test (devised)
7. Visual Discrimination test (devised)
8. Wepman Test of Auditory Discrimination (modified)
9. Vocabulary (WPPSI)
10. Draw-A-Person scored by Koppitz System
11. Preschool Speech and Language Test (Fluharty, 1974)

The following two profiles (Zeitlin, 1975) describe children who are in the same class but whose results indicate the need for very different learning prescriptions:

Robert's birthday is September 4. He scored 54 on the ZEIS. In the baseline diagnosis, his results were:

Vision— acuity 20/70 — 20/30
            fusion test — failed near and far points
            eye muscle balance — questions raised
Hearing — satisfactory
Paiget tests — not conserving
Bender Gestalt Test — 9 errors (average)
Wepman — 8 errors (3 errors average)
Token Test — 27 (Mean 48 — Standard Deviation 8)
Auditory Association — age equivalent 4.5
Sound-Blending — age equivalent 4.2
Visual Discrimination — 3 errors (average)
Draw-A-Person — 1 emotional indicator (average)
                6 body parts (11 average)
Speech — adequate
Perceptual Motor Development — age appropriate

* * * * *

Jack's birthday is July 10. He scored 87 in the ZEIS. In the baseline diagnosis his results were:

Vision — satisfactory

Hearing — satisfactory

Piaget tests — can conserve number, length, liquid quantity
       and substance

Bender Gestalt Test — 8 errors (average)

Wepman — 2 errors (3 errors average)

Token test — 44 (average)

Auditory Association — age equivalent 8.3

Sound-Blending — age equivalent 7.1

Visual Discrimination — 2 errors (3 errors average)

Vocabulary — 19 (Mean 10 — Range 1-19)

Draw-A-Person — emotional indicators 1
            body parts — 11 (average)

Speech — adequate

Perceptual Motor Development — age appropriate

Robert was seen by the child study team for a diagnostic work-up with the following results:

The background history taken by the nurse/teacher showed that he is the youngest of six children ranging in age to twenty-three years. Two of the older children and the mother had reading difficulty. A brother who is a year older is in the resource room program because of learning problems. Motor development as diagnosed by the Purdue Motor Survey was average. IQ as measured by the WPPSI was average with strength in arithmetic and similarities. Vocabulary was much better than in the screening and was in the average range. The Animal House subtest was the most difficult for him, since he had to work steadily at a timed task and to remember what he was being asked to do. A language sample showed him to be within the average range for language usage. The Roswell Chall Test of Auditory Blending showed that he had much difficulty in this area. In general, results showed that he had fair to good visual memory; had difficulty generalizing, i.e. he responded much better to concrete clues; and often responded to parts of a word or phrase rather than the whole. He was slow in processing information and became confused with increased complexity. He showed beginning ability to compensate by use of verbal and motor mediators. At present he shows no interest in learning to read and has difficulty with the classroom routine. He is accepted and well liked by the children in the classroom.

Robert will be helped to establish work patterns by use of short uncomplicated instructions which give a task one step at a time. Classroom instruction will involve concrete manipulative material as much as possible. Reading readiness activities will be multisensory.

Jack had "cracked the code" and was reading a little in kindergarten. At the beginning of first grade he is in a reading group working in a primer of a modified basal series. He is described by his teacher as creative in that he makes up fantastic stories, and uses materials, and illustrates stories very creatively. His writing is "atrocious." He works better on a one-to-one basis than in a group. The teacher sees him as a child who does not always enter the group by choice. He can conceptualize and problem-solve on a more advanced level than most of his peers. He is given special tasks to work on.

Robert and Jack's classroom is structured so that both of their needs can be met. While there are many activities that need to be different, there are also many that they can do together.

The movement toward personalizing learning is slow, but each year the staff becomes more proficient as they have more experience designing and implementing appropriate experiences within the context of total classroom functioning.

This chapter has described seven screening programs. Each program has characteristics that are worthy of consideration in developing a screening program.

Chapter Eight

ABUSES AND MATTERS OF CONCERN IN KINDERGARTEN SCREENING PROGRAMS

SCREENING programs are often victims of the same forces which create the need for the program in the first place: lack of knowledge; attitudes and values detrimental to children; politics; and lack of money, personnel, and resources. The goal to help each child experience success in learning assumes a child-centered approach. In reality this is not always the case. Some programs are based on assumptions about children that theory and experience do not support, others reflect lack of knowledge and/or experience, while others are influenced by the biases and politics of their communities.

Screening can be a negative rather than positive force when the program incorporates any of the following abuses:

1. using screening as diagnosis, i.e. making important decisions on a child from too little, inadequate or inappropriate information, or from only a single involvement;
2. using screening to exclude children;
3. using screening to place labels that stigmatize children;
4. not recognizing the impact of cultural differences;
5. not recognizing the impact of bilingualism;
6. using screening as a program in isolation, i.e. having no goals and objectives, and having no follow-through program;
7. using screening to reinforce and justify existing curriculum-centered programs and to explain the failure of children who do not fit in;
8. focusing on weaknesses of children and ignoring their strengths;
9. allowing attitudes and values of the assessors which are

175

not supportive of the child;
10. using screening to create and implement checklist curriculums.

Screening as Diagnosis

Screening precedes diagnosis, and it serves the child's needs in a different way from diagnosis (see Chapter 2). In many screening programs the information gathered is assumed to be adequate to make educational decisions about the child. The results may be placed on a checklist which indicates that a child is deficient in a particular area, and without further investigation the teacher is expected to remediate in that area. It is not appropriate to say without further diagnosis that the screening shows the child to be low in perceptual motor skills; therefore teachers should remediate in that area. It is not uncommon to find children who function effectively despite specific defects or problems because they are able to compensate. Even when it is appropriate to remediate, screening alone does not provide enough information. For example, if a child misses all questions pertaining to memory for sentences, the examiner would check auditory memory problems. The child may have a hearing problem, a head cold, or may not have understood what was asked of him.

In some programs the screening team meets after the screening and decides on the basis of the screening data what is the best program for the child. The author has observed a screening program where the child goes to five stations within a twenty-minute period. The first station tests speech and language; the second uses the auditory reception subtest of the ITPA as a test of the child's "ability to decode." The third station tests gross and fine motor coordination, the fourth is kinesthetic-conceptual, and the fifth has the child copy nine figures from the Visual-Motor Integration test. Each examiner fills out a form. That afternoon the examiners meet and fill out a checklist which says "This child evidenced some weakness," and lists for check-off six different categories under language area and eight categories under non-language area. Underneath this, there is a checklist of activities to be used including the assignment of this kindergarten child (screening is in October) to one of five different reading and/or readiness programs, and so the child is locked in by the need for instant solutions or prescriptions.

In another school district children whose birthdays fall in the last three months of the year and who score below a set figure are placed, without additional assessment, in what is called a *developmental kindergarten* but is actually a prekindergarten program. This may be an excellent solution for some children, but certainly not for all.

The behavior of four- and five-year-olds is variable and is easily influenced by relatively superficial things. One sample of behavior, seeing a child in one situation, may raise questions of concern but can never give adequate data to make an educational plan. Screening, by definition, is a filtering process, a first step. The complex understanding of a child's learning process cannot be dealt with just in a screening.

Screening to Exclude

On the basis of a screening, some school districts will tell the parents that the child is "not ready" and they should bring him back next year. Most states do not have mandatory schooling before age six or seven.

The story of a young boy was headlined in a national newsweekly as "A Failure at 5?" (*Newsweek*, 1975). The parent said that in May she took her young son to the local elementary school where he was due to start kindergarten that fall. He was given the Denver Developmental Screening Test, a test of twenty minutes duration. The parents were advised that he did not do well on the test and should delay entrance to school for a year. The school reported that five out of eighty-seven children tested "failed" the test. Besides the absurdity of making such an important decision on the basis of a screening, the assumption that "waiting another year" will solve all problems is not often valid. There are children whose development is adequate, but whose maturation process is immature, who would not be harmed and maybe helped by another year at home, assuming that the home is supportive and stimulating. More often, children who initially are identified as potential high risk need the help they can receive by involvement in an educational program. No decision can be made without knowledge of why the child did not do well on the screening.

In the event that a school district chooses to exclude a child from entering school because of his performance on the screening assessment, it must accept the responsibility of providing an alternative experience for that child on his level of competence.

Labeling Children

An area of controversy and concern is the labeling of children as a result of the screening process. The concern was deemed so important that in 1972 the Department of Health Education and Welfare in the Federal government established a commission to study the issues in classification of children (Hobbs, 1975).

Some of the assumptions of their study are relevant to the labeling issue in kindergarten screening.

1. Classification of exceptional children is essential to get services for them, to plan and organize helping programs, and to determine the outcome of intervention efforts.
2. Public and private policies and practices must manifest respect for the individuality of children and appreciation of the positive values of their individual talents and diverse cultural backgrounds. Classification procedures must not be used to violate this fundamental social value.
3. There is a growing public concern over the uses and abuses of categories and labels as applied to children, and there is. widespread dissatisfaction with inadequate uncoordinated, hurtful services for children.
4. Categories and labels are powerful instruments for social regulation and control, and they are often employed for obscure, covert, or hurtful purposes: to degrade people, to deny them access to opportunity, to exclude "undersirables" whose presence in some way offends, disturbs familiar custom, or demands extraordinary effort.

Not to label is impossible. As soon as a symbol or word is used to describe a person or a behavior, that is a label. The issue is the impact and implication of the words or label that is used. Labels can be categorized as "good labels" and "bad labels." Practically speaking, "good labels" are those that can be used to open doors for a child and increase the chances of marshaling resources on his behalf. "Bad labels" are those that close doors to the child, that place him in inferior programs and subject him to unpleasant or humiliating experiences and attitudes.

Whether the label is good or bad may vary with the culture and the values and attitudes of those who respond to the label.

In American education, the Anglo-American values seem to predominate and set the criteria for acceptance, some of which are:

1. to be physically whole, healthy, and attractive;
2. to be efficient in the use of one's time and energy;
3. to control distracting impulses and to delay gratification in the services of productivity;
4. to value work over play;
5. to be white, native born, Protestant;
6. to inhibit aggressive behaviors except in specifically defined situations;
7. to be fluent in American English (Hobbs, 1975).

Cultural norms are changing, but more often than not the child who does not conform to these norms is labeled as different, usually with a negative connotation.

Labeling is the assigning of a category and publicly communicating it. There is a tendency to blame the label for the problems of the child rather than the behavior of the child or the attitudes, feelings, and behavior of others who interact with the child. In many situations, those obviously in need of services are probably informally labeled by others and subjected to various forms of ridicule and failure prior to being formally classified. The effects of the prelabeling experiences on a child's self-concept and his social interaction tend to be confounded with the effects of receiving an official label. Labeling focuses on the child's weakness without regard to his strengths and compensating abilities.

Attaching labels which connote educational deficiency and inability to learn such as "educable mentally retarded," "learning disability," "cultural disadvantaged" may provide teachers with an excuse for failure to teach the child. By attributing school failure to some unalterable attributes of the child, labels allow teachers to dismiss the possibility that their teaching is one cause of the child's failure to progress. There is a tendency in some schools to label children, to fit them into a category, and then teach to the category.

The concept of the self-fulfilling prophecy is seen as one result of labeling (Rosenthal and Jacobson, 1968). There are some who feel that teachers shouldn't screen, and that the initial results should be withheld from them so as not to influence the teacher's response to the child. Testing is often used to predict rather than describe. There is some evidence that in certain circumstances teachers who hold favorable expectations for their pupils actually attempt to teach more than teachers who have been led to believe that their pupils are poor learners (Jones, 1972).

The concern about the labeling and its abuses generates much emotion among many concerned people. Words can be very powerful. Sometimes the issue of labeling is used to maintain the status quo. A group opposed to a program by invoking the labeling issue and generating a lot of heat may obscure the basic issue of trying to help children, and defeat a program but offer no alternatives.

Labels can be useful if they bring attention to a group of children who have special needs which have not been met. They may help parents, teachers, and children to understand why certain children function in atypical ways. Perhaps if the label focused on the educational need rather than the etiology it would facilitate getting the child help with less stigma attached.

There is nothing a teacher can do about mental retardation or deafness; there is however, a great deal a teacher can do about problems in social behavior, reading skills, or ability to communicate. Hobbs (1975) suggests two major categories of classification in accordance not with the types of disability but with kinds and duration of services needed: (1) children in need of special assistance, and (2) children in need of prolonged assistance. The term *high risk,* as used in this book, is seen as a service-oriented label designating an educational need for intervention.

Screening and Cultural Differences

Those children characterized as culturally disadvantaged not only come from cultures that are different but are also predominately from the lower socioeconomic class.

A central characteristic of a culture is that it is encompassing, that is, it constitutes a total design for living that shapes a people's behavior, beliefs, and values in every phase of life. It is difficult to conceive of a large group of people as culturally deprived or disadvantaged because every group maintains a culture. Their cultural norms may be different from those upon which education in America is based. These differences, usually perceived as deviations from the norm, result in biases and behaviors which may have negative implications for the culturally different child and often result in stigmatizing labels and inappropriate expectations. Bryen (1973) says that "being culturally disadvantaged is a social condition which is created, managed, and maintained by both social and professional institutions. The defining of large segments of our black population 'culturally disadvantaged' not only results in differential perceptions and expectancies, but in fact influences their self-evaluation, school achievement, and life chances."

When screening programs do not recognize the impact of cultural differences, they may additionally reinforce and perpetuate the many negative aspects of the problem. Research studies have found that a disproportionate number of children from minority groups in comparison to the total population have been classified with labels indicating deviant functioning.

In 1973, black children in San Francisco schools were greatly overrepresented in special classes. Although they comprised 27.8 percent of the total student population, they constituted 47.4 percent of all students in educationally handicapped classes and 53.3 percent of those in EMR classes.

In a Riverside, California study of persons identified as mentally retarded, there were 300 percent more Mexican-Americans and 50 percent more blacks but only 60 percent as many whites as would be expected from their respective proportions in the community (Mercer, 1972).

The term "six-hour retarded" has been introduced to refer to the low socioeconomic child who is presumably demonstrating adequate adaptive behavior in his community or neighborhood but who is concurrently identified as "educable mentally retarded" for the purposes of school placement.

Hobbs (1975) says that "classification arises from and tends to perpetuate the value of the cultural majority often to the detriment of individual children or classes of children."

In this light classification is a form of social control. It institutionalizes the values of the cultural majority, governs the allocation of resources and access to opportunity, protects the majority from undue anxiety, and maintains the status quo of the community and its institutions.

Screening tests as well as other standardized tests are criticized as reflecting the bias of the dominant culture and therefore discriminating against the culturally different child. Cultural attitudes and behavior expectations of minority cultures may be different and influence test-taking behavior, including the interaction between the examiner and the examined. Testing is seen as another tool to perpetuate negative stereotypes of blacks by demonstrating failures and inabilities (Gay, 1973). It is felt that when minority group children are tested the results are misused to denigrate their dignity and to severely limit their educational opportunities. The tests are seen as reflecting only middle class values and attitudes and not reflecting minority group children's linguistic and cognitive abilities and cultural experience (Oakland, 1973). A large amount of data exists relevant to the various cognitive and language skills of culturally different children. These differences are not always recognized when tests are standardized and use only samples of children representative of the middle class culture. Some of the resulting problems for the culturally different child are that the tests can be biased by being outside the experience of the testee. For example, on the PPVT there are pictures requiring such answers as "wiener" or "hydrant," etc. Either the words or the picture may be alien to many poor and/or rural children. On the Stanford Binet Test, the child is asked to identify which picture answers the question "where does milk come from." The urban poor child may never have seen the cow. The verbal style required by the test can be culture-specific and therefore alien. This may contribute to a communication breakdown and the child may not understand what he is expected to do. Cultural patterns of interacting with adults may influence test-taking results. American middle class children are accustomed to answering questions; being interrogated by family, friends, and strangers; being tested, surveyed, and polled. There are cultures in which the questioning of behavior among unrelated adults is not tolerated and to ask an adult to repeat a statement is an insult (Adler, 1973). Direct questioning from adults to children tends to be associated, by black children, with prospective threat and some association of wrongdoing (Gay, 1973).

A study was conducted to determine if performance deficits of the economically disadvantaged were due to motivational factors. The test was given to eighty-two children between four and five-and-a-half years old. Some were involved in Head Start programs, and others were in a tuition nursery school. The PPVT and the Stanford Binet test were administered. The results showed that the disadvantaged scored lower on the Peabody than on the Stanford Binet because of a linguistic deficit. Reasons given for the results were that more verbal ability was needed for the Peabody, and, also, the Head Start children had a fear of the examiner. A retest showed a ten-point increase for the disadvantaged children's scores compared to the retest for the middle class children. The increase was credited to a familiarity with the examiner and not as improvement in cognitive functioning. These findings support the view that the disadvantaged children approach test situations with wariness which results in lower scores (Zigler, 1973).

In recent years, legal challenges have been made in regard to placing minority children in special education programs based on testing which did not accurately measure their abilities. Lawyers representing black and Mexican-American clients have successfully argued in court that present assessment procedures violate the rights of minority children. Many parents of minority group children are less willing to accept without question the results of school-administered tests.

Children who are culturally different are affected by the prejudices and misperceptions imposed on them by those who are unfamiliar or hostile to them. This is evidenced in the interaction

between child and middle class teacher and/or examiner. In an
attitude study, 288 teachers from sixteen states were given nine
hypothetical but realistic profiles of children with IQ's from 68 to
81. The nine profiles represented the three levels of social class.
The teachers were asked to rate each child according to the appropriateness of the mental retardation level. A disproportionate
number of children from the lower socioeconomic class were seen
as being appropriately labeled as mentally retarded.

The importance of cultural bias is related to use of the results of
the screening. When local norms are used then the normative data
reflects the make-up of the specific community, and the use of the
results is more appropriate to determine the child who has a
special need in that community. Criterion-referenced tests which
are designed to meet the needs of a particular group or program
are deemed by some to be fairer than normative tests.

Screening and Bilingualism

This abuse overlaps and is closely related to cultural differences. The focus is on high risk children whose primary language
is not English and who, as a group, are having less success in
school. A study of children who did not speak English when they
entered school in 1966 showed that by 1975, 10 percent of them
dropped out of school. Of those still in school, 64 percent were
reading below grade level and 10 percent were at least two years
behind in grade placement (Montoya, 1975). Similar problems are
experienced by those who speak a different dialect or "nonstandard" English. A dialect includes differences in every aspect
of speech such as differences in vocabulary or arrangement of
words in an utterance, and the words or sounds that are accented
(Davis, 1969). Black English is the most controversial, and has the
greatest potential for misinterpretation and abuse. It is a dialect
that is spoken by many low socioeconomic black children, and
makes it difficult to differentiate in a standardized assessment
between children who have a language deficit and those who
speak the black dialect rather than standard English. A few examples of the differences are:

	Standard English	*Black English*
linking verb	He is going	He goin?
subject expression	John lives in New York	John, he live in New York
verb form	I drank the milk	I drunk the milk
negation	I don't have any	I don't got none

Research varies in supporting or rejecting the hypothesis that black children do poorer on tests because they speak dialect in an institution based on standard English (Bartel, 1973), though research in language development usually shows these children to be somewhat retarded in developing control of a standard dialect (Hess, 1974).

Dialect differences seemed to also influence the learning problems of the Nez Perce (North American) Indian children. In a study comparing kindergarten Indian children and white children who attend the same reservation school, it was found that there were significant differences between the two populations in their use of receptive vocabulary, and receptive and expressive syntax (Ramstad, 1974).

In screening, many of the existing instruments are unable to account for the language and dialect differences, and the negative interpretations of these tests are made without recognition of their potential impact on the child. These children often have strengths not identified by verbal tests. In a study of 225 Puerto Rican Head Start children (ages four-and-one-half to six) who were given the Vane Kindergarten Screening Test, it was found that there was no significant difference between this group and the standardization sample in full scale score, but the children had a lower mean on vocabulary and a higher mean on the nonverbal subtests.

There has been an attempt to develop so-called "culture fair" tests which primarily include performance rather than verbal items as a standard strategy for avoiding cultural context. Because heredity and environment interact at all stages of development, it is futile to devise a test free of cultural influence. No one test can be fair to all cultures since it is unlikely that any test can be equally fair to more than one cultural group. It also cannot be assumed that nonverbal items measure the same thing as do verbal items; in fact, nonverbal items may be more culturally loaded than verbal ones. Any one test which measures only commonalities among cultures might be measuring trivial functions and thereby missing the significant intellectual functions of all cultures (Bartel, 1973). In considering the question of the cultural fairness of tests, one has to first determine the purpose of the testing, then determine the relevance of the issue of cultural fairness. The second issue often obscures the first (Drew, 1973). Basic to kindergarten screening is the intended use of the results. Some tests described as culture fair and age appropriate for kindergarten children are:

- Culture Fair Intelligence Test (Cottell and Cottell, 1963),
- The Progressive Matrices (Raven, 1963), and the
- Goodenough Harris Draw-A-Man Test (Harris, 1963).

The author is not aware of any existing tests assessing the linguistic competence of speakers of Black English. The Head Start Test Collection (Rosen and Horne, 1971) includes an annotated bibliography of tests for Spanish-speaking children. Several seem appropriate for kindergarten screening and diagnosis.

Walker Readiness Test for Disadvantaged Preschool Children

A nonverbal instrument designed to assess a child's readiness to enter public school programs. Two forms are available. Form A identifies areas of weakness and facilitates the establishment of individual remedial programs. Form B, administered some time after Form A, assesses the efficiency of the program used and the child's progress. Both forms have fifty multiple choice items and are arranged into four parts: likenesses, differences, numerical analogies, and missing parts. Instructions are in Spanish, English, and French. For each item, the child selects the correct answer from four pictures. The test is individually administered and training is not necessary.

Short Test of Educational Ability

This test contains five subtests, including "What Would Happen If," "How Would You," "Spatial Relations," "Verbal Meanings," and "Number Series." Level I is appropriate for Grades K-1 and consists of subtests 1-3. The test takes approximately thirty minutes to administer and does not require the child to read. There are parallel editions in English and Spanish.

Wechsler Intelligence Scale for Children
(Escala de Inteligencia Wechsler Par Ninos)

This Spanish edition of WISC is appropriate for children aged five to fifteen. It should be individually administered by a trained examiner. The instrument consists of twelve tests divided into two subgroups. The verbal scales include general information, general comprehension, arithmetic, similarities, vocabulary, and digit span. The performance scales include picture completion, picture arrangement, block design, object assembly, and coding or mazes. Intelligence quotients, obtained by comparing each subject's performance with scores of individuals in a single age group, are utilized.

Many nonverbal tests described in Chapter Four can be used when the instructions are translated into Spanish.

A landmark legal case in the State of California, *Diane vs. State Board of Education* (1970) dealt with the placement of children in special education based on tests administered in English to those whose primary language is Spanish. Two points in the case settlement that are relevant to kindergarten screening are:

1. All children whose primary home language is other than English must be tested in both their primary language and in English.
2. Such children must be tested only with tests or sections of tests that do not depend on such things as vocabulary, general knowledge, general information, and other similar unfair verbal questions.

Screening as a Program in Isolation

A major and common abuse of screening is to use it as if it were an end in itself. This can happen for many reasons. When there are no goals and objectives (see Chapter 3), the screening may not relate in any planned way to the educational program of the school. This can happen through lack of knowledge and experience or lack of communication between those who initiate the screening and those responsible for the follow-through. There may be a felt need for a follow-through program but no funds or human resources.

Screening as a program in isolation is either useless and a source of frustration for many because nothing is done with the results, or what is even worse, when the results are not used for follow-through but are used for excluding children, as a political football, or as part of a power struggle.

Screening to Justify Existing Programs

Schools with a curriculum-centered approach to teaching may use screening to focus on those children whose development and abilities do not match the curriculum expectations of their program. Screening without follow-through is used to predict a child's success rather than for his education planning.

A school can say "See, we've screened the children and we have all these problem children. What can you expect of us? If we didn't have them we could really teach." When these attitudes and values pervade, then screening becomes one more tool to reinforce a rigid curriculum-centered approach and a tool to justify the failure of those that don't make it.

Focus on Weakness

Another concern is the development of a problem orientation. In emphasizing only weaknesses and remediation rather than including identification and utilization of strengths, the problem rather than the whole child is responded to.

Attitudes and Values of the Assessor

The personnel who do the testing may influence the results. This may be a greater problem when the examiner and the child are from different cultural or language backgrounds. An examiner who is not sensitive or has difficulty interacting with young children can bias the results. The child may be seen as untestable or the interaction can trigger negative behavior or responses on the part of the child. Inadequately trained nonprofessionals may have anxiety about their own functioning and transmit this to the child, or may have expectations that are inappropriate for children of that age and stage of development. If the examiner is a specialist and biased in some way, the authority of his or her action may influence the perceptions of others who are interacting with the child.

Screening to Create a Checklist Curriculum

The use of the screening and diagnostic data to develop appropriate curriculum is an art in its infancy. Many programs, often those with long and complex screening, use the collected information without any subsequent diagnosis to develop a checklist for each child; it then becomes the core of the kindergarten curriculum. It is based on the assumption, not supported by theory, that a child needs to be proficient in everything. It is a product, not process, approach which develops many splinter skills and cheats the child and the teacher of a meaningful kindergarten experience. One school district, which had a screening over an hour in length resulted in a several-page checklist which supposedly described the child. This checklist became the curriculum and was also used as the report card. The teachers were given materials and activities to work with for each item on the checklist. The feedback from the teachers was that this procedure kept them frantic, dissatisfied and endlessly keeping records. The parents were confused and tried to "train" their children to pass some of the activities, and as usual the children were the victims.

The abuses of kindergarten screening often reflect the abuses of our total educational system. Other abuses stem from the lack of knowledge and experience with the concept of early identification and personalized learning. It is the responsibility of those in charge of kindergarten screening to see that these abuses are eliminated or at least modified as much as is humanly possible.

Chapter Nine

OTHER EARLY
IDENTIFICATION PROGRAMS

$\mathbf{K}$INDERGARTEN screening is only one of many possibilities for early identification of potential high risk learners. The school is the one place to which all children must go; therefore they are available for screening programs. There are many advocates of earlier identification and intervention with those children whose development and experience make it extremely difficult or impossible to meet the expectations of the society they live in and the schools they will attend. If one could imagine a continuum of disability, there are those children who are so severely or obviously handicapped at birth that doctors and parents have no difficulty recognizing the problem. Children with incomplete limb development, severe physical disorders, or evidences of Down's Syndrome are quickly identified as compared to the child who is seen as competent and healthy but seems unable to learn to read. The extremely handicapped child may never enter a school system but requires early intervention and educational planning so that he can function as competently as possible. As we move up the continuum of disability, very early identification becomes more difficult and controversial.

Medical Screening

Medical screening has several possibilities:

1. to screen for illness and medical disorders with recognition of their impact on child's ability to learn;
2. to have physicians and health clinics do educational screening as part of their health examination;
3. to use medical information as the entire screening or as a part of the screening.

Medical screening from birth can identify, improve, remediate, and/or prevent many physical factors which influence the learning process. Phenylketonuria (PKU) is an example of a disease which can cause severe retardation unless detected and treated early. A simple test of the urine shortly after birth can detect its presence.

The first five years of a child's life are critical for intellectual and physical development, yet it is over this age span that society's capacity for identifying and treating developmental disorders is at its weakest. First awareness must come from the parent or the family doctor. Even the best intentioned parents sometimes ignore early signs of deficiency because they hope that the child is just a slow developer and once in school will catch up. The doctor may look after disease and overlook developmental milestones or lack of them. A large number of children, particularly in high risk, low income neighborhoods have little access to medical services.

Mass medically based screening and assessment and intervention programs of young children, from birth to five years old, are being explored through federal programs. The development of an "at risk" register of vulnerable children to be kept in each locality has been considered (Alberman and Goldstein, 1970). This register would select a group of infants who, because of specific characteristics, are more likely to evidence handicapping conditions. Children who fell into five main categories might be considered "at risk":

1. children with a family history of an hereditable disease, such as congenital deafness;
2. those with a history of abnormalities in prenatal life, for example, the effects of maternal rubella;
3. those with abnormalities of the perinatal period, for example, abnormal forms of delivery and prematurity;
4. children with a history of abnormal behaviour in the postnatal period which might be associated with or cause chronic mental or physical handicap;
5. children whose developmental progress, as recognized by the mother or by routine periodic developmental screening examinations, deviated from the normal pattern (Sheridan, 1962).

In 1972, a conference sponsored by the U. S. government was held on Screening and Assessment of Young Children at Developmental Risks. Over 100 people from all over the world who were either involved in this area or who represented agencies with an inherent interest in the topic were invited to participate. A monograph by John Meier (1973) drew together the literature from the field and the input of the participants. Developmental risk was defined by the 1970 Developmental Disabilities Act (PL91-517) as any person who has mental retardation, cerebral palsy, epilepsy, or other neurologically based conditions related to mental retardation, which are of an enduring nature and have their onset before age eighteen.

The monograph includes those conditions mentioned in the preceding definition plus any other conditions which are likely to prevent a child from achieving optimum growth and development in any of the social, emotional, intellectual, linguistic, or physical realms considered singly or in combination. This broader definition, therefore, includes those children who predictably will function at a less than normal developmental level because of various inborn and/or environmental deficiencies involving adequate nutrition, intellectual stimulation, language models, or emotional and social experiences. The broader definition is more closely related to the whole range of possibilities related to child failure in school.

The conference addressed "the feasibility, design, and implementation of a massive screening and assessment system to detect infants and children at risk of being or becoming developmentally disabled while they are very young and presumably most amenable to treatment and habilitation" (Meier, 1973). Some conclusions were that:

1. Early identification can be regarded as a sound, if as yet unproven, basis for the management of childhood handicap.
2. It is extremely important that the search for a delay in development among normal children is seen as a part of a larger "well-child" orientation to community child health.
3. Satisfactory techniques for developmental assessment now exist. Training in developmental medicine, both at under-

graduate and postgraduate level, is as yet inadequate to meet the demand.

Medical screening gained impetus through the 1967 Amendments to Title XIX of the Social Security Act which requires that states with Medicaid programs (which includes every state but Arizona) provide screening, diagnostic services, and treatment to all Medicaid-eligible children under age twenty-one. The screening is to include batteries of tests for physical defects; ear, nose, mouth and throat examinations (including inspection of teeth and gums); screening tests for cardiac abnormalities, anemia, sickle-cell trait, lead poisoning, tuberculosis and diabetes; a record of immunizations; and an assessment of nutritional status. In addition, the statute mandates screening for "mental defects." This program, which covers several million young children, was slow in getting underway. In 1972, as part of the Social Security amendments, Congress imposed a stiff financial penalty of one percent of Federal Aid for Dependent Children funds on states that failed to comply with the law. In 1975, the Department of Health, Education, and Welfare contracted with the American Orthopsychiatric Association to develop guidelines for a massive psychological screening program for Medicaid-eligible children.

At the state and local levels, screening clinics affiliated with health departments are held on a regular basis. To encourage pediatricians to include developmental screening in their examinations, the Committee on Children with Handicaps of the New York chapter of the American Academy of Pediatrics developed a one-page instrument called *The Rapid Developmental Screening Checklist* (Giannini et al., 1972) (see Figure 32).

Another screening instrument designed for use by doctors while doing physical examinations on five-year-olds is the Preschool Readiness Experimental Screening Scale (The Press) (Rogers, 1972). It consists of five questions which give a numerical score relating to school readiness. A low score is seen as a signal to refer the child to a school psychologist or diagnostic center for further evaluation.

Mary S. Hoffman developed a Learning Problem Indication Index which she feels could enable a physician to identify, as early

RAPID DEVELOPMENTAL SCREENING CHECKLIST*

This checklist is a compilation of developmental landmarks matched against the age of the child. These are in
easily-scored question form and may be checked "YES" or
"NO" by a physician or his aide, by direct observation.

"NO" responses at the appropriate age may constitute a
signal indicating a possible developmental lag. If there
is a substantial deviation from these values then the child
should be evaluated more carefully, taking into consideration the wide variability of developmental landmarks.
(Adjust for prematurity, prior to two years, by subtract-
ing the time of prematurity from the age of the child,
e.g. a two-month-old infant who was one month premature
should be evaluated as a month-old-infant).

It is our hope that the early recognition of such lags
would lead to early diagnosis and treatment, the results
of which can be very helpful to many of these children.

NAME:_____ D.O.E.:_____ 1st Visit:_____

AGE   DATE

1 month - Can he raise his head from
           the surface while in the
           prone position?   __YES __NO
           Does he regard your face
           while you are in his di-
           rect line of vision?   __YES __NO
2 months - Does he smile and coo?   __YES __NO
3 months - Does he follow a moving
           object?   __YES __NO
           Does he hold his head
           erect?   __YES __NO
4 months - Will he hold a rattle?   __YES __NO
           Does he laugh aloud?   __YES __NO
5 months - Can he reach for and hold
           objects?   __YES __NO
6 months - Can he turn over?   __YES __NO
           Does he turn toward sounds?   __YES __NO
           Will he sit with a little
           support (with one hand)?   __YES __NO
7 months - Can he transfer an object
           (from one hand to another)?   __YES __NO
           Can he sit momentarily with-
           out support?   __YES __NO
8 months - Can he sit steadily for
           about five minutes?   __YES __NO
9 months - Can he say "ma-ma" or
           "da-da"?   __YES __NO
10 months - Can he pull himself up at
            the side of his crib or
            playpen?   __YES __NO
11 months - Can he cruise around his
            playpen or crib, or walk
            holding on to furniture?   __YES __NO
12 months - Can he wave bye-bye?   __YES __NO
            Can he walk with one hand
            held?   __YES __NO

*(Giannini, Margaret J., 1972)

Figure 32.

AGE   DATE

Does he have a two-word vocabulary	__YES	__NO
15 months – Can he walk by himself?	__YES	__NO
Can he indicate his wants by pointing and grunting?	__YES	__NO
18 months – Can he build a tower of three blocks?	__YES	__NO
Does he say six words?	__YES	__NO
24 months – Can he run?	__YES	__NO
Can he walk up and down stairs holding rail?	__YES	__NO
Can he express himself (occasionally) in a two-word sentence?	__YES	__NO
2½ years – Can he jump lifting both feet off the ground?	__YES	__NO
Can he build a tower of six blocks?	__YES	__NO
Can he point to parts of his body on command?	__YES	__NO
3 years – Can he follow two commands involving "on", "under", or "behind"? (without gestures)	__YES	__NO
Can he build a tower of nine blocks?	__YES	__NO
Does he copy a circle?	__YES	__NO
4 years – Can he stand on one foot?	__YES	__NO
Can he copy a cross?	__YES	__NO
Does he use the past tense, properly?	__YES	__NO
5 years – Can he follow three commands?	__YES	__NO
Can he copy a square?	__YES	__NO
Can he skip?	__YES	__NO

as the age of two, the child with low training potential, and distinguish children whose academic failure results from a neurological dysfunction (Hoffman, 1971). Table XII is a revised version of the Index.

It is suggested by the authors that this index could also be used as part of a school screening program.

Infant Screening

Screening of young children not old enough for school entry has been very limited. A few of the programs described screen three-year-olds. This is usually a secondary goal with preference

TABLE XII

Learning Problem Identification Index*

Score one for each positive point
(Abnormality in a child's history)

Perinatal History

Prematurity
Prolonged labor
Difficult delivery
Cyanosis
Blood incompatibility
Adoption
Problems during pregnancy
Low birth weight

History of Developmental Abnormalities

Creeping (late or abnormal)
Walking (late)
Tip-toe walking (prolonged)
Speech (late or abnormal)
Ambidexterity (after the age of 7 years)

Interpretation of Scores:

1 or 2   - Suspicious
3   - Deserves more study
4 or more - Further study mandatory

*Bobbie L. Wilborn and Don A. Smith, "Early Identification of Children with Learning Problems," *Academic Therapy*, 9:5 (Spring 1974), 369.

given to the four- and five-year-old. When three-year-olds are screened it is usually initiated by the parent or a preschool program because of a specific concern. The few screening programs in the literature for children younger than age three are medically based. Research on infant development is limited but there is an increasing amount of it. Screening and diagnostic tools for this age range are even more limited than in the three- to six-year-old range. Meier (1973) includes an annotated index for selected developmental screening tests and procedures for young children in his book. The tests are categorized in the five developmental domains and start in the physical domain at preconception and at birth in other domains. Two tests which assess the infant at birth or shortly thereafter are the Apgar Test and the Brazelton Test.

The Apgar Test (Apgar, 1953) assesses the physical condition of a baby at birth. The five conditions rated are as follows: heart rate, respiratory efforts, reflex irritability, muscle tone, and color. A rating made one minute after birth is most useful in indicating the need for prompt treatment. A five-minute rating is more predictive of survival probability or significant neurologic damage.

The Brazelton Test (1961) is a scale to detect mild neurological dysfunction based on the infant's ability to interact with objects and people.

Infant tests of cognitive development are very low in predictive ability, as they have been traditionally based on sensory motor functioning and are therefore more highly related to subsequent sensory-motor development than to intelligence and thinking. Two infant tests that have been subjected to extensive standardization procedures are the Cattell Infant Intelligence Scale (Cattell, 1960) and the Bayley Scale of Infant Development (1969).

The Cattell Scale measures intelligence in children from age two months to thirty months. The scale has five items and one or two alternates for each age level. The levels are at one-month intervals from two to twelve months of age, two-month intervals from twelve to twenty-four months, and three-month intervals from twenty-four to thirty months. The score obtained is the child's mental age. A number of props are needed. The test is untimed and individually administered by a trained administrater. It takes about twenty to forty minutes to give.

The Bayley Scale assesses developmental status in infants from birth to thirty months of age. The mental scale measures sensory-perceptual acuities and discriminations; early acquisition of object constancy and memory, learning, and problem solving ability; vocalizations and the beginning of verbal communication; and early evidence of the ability to form generalizations and classifications. The motor scale measures the degree of control of the body, coordination of the large muscles, and finer manipulation skills of the hands and fingers. Each of these items has an age placement to the nearest one-tenth of a month and an age range. The last part of the test is an Infant Behavior Record, consisting of thirty ratings, which is completed by the examiner, after the scales have been administered, on the basis of his observations. It deals with social orientation, emotional variables, object relations, motivational variables, activity, reactivity, sensory areas of interest displayed, and general evaluations. The test is untimed (although certain items are timed) and individually administered. Training is needed. The mother (or mother substitute) is present during the test. Average testing time for the Mental and Motor Scales is forty-five minutes (Guthrie, 1971).

Infancy is viewed by many as the new educational frontier. Bloom (1964) estimates that 50 percent of intellectual development occurs between conception and age four. He says that effects of the environment, especially those that can be described as extreme, in terms of either abundance or deprivation "appear to be greatest in the early (and more rapid) period of intelligence development" and further that the evidence so far available suggests that marked changes in the environment in the early years can produce greater changes in intelligence than will equally marked changes in the environment at later periods of development.

The Harvard Preschool Project (White, 1973) is studying development of children from birth to six years. The project started with the study of the overall competence of children who had gotten off to a very good start. They categorized the characteristics that were seen in the most competent six-year-olds. They found that the well-developed three-year-old looked more like the well-developed four-, five- and six-year-olds than did poorly developed six-year-olds. This led to the conclusion that if most of the qualities that distinguish outstanding six-year-olds can be achieved in large measure at age three, then their study at Harvard should concentrate on the zero to three age range. After studying the literature they concluded that "it appeared that under the variety of early rearing conditions prevalent in modern American homes, divergence with respect to the development of educability and overall competence first becomes manifest during the second year of life and becomes quite substantial in many cases by three years of age." Two major factors seem to underly the effectiveness of early child rearing: how the parents respond to the child's development of locomotor ability (walking) and the development of language.

With the increased awareness of the importance of the early years, educational programs are being implemented with populations that are seen as potential high risk. Head Start, which began in 1965 is probably the best known. It annually serves 350,000 children, four-fifths of them on a full-year basis. The Economic Opportunity Act of 1964, as amended in 1967, required Head Start to offer comprehensive health, nutritional education. It also called for direct participation of parents in running the program. Regulations require that each Head Start child receive a medical and dental examination and a hot meal each day. These procedures alone have made Head Start the first organized national program to deliver standardized health care to young children in poverty areas. A controversial aspect of Head Start has been the difficulty of measuring gains made by the children in the program. Initially, growth was measured by the much criticized method of IQ points gained. Head Start and other preschool programs have spawned the development of many new assessment measures.

Federal funding has supported the development of preschool programs for the handicapped. The PIE project (Preschool Instruction for the Exceptional) in the Northern Valley Schools in New Jersey (Ciccaricco, 1975) is a nursery program for severely handicapped children that uses the personalized learning model as the process for meeting the very diverse needs of the handicapped children.

The Pennsylvania Research in Infant Development and Education Project (1972-73) is an educational effort to accelerate the development of children from a variety of cultural and socioeconomic backgrounds.

"It represents a cooperative effort by college, community, private and state agencies to stimulate the development of children, 12 to 52 months of age, by providing developmentally enriching experiences in a controlled environment which enhance the growth of sensory, conceptual and language abilities." The Project had seven components, three of which will be described (Dusewicz, 1973a).

The Center Early Learning Program is a two-year program. Level I or infant group is for the age range from twelve to twenty months by October 1 and Level II is the toddler group. Children are enrolled only at the infant level. About 80 percent of the twenty-five children in each group come from families that are in the low income category. Each group attends a half-day session five days a week during the college school year; Level I in the morning, Level II in the afternoon.

> The program curriculum is designed to provide a structured sequence of developmental activities in which new abilities are continually built upon the foundation of abilities which already have been mastered. Curriculum activities begin in the first year with a concentration in the sensory and perception areas progressing later to the conceptual and language areas, and finally to more academic areas of reading and math instruction (Dusewicz, 1973a).

Pre- and post-tests of five measures including the PPVT and the Vineland Social Maturity Test show significant gains.

The Home Early Learning Program is directed to the same population as the Center Early Learning Program and has the same goals. Two 40-minute visits are made each week by the child's teacher during the months from October to April. For each visit the child and teacher work with a selection of teaching materials to assist the child in attaining specific learning objectives. The teachers who visit the homes are all undergraduate students at West Chester College employed through the college work-study program. Pre- and post-tests over the four years the program has been in operation are equally significant as those of the Center Early Learning Program (Dusewicz, 1973b).

The Parent Involvement Program is an effort toward teaching parents of disadvantage children about child development in general and the types of activities that they can conduct in the home with their children to help them develop. The program is operated on a home visit basis, with a tutor devoting one hour per week for each parent. Evaluation of the program was through a survey questionnaire. It was felt that the major objective of the program had been reached because there was a large increase in the amount of interaction which occurred between the mother and her preschool child. The mother was also a little more understanding of the child's behavior in certain situations. Some of the mothers, by the end of the program, found themselves interested in a possible vocation relating to working with preschool children (Dusewicz, 1973c).

Home-based programs for young children encourage the

parent to become more intimately involved with their child. There is a spin-off in several directions. The parent acquires knowledge and experience that can be applied to other children in the family; it also helps to improve the mother's image of herself as a parent and a person, and as evidenced in the West Chester Parent Involvement Program, it may also have vocational implications. For the young handicapped child and his parents, home-based programs have great relevance.

The Portage Project in Portage, Wisconsin is an intervention program serving seventy-five preschool multiply handicapped children living in a rural area. The children range in age from birth to six years. All instruction takes place in the child's home. Individualized curriculum is prescribed and demonstrated by a home teacher who visits each parent and child one day a week for one and one-half hours for a period of nine and one-half months. During the week the parents teach the prescribed curriculum and record the child's resultant behavior on a daily basis.

Each child's curriculum is based on his present behavior, not his disability label. The project staff devised an Early Childhood Curriculum Guide (Shearer et al., 1972a) which is in two parts: (1) a Developmental Sequence Checklist, which lists sequential behaviors from birth to five years of age in five developmental areas: cognitive, language, self-help, motor, and socialization; (2) a set of curriculum cards to match each of the 450 behaviors stated on the checklist, using behavioral objectives to describe the skill and suggesting materials and curriculum ideas to teach each of the 450 behaviors.

The average IQ of the children in the project was 75 as determined by the Cattell Infant Test and the Stanford Binet Intelligence Test. The average child in the project gained thirteen months in an eight-month period, 60 percent more than his counterpart with a normal intelligence (Shearer, 1972b).

Developmental theory and research support earlier identification of children with special needs, but it is not always possible to reach all of these children early, particularly those whose families move a great deal or are not aware of community resources.

Silver and Hagin (1975) developed SEARCH, an instrument to

be used "for scanning large numbers of school children to detect those with learning problems and those with potential for emotional decompensation." It is an individual test which is administered at the end of the kindergarten year or the beginning of first grade. It has ten component subtests and requires twenty minutes to administer and score. The scores are translated into stanines. Children identified by SEARCH are a heterogenious group. Clinical services are seen as necessary to make individual diagnosis.

In a pilot study in New York City it was found that SEARCH scores can predict vulnerability or lack of it with a high degree of accuracy. The score range can also be a predictor of the type of vulnerability. It was found that scores in the three lowest stanines suggest the need for neuropsychiatric consultation, that educational intervention alone may be inadequate. A prescriptive program, TEACH, is in process of development which helps the teacher capitalize on the information generated by SEARCH. Preliminary results (Hagin, 1975) indicate that children in this first grade pilot program have shown significant gains over their counterparts in the control group.

The vulnerability of the potential high risk child is often evident at a very young age. Certain children may be helped more by earlier identification and intervention programs, though there is the same potential for abuse which exists in kindergarten screening.

Chapter Ten

EVALUATION AND FUTURE GOALS

$\mathbf{K}$INDERGARTEN screening is a tool which, when used appropriately, helps the educator to plan more effectively for each child. It is part of the total educational process, but it can never be a substitute for good teaching or a sound educational program.

What can be accomplished by prekindergarten and kindergarten screening? Early identification of children who may have special needs changes the focus to prevention of problems rather than remediation. Screening generates and reenforces an awareness of the range of individual differences among young children coming to school and hopefully causes school personnel to reexamine their expectations and curricular goals for their primary grades. Screening facilitates communication that is child-centered between teachers, specialists, administrators, and parents. This increased communication may result in more involvement by the parent with the school and increased understanding of their child in relation to his educational needs. Communication among educators may also facilitate a multidisciplinary approach for helping children with special needs and a search for learning of more effective ways for these children to experience success in school.

Kindergarten screening has the potential to facilitate these positive results. Different programs have achieved many of them but on the other hand many things have impeded achieving such results. Some of these factors are directly related to screening and others to the wider milieu, of which screening is a part. While there has been much change from the attitude of "Leave the child alone and he will outgrow his problem," there is not common agreement on what age to begin the identification process and the method to be used. This controversy exists at all levels: local, state, and national.

At the time this book was written many states had or were

considering laws mandating early identification programs. The federal government is seeking to implement psychoeducational screening for those children covered under Title XIX of the Social Security Act through a program known as Early and Periodic Screening, Diagnosis, and Treatment (EPSDT). School districts throughout the country are devising and implementing programs, often with the assistance of state and federal funding. Enough programs exist to allow for an informal assessment of strengths and weaknesses. There are no statistics that document changed attitudes toward children with special needs, or the number of changes in curriculum or inservice courses held as a result of screening programs. There are statistics in some programs that document improved functioning of children who benefited by early identification and follow-through programs. The current trend seems to favor initiating screening but at the same time recognizing the concomitant problems and concerns, and the need to do something about them.

Concerns Related to the Screening

In the screening process, the major problems are definition and instrumentation. What does the high risk learner look like and how do we assess those characteristics? Using the concept of mismatch, how do we determine the cutoff point at which a potential problem exists? This has been resolved in some communities by using a percentage as a guideline, usually 10 to 15 percent. Another way has been to establish a "watch and wait" category for those children lower on the continuum of potential risk. The choice of a cutoff point may influence the number of false positives and negatives that occur in the screening. The false positives are those that are identified as potential high risk but in fact are not. This category is of less urgent concern because subsequent diagnosis will clarify the status of these children. The false negatives are those that are potential high risk but are not identified by the screening. If a screening is to be fruitful, the cutoff point for follow-through must be high enough to minimize the number who fall into this category.

To describe the potentially unsuccessful learner, one must

know the characteristics of the successful learner. In order to know this, success must be defined in terms of curricular and behavior expectations. This possibility is complicated by the fact that many schools espouse curricular goals that sound flexible and child-centered but in fact classroom expectations are lock-stepped and rigidly achievement oriented.

If the characteristics of the successful and unsuccessful learner in a school system are contrasted, then consideration can be given to identification of those areas of contrast. For example, if most successful first grade children have good auditory memory and most unsuccessful first graders do not, then this might be an area for assessment. This rational possibility to determine what to assess is compounded by many things. The knowledge of how children learn is based on a variety of theoretical assumptions rather than a single body of facts. Developmental theory confirms the observations in the classroom that there is a wide variation in how children develop within themselves and as compared to others.

Situational and environmental factors influence how a child's inherent abilities develop. The problem of definition includes definition of high risk and of the areas of development and experience of this child.

Assuming definitions have been agreed upon, how are these characteristics to be assessed? Assessment can only be done in areas that can be defined and measured. For example, perceptual development is defined in terms of many concepts such as body image, laterality, directionality, and so forth. These concepts lend themselves to commonly agreed upon operational definitions which are measureable. At least equally important to the learning process is motivation, which is much harder to define and measure and therefore is often not included in assessment.

These two basic problems can be compounded by other decisions related to the actual screening, such as who does the screening and where, and when it takes place. The attitudes and values of those who plan and implement the screening also may influence the results.

Concerns Related to the Screening Program

A screening program can be cause for concern. Chapter Eight

described some of the major abuses that can cause a screening program to have a negative rather than positive impact. There are other concerns that warrant consideration as they influence the adequacy of a program. A major concern is the lack of adequate knowledge of what is the best educational program for children who have special needs. A successful prescription for one child may not work for a child who seems to be similar. In the various pilot screening programs, a wide variety of materials and strategies have been used with varying degrees of success.

Unrealistic expectations for the child and for the program create an environment in which success for all children is not possible. An example of an unrealistic expectation would be to have as a goal to raise a child's IQ rather than to improve his achievement. If the program is oversold, then anything less than a miracle will cause dissatisfaction with the program and with the children involved. There is often the covert expectation that anything short of making the atypical child typical is failure. It is helpful to specify and publicize objectives that are possible to achieve within a stated time period. These objectives and the goals that they are part of need to be consistent with the educational philosophy that the school is actually operating from. Often, unrealistic expectations stem from either lacking or conflicting philosophies within a system.

Unwillingness of educators to do risk-taking and learning through evaluation of their efforts is a concern. In starting a new program, it is not always possible to meet the needs of each person involved, or be aware of every possible pitfall or plan for every contingency. The needs of the child should come first. Educators need to be more willing to admit that in the learning process mistakes are made and that it is valid to learn from these mistakes.

In launching a screening program, how ready should a program be before it is presented and implemented? This is a question without a definitive answer. Because knowledge and experience with screening programs is in its infancy, taking risks is necessary. A committee can never know all the answers to all the questions. When it has done the best job it feels capable of, then the program needs to be field-tested for critical feedback. It is through feedback that programs improve and the body of knowledge is expanded. For a program to be ready, it must have a built-in method for evaluation. A dilemma occurs in many programs; initially the program is developed with the awareness of the imperfect state of knowledge in the field, but upon implementation, the results are used as if they were indisputably correct.

Too long or too complex screening can hamper a program. The collection of too much data and data for which no use is planned is a waste of everybody's time. Data of a personal, but irrelevant, nature serves no useful purpose and may create feelings of antagonism on the part of the parents toward the school. Some information may feed into the prejudices of the educators and influence their attitude toward the child.

When relevant information of a personal nature is sought, it must be made clear to the parents that they have the right not to share it, and the right to know why the information is requested, and how it is to be used.

Collection of insufficient background data can impede educational planning. A child may not be open to learn because he is hungry, tired, unhappy, allergic, or any of the many other nonschool-related factors that influence the child's functioning. Background information helps raise relevant questions even though it is not always possible to do anything about it. For example, an extra classroom snack or a short nap may be part of a child's prescription.

There is concern as to whether screening is too overwhelming as the child's first experience in school. This depends on how sensitively children are interacted with and the type of environment in which the screening is conducted. An unwilling child should be encouraged but never forced to participate.

Screening programs, particularly in the follow-through phase, are hampered by the lack of resources, time, money, and skills to personalize learning. This may be due to the total lack of resources in a school and community or because of the priorities set for their use. Many feel that it is not realistic to become involved in new programs when there are so many problems in existing programs. For example, given a limited number of resources, do you set priorities to help the children who are presently failing or do you give priority to those children who haven't failed yet but will without the extra attention that a screening program provides?

The follow-through program is the source of many concerns. In many programs, there is focus on short-term involvement such as a summer program or a part or all of the first school year. For some children, this may be adequate; for others, ongoing support is necessary. In some programs placement is the end product, often in a situation of limited options, none of which may meet the child's need. The concept of mainstreaming, compounded by the confusion of unclear definition, has created problems of where and how a child's special needs are met.

Screening and diagnosis should not lead to checklist curriculums, but there needs to be a relationship between what is known about the child and the educational experiences planned. In this situation, packaged programs and kits have been both a help and a hindrance. They are a help in that they provide the neophyte with teaching tools and materials and the security of the implied expertise of the creator of the program. The hindrance is that there is a tendency to put an entire class or group through a program whether it is necessary or not. Thus, there is movement away from the needs of specific children. Use of packaged programs and kits are often disproportionately expensive and their use tends to reduce the use of the teacher's knowledge and creativity. Many programs are based on the inappropriate assumptions that in order to learn effectively the child has to be good at everything or that there is one "true" answer. Often more splinter skills than generalizable knowledge are learned. There is a flight to packaged materials when screening and diagnosis fail to provide recommendations which are specific enough to help the teacher utilize her existing knowledge. Intelligently used, packaged programs can help, but they should be only part of a larger program.

Critical to any educational program is the competence, attitude, and enthusiasm of the teacher. It is upon his or her shoulders that ultimately the implementation of any program rests. Teachers, like children, are the products of their own background experience. This includes their ethnic and socioeconomic background, their reasons for wanting to be a teacher, their experience as a student, and their teacher training. In too many teacher training programs there is a sharp delineation between so-called "regular" and "special" education, as if they drew from radically different bodies of knowledge. This creates a schism and a sense of inadequacy in the classroom teacher of his ability to deal with children who do not conform to the established norm. The bond between the two fields is good teaching practice and the ability to implement flexible classroom procedures.

When teachers have not had the necessary training to be comfortable with children with a wide range of needs, it is necessary for the schools to plan to help and support the teachers. The way in which resource people are used will influence the total program. If their use is limited to removing children from the classroom for remediation, then the classroom teacher is led to expect that she has no responsibility for that aspect of the child's program. Communication between the specialist and the classroom teacher is as critical as communication among the specialists and with administrators. When this does not occur, the results for the child are as fragmented as a blind man's description of an elephant.

The final school-related concern is the need for cricital and ongoing assessment of every facet of a program. In too many schools this is seen as a luxury for which there is no time, or the program becomes so bound up in someone's ego or power needs that any criticism would be received with hostility.

Broader Issues Relating to Screening

Screening is only a small part of the total educational process. It reflects, and is influenced by, the broader issues of the society and institutions of which it is a part. The attitudes, values, and norms of a society establish the concepts of good and bad or desirable and undesirable. In Chapter Eight the issue of labeling was discussed. The most negative implication occurs when labels are used to stigmatize or exclude. The most positive occurs when labels are used to facilitate funding and sound educational planning. Too often, the issue of labels is used as an emotionally loaded device to cloud the issue and delay dealing with a problem or avoiding it.

Political and territorial issues may influence screening programs. Education is a multibillion dollar industry and subject to all the forces therein such as unions, economic survival through various sources of funding, and pressures of many special interest groups. Teacher's unions are insisting that education and involvement with young children belong in the schools; others feel it to be the province of the government and community agencies.

Communities differ in their awareness and their ability to become involved with preschool children. Programs increase their effectiveness when there is a cooperative effort between the schools and the community agencies.

All too often, money is a critical issue, both in its availability and the priority for its use. An argument for screening is that it is more cost effective to prevent than remediate. The cost of maintaining a minimally or nonfunctioning person is a great financial as well as emotional burden on a society. Any steps to increase a person's potential to contribute to society would seem to be economical.

A most difficult issue to resolve is how much can each child be expected to achieve? When can one say that this child is doing the best he is able? Is it meaningful to expend a set amount of money to help one child move an inch, when the same expenditure would help another child to move a foot? How does one deal rationally with the emotionally packed issue of individual differences and realistic and unrealistic expectations?

RESEARCH. As in other facets of education, many of the issues of screening could be confronted more realistically if there were a larger body of research to draw from. The basic assumption of screening is that potential high risk children can be identified early and that intervention will make a difference. More knowledge is needed to support this assumption and more tools are needed to act from it.

Some suggested areas for research are as follows:

1. identification of predictors which facilitate and interfere with learning the characteristics of potential high risk children;

2. development of programs and materials to help the potential high risk child to learn more effectively;
3. longitudinal studies of children involved in screening programs;
4. development of more valid and reliable assessment instruments;
5. culture-fair tests;
6. comparisons of effectiveness of various assessment techniques;
7. impact on child of examiner of different culture or sex;
8. impact of different methods of test administration, i.e. one examiner or several stations;
9. determining appropriate learning experiences for identified problems;
10. role of alternative environments in prescription;
11. relationship between parent expectation and child's success in classroom;
12. relationship between parent involvement and child's success in classroom;
13. impact of teacher attitudes on potential high risk learner;
14. determining age that is most appropriate for early identification;
15. determining cost benefits for preschool identification and intervention programs as opposed to a later screening and identification;
16. better designed pilot screening programs for feedback of what works.

From Here to Where?

Each child has a past, a present, and a future. The past needs to be known to the degree that it helps to understand the present and plan for the future. The same is true for screening. Statistical evidence and the experiencing of frustration and failure have created a need to focus on the issue of prevention rather than on remediation or continued failure. Early identification of young children is one way of dealing with this issue, and screening is one tool. Screening programs are only a piece of a larger system of educational, health, and community services for children. They must be responsive to and not exist independent of the total system.

A start has been made to identify and develop programs for potential high risk learners. At the time of this writing the momentum toward screening is increasing, as are the controversies surrounding it. What does the future look like?

Government involvement at the federal and state level is increasing through legislation and supportive funding. Because school-age populations are declining, school space and personnel are becoming increasingly available. The issue of who should implement screening programs resembles a territorial imperative as the schools and other agencies vie for control of the education of preschool children.

Those involved in screening are attempting to describe an ideal screening program. Meier (1975) says that screening should be viewed as a continuous process beginning at preconception and repeated during the course of the preschool and school years. The purpose of repeated screening at regular intervals is to identify conditions that might have been missed originally, might present themselves at a later age, as well as those that might have improved over time and should be removed from surveillance.

Denhoff (1971) says that an ideal early identification program for high risk children should begin during the neonatal period with the tagging of these infants. It should continue during the infancy and preschool years with the follow-up of these babies as well as the identification of other children by an aware parent and the professional community. A general screening of all children should take place before they enter kindergarten. Identified high risk children should be followed through the primary school years with a range of educational and medical services.

However screening is conceptualized, there seems to be a role for the school and a need to look at children carefully before they start their schooling. As a start, the area of greatest need is to help those children where the mismatch is greatest. There has to be continuous assessment of how the school, teamed with the parents and community agencies, can meet the needs of all children. Kindergarten screening is a start; flexible and personalized learning programs for all children are a goal. There is a need to match what the child is able to do to what we are asking him to do.

BIBLIOGRAPHY

"A Failure at 5," *Newsweek*, p. 48, July 14, 1975.

Adelman, H. S.: The not too specific learning disability population. *Exceptional Child*, 37:528-33, 1971.

Adler, Sol: Data gathering: the reliability and validity of test data from culturally different children. *Journal of Learning Disabilities*, 6:429-34, Aug./Sept. 1973.

Alberman, E. D. and Goldstein, H.: The 'At Risk' register — A statistical evaluation. *Br J Prev Social Med*, 24:129-35, Aug. 1970.

American Academy of Pediatrics: Statement on Early Identification of Children with Learning Disabilities: The Preschool Child, 1973.

Ames, Louis Bates, Gillespie, Clyde, and Steiff, John: *Stop School Failure*. New York, Har-Row, 1972, p. 170.

Apgar, Virginia: Apgar Test. Unpublished testing material, 1953.

"Arlington Specialist Helps the Handicapped," *Mid-Hudson Channel*, June 1972.

Bangs, T.: Disorders of the Preacademic Child. *Language and Learning*. New York, Appleton, 1968.

Barnhart, C. L. (Ed.): *American Collegiate Dictionary*. New York, Random, 1963, pp. 333, 1090.

Bartel, Nettie R., Grill, J. Jeffrey, and Bryen, Diane: Language Characteristics of Black Children: Implications for Assessment. *Journal of School Psychology*, 2:351-64, 1973.

Bartlett, Charles H.: The Educational Evaluation in an Interdisciplinary Setting: A Developing Concept. In Kirk, S. and McCarthy, J. (Eds.): *Learning Disabilities: Selected ACLD Papers*. Boston, Hm, 1975.

Bannatyne, A. D.: The slow developer. *Academic Therapy*, 5:255-57, Summer 1970.

Bayley, N.: *Bayley Scales of Infant Development*. New York, The Psychological Corporation, 1969.

Belmont, I., Flegenheimer, Hannah, and Birch, Herbert: Comparison of Perceptual Training and Remedial Instruction for Poor Beginning Readers. *Journal of Learning Disabilities*, 6:230-35, April 1973.

Bernstein, B.: *Family Role Systems, Socialization and Communication*. Paper presented at the Conference on Cross Cultural Research into Childhood and Adolescence, Univ. of Chicago, 1964.

Bloom, Benj. S. et al.: *Compensatory Education for Cultural Deprivation*. New York, HR & W, 1965.

215

Bloom, Benj. S.: *Stability and Change in Human Characteristics*. New York, Wiley, 1964.

Bloom, Benj. S. (Ed.): *Taxonomy of Educational Objectives Handbook I: Cognitive Domain*. New York, McKay, 1956.

Bradley, Estelle: Screen Them Early. *Academic Therapy, 10*:305-8, Spring 1975.

Brazelton, T.: Psychophysiologic reactions of the Neomate: The value of the observations of the neomate. *Journal of Pediatrics, 38*:508, 1961.

Bryant, N.: Some Conclusions Concerning Impaired Motor Development Among Reading Disability Cases. *Bulletin of Orton Society, 14*:16-7, 1964.

Bryen, Diane and Bartel, Nettie: The Disadvantaged is a Social and Professional Phenomena. *Journal of School Psychology, 11*:387-401, 1973.

Buros, O. K. (Ed.): *7th Mental Measurements Yearbook*. Highland Park, New Jersey, Gryphon Press, 1972.

Caldwell, B. M.: A Decade of Early Intervention Programs, What We have Learned. *American Journal of Orthopsychiatry, 44*:491-96, 1974.

Caldwell, Bettye: Cooperative Preschool Inventory. Educational Testing Service. Princeton, New Jersey, 1970.

Cattell, P.: *Cattell Infant Intelligence Scale*. The Psychological Corporation, New York, 1960.

Cattell, Raymond: *Culture Fair Intelligence Test*. Institute for Personality and Ability Testing. Champaign, Illinois, 1963.

Cennamo, Elizabeth, school psychologist, South-Western City School District, Grove City, Ohio. Personal correspondence, 1975.

Chalfant, J. C. and Flathouse, V. E.: Auditory and visual learning. In Myklebust, H. (Ed.): *Progress in Learning Disabilities, Vol. 2*, New York, Grune, 1971.

Chess, S.: *An Introduction To Child Psychiatry*. New York, Grune, 1969.

Ciccoricco, Edward et al.: *Preschool Instruction for the Exceptional (PIE) Project Report 1974-75*. Northern Valley Schools, Closter, 1975.

Colorado Division of Special Services, *Report of a Title VI, ESEA, Summer Screening Clinic Sponsored by El Paso County School District #11, and the Colorado Department of Education*, Colorado Springs, 1968.

Cowgill, Mary, Friedland, Seymour and Shapiro, Rose: Predicting Learning Disabilities from Kindergarten Reports. *Journal of Learning Disabilities, 6*:577-82, Nov. 1973.

Cohen, Dorothy and Stern, Virginia: *Observing and Recording the Behavior of Young Children*. New York, Teacher's College Press, Columbia University, 1958.

Davis, A. L.: American Dialects for English Teachers. Interim Report, Illinois State-Wide Curriculum Study Center, ERIC ED 032 298, 1969.

De Hirsch, K.: Learning disabilities: An Overview, *Bulletin of New York Academy of Medicine, 50*:April 1974.

De Hirsch, K.: Learning disabilities: An Overview. International Conference of Assoc. of Children with Learning Disabilities. New York, 1975.

De Hirsch, K., Jansky, J., and Lanford, W.: *Predicting Reading Failure*. New York, Har-Row, 1966.

Denhoff, E., Hainsworth, P., and Hainsworth, M.: Learning disabilities and early childhood education: An information processing approach. In Myklebust, H. (Ed.): *Progress in Learning Disabilities, Vol. II*. New York, Grune, 1971.

Deutsch, M.: The role of social class in language development and cognition. *Amer. Journal of Orthopsychiatry, 35*:78-88, Jan. 1965.

DIAL, Learning Disabilities/Early Childhood Research Project, Office of the Supt. of Public Instruction, State of Illinois, 1972.

Diana vs. State Board of Education, C-70 37FFP, District Court for Northern California, February, 1970.

DiNola, Alfred, Kaminsky, Bernard and Sternfeld, Allen: *Preschool and Kindergarten Performance Profile: Teacher's Manual*. Ridgefield, Educational Performance Association, 1970.

Drew, Clifford, Jr.: Criterion referenced and norm referenced assessment of minority group children. *Journal of School Psychology, 2*:323-29, 1973.

Dubnoff, B.: Early Detection and Remediation of Learning Disabilities. In Oglesby & Sterling (Eds.): *Proceedings, Bi-Regional Institute on Earlier Recognition of Handicapping Conditions in Childhood*, 131, 1970.

Dusewicz, Russell and O'Connell, Mary Ann: Center Early Learning Program. Unpublished paper, Bureau of Research and Related Services, West Chester State College, West Chester, 1973a.

Dusewicz, Russell and O'Connell, Mary Ann: Home Early Learning Program, Unpublished paper, Bureau of Research and Related Services, West Chester State College, West Chester, 1973b.

Dusewicz, Russell and O'Connell, Mary Ann: The Parent Investment Program, Unpublished paper, Bureau of Research and Related Service, West Chester State College, West Chester, 1973c.

Egan, D. et al.: Developmental Screening 0-5 years. *Clinics in Developmental Medicine*, No. 30. London, Spastics International Medical Publishers, Heinemann, 1969.

Elkind, D.: Increasing and realizing human potentials. *Childhood Education, 47*:7, 346-48, 1971.

Erikson, Erik: *Childhood and Society*, 2nd ed. New York, Norton, 1963.

ESEA, Early Prevention of School Failure: Peotone, Illinois, 1971, p. 4.

Ferguson-Florissant School District, *Parents as Partners in Early Education*. Title III, Ser. 306, ESEA, Ferguson, 1974.

Farrald, Robert and Schamber, Richard: *ADAPT — A Diagnostic and Prescriptive Technique*. Sioux Falls, Adapt Press, Inc., 1973, p. 7.

Feshback, Seymour, Adelman, Howard and Fuller, Williamson: Early Identification of Children with High Risk of Reading Failure. *Journal of Learning Disabilities, 7*:639-44, Dec. 1974.

Fluharty, Nancy Buono: Preschool Speech and Language Screening Test. *Journal of Speech & Hearing Disorders, 39*:75-88, Feb. 1974.

Forress, Steven: Implications of Recent Trends in Educational Learning Disabilities. *Journal of Learning Disabilities,* 7:Aug./Sept. 1974.

Frostig, Marianne et al.: Frostig Program for the Development of Visual Perception, Chicago, Follett, 1964.

Frostig, Marianne and Maslow, Phyllis: *Learning Problems in the Classroom.* New York, Grune, 1973.

Furth, Hans G. and Wacks, Harry: *Thinking Goes to School.* New York, Oxford Pr, 1974, p. 25.

Gay, Geneva and Abrahams, Roger: Does the Pot Melt, Boil or Brew? Black Children and White Assessment Procedures. *Journal of School Psychology,* 2:341-50, 1973.

Gesell, A. and Amatruda, E.: *Developmental Diagnosis,* 2nd ed. New York, Hoeber, 1947.

Getman, G. N. and Kane, E. R.: *The Physiology of Readiness: An Action Program for the Development of Perception in Children, Programs to Accelerate School Success,* P.A.S.S., Minneapolis, 1964.

Giannini, M. et al.: The Rapid Developmental Screening Checklist. American Academy of Pediatrics, New York, Feb. 1972.

Goldberg, Herman K. and Schiffman, Gilbert: *Dyslexia, Problems of Reading Disability.* New York, Grune, 1972.

Goodman, K.: Reading: The key is in the children's language. *Reading Teacher,* 25:505-08, 1972.

Gray, S. W. and Klaus, R. A.: The Early Training Project: A Seventh Year Report. *Child Development, 41*:909, 924, 1970.

Green, Orville, C. and Perlman, Suzanne, M.: Endocrinology & Disorders of Learning. In Myklebust, H. (Ed.): *Progress in Learning Disabilities, Vol. II.* New York, Grune, 1971, pp. 1-17.

Grotberg, Edith: Identification of Preschool Learning Disabled Children — Is it Possible? Unpublished lecture presented 1975, International Conference ACLD, New York, Feb. 26, 1975.

Guthrie, P. D.: *Head Start Test Collection.* Educational Testing Service, Princeton, 1971.

Hagin, Rosa: Personal Communication with the author, Oct. 1975, SEARCH.

Hainsworth, Peter K. and Hainsworth, Marian: *Preschool Screening Systems: Start of the Longitudinal-Preventive Approach.* Pawtucket, Rhode Island, 1974.

Hainsworth, Peter K. and Siqueland, M. L.: *Early Identification of Children with Learning Disabilities.* Crippled Children and Adults of Rhode Island, Inc., 1969, p. 5.

Hainsworth, Marion L., Hainsworth, Peter K., and Siegal, Judith: *Information Processing Curriculum, Vol. I.* Developed Under Title VIG, Rhode Island Dept. of Education, 1972-74.

Halliwell, Joseph and Solan, Harold: The effects of a Supplemental Perceptual Training Program on Reading Achievement. *Exceptional Children, 38*:613-20, April 1972.

Hammill, Donald and Bartel, Nettie: *Teaching Children With Learning and Behavior Problems.* Boston, Allyn, 1975.

Haring, Norris G. and Ridgway, Robert W.: Early Identification of Children with Learning Disability. *Exceptional Child, 33*:387-95, 1967.

Harris, Dale B.: *Children's Drawings as Measures of Intellectual Maturity.* New York, Har Brace World, 1963.

Havard, Janice: Allergies Create Problems. *Journal of Learning Disabilities, 6*:492-500, Oct. 1973.

Hawley, Clyde and Buckley, Robert: Food Dyes and Hyperkinetic Children. *Academic Therapy, 10*:27-32, Fall 1974.

Heath, Earl J.: In Service Training: Preparing to Meet Today's Needs. *Academic Therapy, 9*:267-80, Spring, 1974.

Hess, Karen M.: The Nonstandard Speakers in our Schools, What Should be Done? *Elementary School Journal, 74*:283, 1974.

Hildreth, G. H., Griffiths, N. L. and McGauwran, M. E.: *Metropolitan Readiness Tests.* New York, Har Brace J, 1969.

Hobbs, Nicholas (Ed.): *Issues in the Classification of Children.* Vol. 1 & 2, San Francisco, Jossey-Bass Publishers, 1975.

Hobbs, Nicholas: *The Futures of Children Categories, Labels and Their Consequences.* San Francisco, Jossey-Bass Publishers, 1975.

Hodges, W., McCandles, B., and Spicker, H.: The Development and Analysis of a Diagnostically Based Curriculum for Psychosocially Disadvantaged Children. Final Report, Indiana University, Contract No. OFG-32-24-0310-1011, U. S. Office of Education, 1967.

Hoepfner, Ralph, Stern, Carol and Nummedal, Susan (Ed.): *CSE-ECRC Pre-School Kindergarten Tests Evaluations,* UCLA Graduate School of Education, Los Angeles, 1971.

Hoffman, Mary P.: Early Identification of Learning Problems. *Academic Therapy, 7*:1, 23-35, Fall 1971.

Holliday, Frances B. and Olswang, Lesley B.: *School-Community Programs in Early Childhood Development.* District 65, Evanston Public School Systems, 1975.

Howes, Doris: Vocabulary size estimated from the distribution of word frequencies. In Myklebust, H. (Ed.): *Progress in Learning Disabilities, Vol. II,* New York, Grune, 1971.

Humes, Charles, Miles, Patricia and Savage, William: Early Learning Disabilities Identification: A Report. *Academic Therapy, 10*:419-26, Summer 1975.

Isaac, Stephen and Michael, William: *Handbook in Research and Evaluation.* San Diego, Robert R. Knopp Publisher, 1971.

Iwakami, Eileen: Department of Health, Honolulu. Personal correspondence, June 12, 1975.

Jansky, J.: The Contribution of Certain Kindergarten Abilities to Second Grade Reading and Spelling Achievement. Doctoral Thesis, Teachers College, Columbia, University, 1971.

Johnson, D. and Myklebust, H.: *Learning Disabilities, Education, Principles and Practice.* New York, Grune, 1967.

Johnson, Rosa: *Pre-Kindergarten Screening/Registration Procedure.* Mimeographed Booklet, Horseheads Central School District, Horseheads, New York, Spring 1974.

Jones, R. L.: Labels and Stigma in Special Education. *Exceptional Children, 38*:553-64, March 1972.

Kalstrom, C.: *The Yellow Brick Road.* Learning Concepts, Inc., Austin, 1975.

Kappelman, Murray: Learning Disabilities: A Team Approach to Diagnosis and Prescription. *Educational Leadership, 32*:513-16, May 1975.

Keogh, B. K. and Smith, C. E.: Visual motor ability for school prediction, A Seven Year Study. *Percept Mot Skills, 25*:101-10, 1967.

Keogh, B. K.: The Bender Gestalt as a predictive and diagnostic test of reading performance. *Journal of Consulting Psychology, 29*:83-4, 1965.

Keogh, B. and Becker, L.: Early detection of Learning Problems: Questions, Cautions and Guidelines. *Exceptional Children, 40*:5-11, Sept. 1973.

Kephart, N.: *The Slow Learner in the Classroom.* Columbus, Merrill, 1960.

KIND Program, Wappingers Central School District. Wappingers Falls, Mimeographed Report, 1973.

Kleisinger, G. J.: Individual Readiness and Diagnostic Test for Pre-school Evaluation. *Journal of School Health, 43*:233-35, April 1973.

Koluger, George and Kolson, Clifford J.: *Reading and Learning Disabilities.* Columbus, Merrill, 1969.

Koppitz, Elizabeth M.: *The Bender Gestalt Test for Young Children.* New York, Grune, 1964.

Koppitz, Elizabeth M.: *Children With Learning Disabilities: A Five Year Study.* New York, Grune, 1971, p. 199.

Koppitz, Elizabeth M.: *Psychological Evaluation of Children's Human Figure Drawings.* New York, Grune, 1968.

Krathwohl, David R., Bloom, B. and Masin, B.: *Taxonomy of Educational Objectives Handbook II Affective Domain.* New York, McKay, 1964.

Landsberger, Betty: *Bobbie Goes to Screening.* North Carolina Department of Human Resources, Div. of Health Services, Raleigh, 1975.

Lerner, Janet W.: *Children With Learning Disabilities.* Boston, HM, 1971.

Lessler, Ken: Health and Educational Screening of School Age Children — Definition and Objectives. *American Journal of Public Health, 62*:191-98, Feb. 1972.

Lewin, Kurt: *Field Theory in Social Sciences.* New York, Harper, 1951.

Lindemann, Eliz B., Rosenblith, Judy F., Allensmith, Wesley, Budd, Lindly and Shapiro, Sybil: Predicting School Adjustment Before Entry. *Journal of School Psychology, 6*:24-42, Fall 1967.

Lowell, Robert E.: Reading Readiness Factors as Predictors of Success in First Grade Reading. *Journal of Learning Disabilities, 4*:563-67, Dec. 1971.

Lowenthal, Barbara: What Parents Can do to Help Their Special Preschoolers. *Academic Therapy, 10*:181-85, Winter 1974-75.

Mackie, Romaine: *Special Education in the U.S. Statistics 1946-1949.* New York, Teacher's College Press, 1969, p. 61.

Mager, Robert F.: *Goal Analysis.* Belmont, Fearon Publishers, 1972, p. 35.

Mager, Robert F.: *Preparing Instructional Objectives.* Palo Alto, Fearon Publishers, 1972.

Mallast, Dennis: Principal, W. H. Stevenson Elementary School, Ransomville, New York, personal correspondence, July 18, 1975.

Mallory, Arthur: Commissioner of Education, State Department of Education, Jefferson City, Missouri, personal communication, Sept. 24, 1975.

Mann, Philip H. and Suiter, Patricia: *Handbook of Diagnostic Teaching.* Boston, Allyn, 1974.

Mardell, Carol and Goldenberg, Dorothea: For Prekindergarten Screening Information: DIAL. *Journal of Learning Disabilities, 8:*140-47, March 1975.

Maryland State Department of Education, Division of Instruction: Guidelines — Early Identification and Instructional Programming for Learning Problems, 6, 1975.

Mason, A. W.: Follow-up of Educational Attainments in a Group of Children With Retarded Speech Development and in a Control Group. In Clark, M. and Maxwell, S. (Eds.): *Reading: Conference on Progress in Reading.* Proc. Fifth Annual Study Congress of United Kingdom Reading Assn., Edinburgh, 1967-68.

Mauser, August J.: Learning Disabilities and Delinquent Youth. *Academic Therapy,* 411-32, Summer 1974.

Mauser, August J.: *The Remediation of Learning Disabilities in Juvenile Delinquent Youth.* From selected convention papers on learning disabilities from the Third Annual conference of the Association for Children With Learning Disabilities, Pittsburgh, ACLD, pp. 1-7, 1973.

McCarthy, Jeanne and Kirk, Samuel: A Report to the Stockholders: Overview of Research by the Leadership Training Institute in Learning Disabilities. International Conference, ACLD, New York, Feb. 28, 1975.

Meier, John: Screening, Assessment and Intervention for Young Children at Developmental Risk. Hobbs, N. (Ed.): *Issues in the Classification of Children, Vol. II.* San Francisco, Jossey-Bass Publishers, pp. 497-543, 1975.

Meier, John: *Screening and Assessment of Young Children at Developmental Risk.* The President's Committee on Mental Retardation, Washington, D.C., U.S. Government Printing Office, p. 7, March 1973.

Mercer, Jane: Psychological Assessment and the Rights of Children. *Journal of School Psychology, 11:*130-57, 1973.

Missouri State Department of Education: *Guidelines For an Early Childhood Screening Program,* Jefferson City, 1973.

Missouri, University City School District: *Early Education Screening Test Battery of Basic Skills Development,* Washington, D.C., Bureau of Research, No. BR-6-1328, January, 1969.

Money, J.: On Learning and Not Learning to Read, *The Disabled Reader,* John Hopkins, 21-40, 1966.

National Special Education Information Center, *Closer Look,* 1974. Washington, D.C., U.S. Printing Office, 1974.

Neifert, James and Gayton, William: Parents and the Home Program Approach in the Remediation of Learning Disabilities. *Journal of Learning Disabilities, 6*:2, Feb. 1973.

Noll, J. D. and Berry, W. R.: The Use of the Token Test with Children. *Journal of the Indiana Speech and Hearing Association, Inc.,* Vol. XXVII, 1969.

Novack, H., Bonaventura, E., and Merenda, P.: A Scale For Early Detection of Children with Learning Problems, *Exceptional Children, 6*:98-105, Oct. 1973.

Oakland, Thomas: Assessing Minority Group Children: Challenges for School Psychologists. *Journal of School Psychology, 11*:294-303, 1973.

Oconomowoc Public Schools: *Early Childhood Screening Program,* ESEA Title VI, Wisconsin, 1974.

Oseretsky Tests, The: Educational Test Bureau, Circle Pines.

Peotone, Illinois, ESEA, Early Prevention of School Failure, 1971, p. 4.

Piaget, H.: *Origins of Intelligence in Children.* New York, International Universities Press, 1952.

Poremba, C.: The Adolescent and Young Adolescent with Learning Disabilities: What are His Needs: What are the Needs of Those Who Deal With Him? In *International Approach to Learning Disabilities of Children and Youth.* Selected papers from the Third Annual Conference, ACLD, San Rafael, Academic Therapy Publication, 1967.

Powers, Hugh: Dietary Measures to Improve Behavior and Achievement. *Academic Therapy, 9*:203-14, Winter 1973-74.

Price, Landon Dewey: The Trouble with "Poor Auditory Discrimination", *Academic Therapy, 8,* Spring 1973.

Project First Step, Title VIG, Child Service Demonstration Program, Warwick, School Department, Warwick, Rhode Island, 1974.

Ramey, Craig T.: Children and Public Policy — A Role For Psychologists. *American Psychologist, 29*:Jan. 1974.

Ramstad, Vivian and Potter, Robert: Differences in Vocabulary and Syntax Usage Between Nez Perce Indians and White Kindergarten Children. *Journal of Learning Disabilities, 7*:491-97, Oct. 1974.

Raven, J. C.: *Progressive Matrices.* New York, Psychological Corporation, 1963.

Reger, Roger: A Case Study of the Effects of Labeling. *Journal of Learning Disabilities, 7*:60-61, Dec. 1974.

Report to the New York State Legislature: *A Survey of Educational Screening Programs in New York State School Districts and Boards of Cooperative Educational Services.* Albany, The University of the State of New York, March 1, 1975.

Reynolds, Maynard C.: A Framework for Considering Some Issues in Special Education. *Exceptional Children, 28*:367-70, March 1962.

Rockwood School District: *Parents as Parteners*, Title III, ESEA FY 1973, Portland, 1973.

Rogers, W. B. and Rogers, Robert: A New Simplified Preschool Readiness Experimental Screening Scale (The Press). *Clinical Pediatrics, 11*:558-62, Oct. 1972.

Rogolsky, Maryrose M.: Screening Kindergarten Children: A Review and Recommendations. *Journal of School Psychology*, 7:18-25, 1968-69.

Rosen, Pamela and Horne, Eleanor: *Tests for Spanish Speaking Children: An Annotated Bibliography*. Head Start Test Collection, Educational Testing Service, Princeton, Aug. 1971.

Rosenthal, Robert and Jacobson, Lenore: *Pygmalion in the Classroom*. New York, HR & W, 1968.

Rudder, Carol: School Psychologist, South Western City Schools, Grove City, Ohio. Personal Correspondence, June 7, 1974 and June 4, 1975.

Saphier, J. D.: The relation of Perceptual Motor Skills to Learning and School Success. *Journal of Learning Disabilities*, 6:56-65, Nov. 1973.

Satz, Paul and Friel, Janet: Some Predictive Antecedents of Specific Reading Disability. *Journal of Learning Disabilities*, 7:437-44, Aug./Sept. 1974.

Scagliotta, Edward G.: *Initial Learning Assessment*. San Rafael, Academic Therapy Publications, 1970.

Shearer, D., Billingsley, J., Frohman, S., Hillard, J., Johnson, F. and Shearer, M.: *Portage Checklist and Curriculum Guide to Early Education*, Cooperative Educational Service Agency #12, Portage, 1972a.

Shearer, Marsha and Shearer, David: The Portage Project: A Model for Early Childhood Education. *Exceptional Children, 39*:210-17, Nov. 1972b.

Sheridan, M. D.: Infants at Risk of Handicapping Conditions. Monthly Bulletin of the Health Laboratory Service, London, England, Vol. 21:238, 1962.

Short Test of Educational Ability: Chicago, Science Research Associates, Inc., 1966.

Silver, Archie and Hagin, Rosa: *SEARCH — A Scanning Instrument for the Identification of Potential Learning Disability*. The Learning Disorders Unit, Department of Psychiatry, N.Y.U., Bellevue Medical Center, 1975.

Smith, I. Leon. and Greenberg, Sandra: Teacher Attitudes and the Labeling Process. *Exceptional Children, 41*:319-24, Feb. 1975.

Statistical Abstracts of the U.S.: Washington, D.C., U.S. Government Printing Office, 1966.

TADS, Evaluation — Bibliography. Tadscript #2. Technical Assistance Development System, Chapel Hill, University of North Carolina, 1973.

Terman, L. and Merrill, M.: *Stanford-Binet Intelligence Scale*, Boston, Houghton Mifflin Co., 1960, p. 98.

Vermont Department of Education: Suggested Procedures for Planning Compensatory Early Education Programs (Title I) and Essential Early Education Programs (Special Education), Montpelier, 1975, mimeographed.

Walker, Deborah: *Socioemotional Measures for Preschool and Kindergarten*

Children. San Francisco, Jossey-Bass Publishers, 1973.

Walker, W.: *Walker Readiness Test for Disadvantaged Preschool Children.* Regional Research Program, Kansas City, 1969.

Ward, Maryane, Cartwright, G. Philip, Cartwright, Carol and Campbell, Judith: *Diagnostic Teaching of Preschool and Primary Children.* The Pennsylvania State University, 1973.

Wechsler, David: *Wechsler Intelligence Scale for Children (Escala de Inteligencia Wechsler Para Ninos).* New York, Psychological Corporation, 1949.

Wellesley Public Schools, Title VI Project 1968-1970: *Early Identification of Children with Potential Learning Disabilities,* Final Report, 1970.

West, T. and Millsom, C.: Learning Disabilities Funding: Where do We go From Here? *Educational Leadership,* 503-06, May 1975.

White, Burton L. and Watts, Jean Carew: *Experience and Environment Major Influences on the Development of the Child, Vol. 1.* Englewood Cliffs, P-H, 1973, p. 21.

Wilborn, Bobbie and Smith, Don: Early Identification of Children with Learning Problems. *Academic Therapy,* 9:363-71, Spring 1974.

Wunderlich, Ray C.: *Kids, Brains and Learning.* St. Petersburg, Johnny Reads, Inc., 1970.

Zeitlin, Shirley: Diagnostic and Prescriptive Learning: A Formula for Success in School. *The Campus Learning Center Experience,* New Paltz, State U. College, 1973, pp. 67-88.

Zeitlin, Shirley and Nichols, Lois: *A Model for Personalized Learning.* Unpublished paper. New Paltz, State U. College, 1975.

Zeitlin, Shirley: *Baseline Kindergarten Assessment.* Unpublished paper, New Paltz, New York, SUC, 1975.

Appendix A

STATE LAWS FOR EDUCATION AND SCREENING OF HANDICAPPED CHILDREN

Children Eligible For Special Services	Minimum Ages	Mandated Laws For Handicapped	K-Screen Law	K-Screen Pilot Program
ALABAMA Includes but not limited to mild and moderately to severely deaf and hearing impaired, blind and vision impaired, crippled, emotionally conflicted, socially maladjusted, learning disabled, multiply handicapped.	6	X to be implemented (1977)		X
ALASKA Educable and trainable mentally retarded, physically handicapped, emotionally handicapped, learning disabled, multiply handicapped.	legal school age	X	X	X
ARIZONA Educable mentally handicapped, emotionally handicapped homebound or hospitalized, multiply handicapped, physically handicapped, learning disabled, speech handicapped, trainable handicapped.	5	X		
ARKANSAS Retarded, deaf, hard of hearing, speech impaired, visually handicapped, emotionally disturbed, crippled, learning disabled, other health-impaired children with mental, physical, emotional or learning problems requiring special education services.	6	X (1979)		
CALIFORNIA Deaf or hard of hearing, blind, or partially seeing, orthopedically	3	X		X

Children Eligible For Special Services	Minimum Ages	Mandated Laws For Handicapped	K-Screen Law	K-Screen Pilot Program
or health impaired, aphasic, speech handi- capped, children with physical illness or condition making at- tendance in regular classes impossible or inadvisable, multiply handicapped, physically handicapped.				
Educationally handi- capped and mentally retarded.	legal school age			
COLORADO Physically handicapped Educable mentally handicapped	3 5	X		
Educationally handi- capped (emotionally and/or perceptually handicapped)	5			
Learning disabled Trainable mentally retarded.	no age requirement 5			
CONNECTICUT Mentally retarded, phy- sically handicapped, socially or emotionally maladjusted, neuro- logically impaired, learning disabled. Handicapped children beginning at age 3 may receive special education services if their additional at- tainment would be irreparable damaged without it.	5	X		
DELAWARE Physically handicapped, maladjusted, mentally handicapped, learning disabled.	4	X		X
DISTRICT OF COLUMBIA There is no statutory reference to special education in the edu- cation law of the District of Columbia. However, Mills v. Board of Education of District of Columbia (1972) required that	school age			

Children Eligible For Special Services	Minimum Ages	Mandated Laws For Handicapped	K-Screen Law	K-Screen Pilot Program
educational services must be provided to all handicapped children.				
FLORIDA Educable mentally retarded, trainable mentally retarded, speech impaired, deaf, hard of hearing, blind, partially sighted, crippled and other health impaired, emotionally disturbed, socially maladjusted, learning disabled.	3	X		X
GEORGIA Mentally retarded, physically handicapped, speech handicapped, autistic, hearing impaired, visually impaired, and any other exceptionality that may be identified.	3	X		X
Special preschool program for deaf, hearing impaired, and speech handicapped.	no age limitation			
HAWAII Children who deviate in physical, mental, social or emotional characteristics to the extent that specialized training, techniques, and equipment are needed for maximum fulfillment.	none	X		X
IDAHO Includes but not limited to physically handicapped, mentally retarded, emotionally disturbed, chronically ill, perceptually impaired, visually or auditorily handicapped, speech impaired.	none	X		
ILLINOIS Physically handicapped, learning disabled, maladjusted, educable mentally handicapped, trainable mentally handicapped, speech	3	X	X	X

Children Eligible For Special Services	Minimum Ages	Mandated Laws For Handicapped	K-Screen Law	K-Screen Pilot Program
defective, and multiply handicapped.				
INDIANA Physical or mental disability as defined by regulations, includes multiply handicapped.	3	X		X
IOWA Crippled, visually impaired, hard of hearing, speech impaired, heart diseased, tubercular, emotionally maladjusted, physically handicapped and children intellectually incapable of regular instructional programs. Children not in state institutions under age 5 may receive services.	5	X		X
KANSAS Developmentally disabled, homebound, crippled, hard of hearing, socially and emotionally maladjusted, visually impaired, speech impaired, cerebral palsied, delicate (including heart conditions), tubercular, and children found by a competent authority to be best educated by special instruction from a special teacher.	birth	X		
KENTUCKY Neurologically impaired, emotionally disturbed, functionally retarded, children with learning disabilities or communication disorders, multiply handicapped, physically handicapped, speech defective, educable and trainable mentally retarded.	birth	X		
LOUISIANA Physically handicapped, slow learners, educable	3	X		

Children Eligible For Special Services	Minimum Ages	Mandated Laws For Handicapped	K-Screen Law	K-Screen Pilot Program
and trainable mentally retarded, deaf and hard of hearing, speech impaired, blind, and/or partially sighted, emotionally disturbed, cerebral palsied, learning disabled, other health impaired.				
MAINE Children able to benefit from an instructional program but who cannot be provided for in regular programs because of physical or mental deviations.	5	X		X
MARYLAND Physically and mentally handicapped Special program: children under age 6 may receive special services if such services would help them to approach a degree of development similar to pupils in regular school programs.	6	X (1979)		X
MASSACHUSETTS School age child who because of temporary or more permanent adjustment difficulties or attributes arising from intellectual, sensory, emotional or physical factors, cerebral dysfunctions, perceptual factors, or other learning disabilities or any combination of these who is unable to make effective progress in a regular school program.	3	X	X	X
MICHIGAN Handicapped including but not limited to mental, physical, emotional, behavioral, sensory, and speech handicaps.	none	X		X
MINNESOTA Deaf, hard of hearing, blind, partially seeing,	4	X		X

Children Eligible For Special Services	Minimum Ages	Mandated Laws for Handicapped	K-Screen Law	K-Screen Pilot Program
crippled, speech defective. Trainable mentally retarded, educable mentally retarded, emotionally disturbed	5 6			
MISSISSIPPI Defective hearing, visually impaired, speech impaired, mentally retarded, physically handicapped.	birth			
MISSOURI Children who deviate from the average in physical, mental, or social developmental characteristics to the extent that they require special education services.	6	X	Guide-lines	X
MONTANA Physically handicapped, includes but not limited to cardiopathic, cerebral palsied, speech defective, and hearing and vision handicapped, educable mentally retarded.	birth	X		X
Trainable mentally handicapped	birth			
Custodial mentally handicapped	legal school age			
State School for the deaf and blind	none			
NEBRASKA Trainable mentally retarded, physically handicapped, crippled, visually handicapped, hard of hearing, speech defective, cardiopathic, tubercular, cerebral palsied, educable mentally retarded, multiply handicapped, emotionally disturbed.	5	X		
NEVADA Vision, hearing, speech, orthopedic, mental and neurological disorders or defects, or any	3	X		

Children Eligible For Special Services	Minimum Ages	Mandated Laws For Handicapped	K-Screen Law	K-Screen Pilot Program
disabling condition caused by accident, injury, or disease.				
NEW HAMPSHIRE	4	X		
Deaf				
Physically, emotionally and intellectually handicapped.	5			
NEW JERSEY Mentally retarded, visually handicapped, auditorily handicapped, communication handi- capped, neurologically or perceptually impaired, orthopedically handi- capped, chronically ill, emotionally disturbed, socially maladjusted, and multiply handicapped. Program may be conducted on a permissive basis to children under 5.	5			
NEW MEXICO Exceptional children are children whose abilities render regular services in the public school inconsistent with their educational needs.	legal school age	X (1977)		
NEW YORK Children who because of mental, physical or emotional reasons, cannot be educated in regular classes.	legal school age	X		X
NORTH CAROLINA Handicapped, crippled, other classes of individuals requiring special types of in- struction.	birth		X	X
NORTH DAKOTA Educable children whose educational needs are not adequately provided for through usual facilities because of physical, mental, emo- tional or social conditions.	6	X		X

Children Eligible For Special Services	Minimum Ages	Mandated Laws For Handicapped	K-Screen Law	K-Screen Pilot Program
OHIO Hearing and vision impaired, crippled, trainable mentally retarded, educable mentally retarded, emotionally handicapped.	5	X		X
OKLAHOMA Educable mentally retarded, speech defective, emotionally disturbed, perceptually handicapped, learning disabled as a result of neurological impairment, multiply handicapped, children with special health problems, children requiring services of a visiting counselor. Deaf-blind, blind and partially blind, hard of hearing and deaf.	4 2	X		X
OREGON Blind, deaf, partially sighted, hard of hearing, speech defective, crippled or physically handicapped, extreme learning problems, neurologically handicapped, emotionally handicapped, trainable mentally retarded. Educable mentally retarded.	birth 6	X	guide-lines	X
PENNSYLVANIA Children who deviate from the average in physical, mental, emotional or social characteristics to extent that they need special education facilities or services.	legal school age	X		X
RHODE ISLAND Mentally retarded, physically handicapped, and emotionally handicapped.	3	X		X
SOUTH CAROLINA Educable mentally	legal school	X (1977)		X

Children Eligible For Special Services	Minimum Ages	Mandated Laws For Handicapped	K-Screen Law	K-Screen Pilot Program
retarded, trainable mentally retarded, emotionally handicapped, orthopedically handicapped, physically handicapped, visually handicapped, learning disabled.	age			
Hearing handicapped.	4			
SOUTH DAKOTA Children with physical or mental conditions that cannot be adequately provided for through the regular public schools.	birth	X	Mandate	
TENNESSEE Educable, trainable, and profoundly retarded, speech and/or language impaired, deaf and hearing impaired, blind and visually limited, physically handicapped and/or other health impaired including homebound, hospitalized, learning disabled includes perceptually handicapped, emotionally conflicted, functionally retarded, socially maladjusted, emotionally handicapped, and any other child whose needs cannot be met in the regular classroom setting.	4	X	X	
TEXAS Hard of hearing, orthopedically handicapped, physically handicapped, mentally retarded, emotionally disturbed, language or learning disabled.	3	X		X
UTAH Children with exceptional physical or mental condition.	5	X		
VERMONT Children with physical	birth	X		

Children Eligible For Special Services	Minimum Ages	Mandated Laws For Handicapped	K-Screen Law	K-Screen Pilot Program
or mental deviations.				
VIRGINIA Mentally retarded, physically handicapped, emotionally disturbed, learning disabled, speech impaired, hearing impaired, mentally handicapped or otherwise handicapped.	2	X		
WASHINGTON Temporarily or permanently retarded in normal educational processes because of a physical or mental handicap or emotional maladjustment or any other handicap, children with specific language or learning disabilities. Programs may be provided to children on preschool level.	legal school age	X		X
WEST VIRGINIA Visually impaired, physically handicapped, orthopedically handicapped, epileptic, mentally retarded, speech handicapped, multiply handicapped, autistic, socially or emotionally maladjusted (including the delinquent), learning disabled, both physically and psychologically, and others which may be identified by the state superintendent of free schools. Programs may be conducted on a permissive basis for children aged 3-6.	6	X		X
WISCONSIN Crippled, cardiac, visually handicapped, auditorily handicapped, mentally retarded, and otherwise physically handicapped.	birth	X	X	

Children Eligible For Special Services	Minimum Ages	Mandated Laws For Handicapped	K-Screen Law	K-Screen Pilot Program
WYOMING Children with mental, physical, psychological, or social maladjustment.	legal school age	X		X

SCREENING PROGRAMS SURVEYED

Alaska	Title VIG Project Denali Elementary School 148 East 9th Avenue Anchorage, Alaska 99503
Connecticut	Fairfield Public Schools P. O. Box 220 Fairfield, Connecticut 06430
Georgia	Gwinnett County Schools Gwinnett Drive Lawrenceville, Georgia 30245
Hawaii	State of Hawaii Department of Health P. O. Box 3378 Honolulu, Hawaii 96801
Illinois	Early Prevention of School Failure Title III ESEA 114 North Second Street Peotone, Illinois 60468
	School Community Program in Early Childhood Development Miller School 425 Dempter Street Evanston, Illinois 60200
Maryland	Maryland State Department of Education Division of Instruction P. O. Box 8717, BWI Airport Baltimore, Maryland 21240
Massachusetts	Hanover Public Schools 848 Main Street Hanover, Massachusetts 02339
	Wellesley Public Schools Wellesley, Massachusetts 02181
Michigan	PREP - Parent Readiness Education Project Redford Union School District 18499 Beech Daly Road Redford Township Detroit, Michigan 48240
Missouri	Parent Child Early Education Program Ferguson-Florissant School District 655 January Avenue Ferguson, Missouri 63135
New Jersey	Cherry Hill Public School Cherry Hill, New Jersey 08002

New York   Arlington Central School District
232 Dutchess Turnpike
Poughkeepsie, New York 12603

Beacon City School District
88 Sargent Avenue
Beacon, New York 12508

North Bellmore Union Free School District
1602 Bellmore Avenue
North Bellmore, New York 11710

van den Berg Learning Center
State University College
New Paltz, New York 12561

Carmel Central School District
30 Fair Street
Carmel, New York 10512

Hilton Central School District
Hilton, New York 14468

Horsehead Central School District
Horsehead, New York 14845

Middletown Public Schools
159 Prospect Avenue
Middletown, New York 10940

Wappingers Central School District
Remsen Avenue
Wappingers Falls, New York 12590

Ohio   United Local Elementary School
Hanoverton
Columbiana County, Ohio 44423

South Western City Schools
465 Kingston Avenue
Grove City, Ohio 43123

Oregon   Union County Intermediate Educational
  District
1605 Adams Avenue
LaGrande, Oregon 97850

HEED - Help Eliminate Early Learning
  Disability
School District # 6
451 North Second Street
Central Point, Oregon 97501

Washington   Intermediate School District No. 111
5601 Sixth Avenue
Tacoma, Washington 98406

Wisconsin   Joint School District # 10
120 East Harris Street
Appleton, Wisconsin 54911

Board of Education
Joint School District No. 1
Green Bay, Wisconsin 54303

Project Right Start
Oconomowoc Public Schools
521 Western Street
Oconomowoc, Wisconsin 53066

Cooperative Educational Service
  Agency 13
908 West Main Street
Waupun, Wisconsin 53963

Appendix C

SCREENING INSTRUMENTS

Published Tests

ABC Inventory
N. Adair and G. Blesch
Research Concepts (A Division of Test Maker, Inc.)
1368 East Airport Road
Muskegon, Michigan 49444

Bannatyne System
A. Bannatyne
Learning Systems Press
P. O. Box 2999
LaFayette, Louisiana 70501

Basic Concepts Inventory
S. E. Engelman
Follett Education Corp.
1019 West Washington Boulevard
P. O. Box 5705
Chicago, Illinois 60657

Daberon
Daberon Research
4202 S. W. 44th Avenue
Portland, Oregon 97221

Dallas Preschool Screening Test
Robert Percival and Suzanne Poxon
Dallas Educational Diagnostic and Development Center
P. O. Box 1254
Richardson, Texas 75080

Denver Developmental Screening Test
W. Frankenburg and J. B. Dodds
Ladoca Project and Publishing Foundation, Inc.
East 51st Avenue and Lincoln
Denver, Colorado 80216

Developmental Test of Visual-Motor Integration
(Beery-Buktenica)
K. Beery and N. Buktenica
Follett Educational Corporation
1019 West Washington Boulevard
P. O. Box 5705
Chicago, Illinois 60607

DIAL Inc.
Mardell & D. Goldenberg
Box 911
Highland Park, Illinois 60035

Draw-A-Person - Koppitz Scoring System
Elizabeth M. Koppitz
Psychological Evaluation of Children's Human Figure Drawing
Grune and Stratton, Inc.
757 Third Avenue
New York, New York 10017

Echoic Response Inventory for Children
C. Stern
10323 Lorenzo Drive
Los Angeles, California 90064

Gesell Developmental Kit
Frances L. Ilg, Louise Bates Ames
Program for Education
Box 85B
Lumberville, Pennsylvania 18933

Goldman Fristoe Test of Articulation
R. Goldman and M. Fristoe
American Guidance Service, Inc.
Publishers Building
Circle Pines, Minnesota 55014

Goldman Fristoe Woodcock Test of Auditory Discrimination
R. Goldman, M. Fristoe and R. Woodcock
American Guidance Services
Publishers Building
Circle Pines, Minnesota 55014

Jansky Modified Screening Index
Bulletin of the Orton Society XXIII, 1973
The Orton Society, Inc.
8415 Bellona Lane
Towson, Maryland 21204

Kindergarten Evaluation of Learning Potential
J. A. R. Wilson and M. C. Robeck
Webster Division, McGraw-Hill Book Company
Manchester Road
Manchester, Missouri 63011

Kindergarten Auditory Screening Test
Jack Katz
Follett Education Corporation
1019 West Washington Boulevard
P. O. Box 5705
Chicago, Illinois 60607

The K-Q Kindergarten Questionnaire
S. Berger, E. Perlman
10 Tyler Road
Lexington, Massachusetts 02173

The Meeting Street School Screening Test
P. Hainsworth, M. Siqueland
Meeting St. School
333 Grotto Avenue
Providence, Rhode Island 02906

Northwestern Syntax Screening Test
Laura L. Lee
Northwestern University
Evanston, Illinois

Peabody Picture Vocabulary Test
Lloyd M. Dunn
American Guidance Service, Inc.
Publishers Building
Circle Pines, Minnesota 55014

Preschool Inventory Revised Edition - 1970
Bettye M. Caldwell
Educational Testing Service, Cooperative Tests and Services
Rosedale Road
Princeton, New Jersey 08540

Preschool Screening System
P. Hainsworth, R. Hainsworth
Box 1635
Pawtucket, Rhode Island 02862

Riley Preschool Developmental Screening Inventory
Clara M. D. Riley
Western Psychological Services
Box 775
Beverly Hills, California 90213

Screening Test for Auditory Comprehension of Language
Elizabeth Carrow-Woolfolk
Learning Concepts, Inc.
2501 North Lamar, N. W.
Austin, Texas 78705

Slosson Intelligence Test for Children and Adults (SIT)
R. L. Slosson
Slosson Educational Publications
140 Pine Street
East Aurora, New York 14052

The Token Test
DeRenzi and Vignolo (1962), "The Token Test: A Sensitive
Test to Detect Receptive Disturbances in Aphasics,"
BRAIN, 85, 665-678.

The Yellow Brick Road
Christine Kallstrom
Learning Concepts, Inc.
2501 North Lamar, N. W.
Austin, Texas 78705

Valett Developmental Survey
R. E. Valett
Consulting Psychologists Press, Inc.
577 College Avenue
Palo Alto, California 94306

The Vane Kindergarten Test
Julia R. Vane
Clinical Psychology Publishing Co., Inc.
4 Covant Square
Brandon, Vermont 05733

Published Teacher Observation Instruments

California Preschool Social Competence Scale
S. Levine, F. F. Elves and M. Lewis
Consulting Psychologists Press, Inc.
577 College Avenue
Palo Alto, California 94306

Child-Early Identification Screening Inventory
Eugene Medvedeff
Westinghouse Learning Corporation
P. O. Box 30
Iowa City, Iowa 52240

Preschool Attainment Record (PAR)
E. A. Doll
American Guidance Service, Inc.
Publishers' Building
Circle Pines, Minnesota 55014

Rhode Island Pupil Identification Scale
H. Novack
R. I. P. I. S.
Box 9311
Providence, Rhode Island 02904

Verbal Language Development Scale
M. J. Meacham
American Guidance Service, Inc.
Publishers' Building
Circle Pines, Minnesota 55014

Unpublished Teacher Observation Instruments

Alaska Learning Disabilities Ranking Scale
Dr. Barbara Smart, Project Director
Title VIG Office - Special Education
Denali Elementary School
148 East 9th Avenue
Anchorage, Alaska

Behavioral Checklist
Dr. Eileen Iwakami - Chief Psychologist
Children's Health Service Division - State of Hawaii
Department of Health
P. O. Box 3378
Honolulu, Hawaii 96801

Maryland Systematic Observation Inst.
Maryland State Department of Education
P. O. Box 8717 BWI Airport
Baltimore, Maryland 21240

Published Parent Surveys

Child Behavior Rating Scale (CBRS)
R. N. Cassel
Western Psychological Services
12031 Wilshire Boulevard
Los Angeles, California 90025

Early Detection Inventory
F. E. McGahan, Carolyn McGahan
Follett Educational Corporation
1019 West Washington Boulevard
P. O. Box 5705
Chicago, Illinois 60607

Preprimary Profile: Introduction to my Child
H. J. Schiff, M. I. Friedman
Science Research Associates, Inc.
259 East Erie Street
Chicago, Illinois   60611

The School Readiness Checklist
John J. Austin, J. Clayton Lafferty
Research Concepts
1368 East Airport Road
Muskegon, Michigan   49444

School Readiness Survey
F. L. Fordan, James Massey
Consulting Psychologists Press, Inc.
570 College Avenue
Palo Alto, California   94306

ZEIS
(ZEITLIN EARLY
IDENTIFICATION SCREENING)
Research Edition

Research Edition

NAME: _____ DATE OF TEST: _____
     (last)   (first)   (year)   (mo.)   (day)

CLASS: _____ EXAMINER: _____ DATE OF BIRTH: _____

CHRONOLOGICAL AGE: _____
               (year)   (month)

Summary Score:

Verbal		Pencil & Paper		Performance	
Information question (1)	6 ___	Draw a Person (6)	16 ___	Gross Motor (10)	10 ___
Vocabulary (2)	10 ___	Copy Form (7)	10 ___	Body Image (11)	8 ___
Language (3)	4 ___	Recall (8)	5 ___	Directions (12)	
Auditory Memory (4)	6 ___	Directions (9)	4 ___	Nonverbal	6 ___
Concepts (5)	9			Verbal	6 ___
Total	(35) ___	Total	(35) ___	Total	(30) ___
				TOTAL	(100) ___

Check characteristics when appropriate:
___Uses self control   Distractable-hyperactive
                                  lacking control

___Independent, confident   Dependent, fearful   ___
___Pleasant, smiling, responsive   Disagreeable, frowning   ___
                                    unfriendly

___Attentive   Inattentive, short   ___
                                    attention span

___Follows directions   Unable to follow   ___
                                    directions

___Cooperative   Uncooperative, dis-   ___
                                    ruptive

___Speech clear, well spoken   Speech difficult to   ___
                                    understand

___Agile   Clumsy   ___

FIGURE DRAWING:
___Excessive amount of   ___3 or more figures drawn
    time   spontaneously
___Refusal to do drawings   ___drawing contains obvious
                                    penis
___Grotesque drawing   ___tiny figures - less than two
                                    inches

COMMENTS: _____

_____

Direct the following questions to the child and record his responses.

1. *Information*
   a. What is your name_____ (2)
      If first name only given, ask: do you have
      another name too?
      First name (1) first and last (2)
   b. How old are you?_____ (2)
   c. On what street do you live?_____ (2)   (6)___

2. *Vocabulary*
   a. What is a hat?_____ (2)
   b. What is a ball?_____ (2)
   c. What is a stove?_____ (2)
   d. What is an orange?_____ (2)
   e. What is a letter?_____ (2)   (10)___

3. *Language*
   a. Present strip one of pictures and say,
      "show me the boat"_____ (1)
   b. Strip two - "show me the cat"_____ (1)
   c. Strip three - ask and point - "what is
      this?"_____ice cream cone_____ (1)
   d. Strip four - "what is this?"____truck_____ (1)   (4)___

4. *Auditory Memory*
   Tell the child the following:
   "I am going to say some words. Listen carefully
   because when I'm finished I want you to say them
   back to me." A child may have two trys - first
   try (2) - second try (1) response must be identical.
   a. He is a big boy_____ (2)
   b. We are going to buy some candy for
      mother_____ (2)
   c. John likes to feed little puppies in
      the barn_____ (2)   (6)___

5. *Concepts*
   a. Place the 9 cubes of one color on the
      table, say: Let me hear you count
      out loud the number of blocks I have_____ (3)
   b. Group the blocks according to color in
      3 groups (9-3-1) and say, "Which group
      has the most blocks?"_____ (3)
   c. Place the 6" pencil and the 3" pencil
      on the table, say to the child, - pick
      up the longer pencil._____ (3)   (9)___

6. *Draw a Person*
   Tell child, "Here is a piece of paper. Make
   a picture of a person, a whole person like
   Mommy or Daddy or a boy (or a girl) like you."

   Head----(2)   Mouth----(2)   Arms----(2)
   Eyes----(2)   Body-----(2)   Hair----(1)
   Nose----(2)   Legs-----(2)   Feet----(1)   (16)___

7. *Copy Forms*
   Say: Here is another piece of paper. Here is
   a shape (show card with shape). Copy one just
   like this on your paper. (present figures in
   order - one at a time)

○   △

+   ◇

▢   (10)___

8. *Recall*
   Give child another piece of paper and say: See
   how many of the shapes we just saw you can
   remember and draw for me now.
   a.--------(1)   d.--------(1)
   b.--------(1)   e.--------(1)
   c.--------(1)   (5)___

9. *Directions*
   Hand child paper with picture of car and ask--
   a. Draw a ball in back of the car_____ (1)
   b. Draw a line from the bottom of your
       paper to the car_____ (1)
   c. Draw a line from the left hand side of
       your paper to the car_____ (1)
   d. Draw an X in the upper right hand corner
       of your paper_____ (1)   (4)___

10. *Gross Motor*
    a. Hop on one foot until I tell you to
        stop (approx. 5 seconds)_____ (2)
    b. Walk on this line like this
        (demonstrate)_____ (2)
    c. Skip to the wall (any point a few feet
        away) well-coordinated_____ (2)
        skip, hop (1)
    d. Say: "Try to catch this beanbag." Easy
        toss from approx. 8'_____ (2)
    e. Say: "Open one hand and close it. Now
        open the other hand and close it. Keep
        going alternating one hand at a time"
        (demonstrate). Child alone for about
        6 seconds._____ (2) (10)___

11. *Body Image*
    Ask the child to stand facing you. Say to the
    child:
    a. touch your mouth_____ (2)
    b. touch your shoulders_____ (2)
    c. touch your eyes_____ (2)
    d. touch your ankles_____ (2) (8)___

12. *Directions - Imitation*
    Examiner stands facing the child and performs
    a series of movements one at a time.
    1) The child repeats the same movements im-
        mediately after the examiner. Say, I'm
        going to do something with my hands and
        you do just what I do. If necessary, tell
        child to wait until you finish showing be-
        fore he starts.
        a. (1) Raise right hand over head,
                 return to right shoulder.

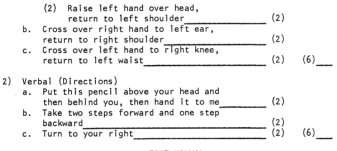

```
    (2)  Raise left hand over head,
         return to left shoulder_____  (2)
    b.  Cross over right hand to left ear,
        return to right shoulder_____     (2)
    c.  Cross over left hand to right knee,
        return to left waist_____     (2)    (6)___

2)  Verbal (Directions)
    a.  Put this pencil above your head and
        then behind you, then hand it to me_____  (2)
    b.  Take two steps forward and one step
        backward_____     (2)
    c.  Turn to your right_____  (2)    (6)___
```

TEST MANUAL

Zeitlin Early Identification Screening (ZEIS)
Research Edition

The ZEIS is a short individually administered instrument which is designed to identify early kindergarten and pre-kindergarten children who
may have special learning needs. It screens out children who need further diagnosis to determine if they are potential high risk learners.

The screening takes fifteen to twenty minutes and consists of twelve
questions relating to language, cognitive development, auditory and visual memory, gross motor, visual-motor development, body image, directionality, and laterality. The sum of these characteristics seems to discriminate between those children who may or may not have special educational
needs. No individual question is intended to be a measure of competence
of an ability, but part of an overall indication of the child's development. The questions are divided into three parts; verbal, pencil and
paper tasks, and nonverbal performance. The ZEIS is scored on the basis
of 100 points. The questions cover a developmental range of three to seven
years with emphasis on four- to five-year-old development. There is a
checklist for recording relevant observable behaviors, i.e. independence-
dependence, speech. A checklist of Koppitz emotional indicators is also
included to be used by the school psychologist to evaluate the figure
drawing question. In addition to its use for individual screening, the
ZEIS gives an overview of the entering kindergarten population.

A light, airy room which is free from distractions is used. Parts one
and two require the child to sit at a desk or table of appropriate height
with the examiner. Part three requires open floor space.

The ZEIS may be given in its entirety by one examiner or at three
stations in one room with the child moving from one examiner to the next
in the sequence of the test. When stations are used they should be suf-
ficiently far apart so as not to distract each child. The pace should
be monitored so there is not more than one child at a station. The screening may be administered by teachers, paraprofessionals, and other educational personnel after one training session.

Directions for Administration and Scoring:

The use of the wording in the test insures standardization of administration. If the child does not seem to understand the directions, they
may be repeated except if specifically indicated not to. Guessing is not
encouraged, nor should any prompting or elaborating be done, which will
give the child additional clues as to what response is expected. For example in the Draw-A-Person (Question 6), after the initial instruction is
given, nothing further relating to the question is said. If the child asks
for feedback, such as "Is this right?" a neutral response such as "What do
you think?" is given.

While there is no time on the test, a child should be discouraged from
lengthy distracting conversation. Note should be made in the comments if
the child needs an excessive amount of time (as compared to most of his
peers) to complete the test. A relaxed, friendly interaction is encouraged.

1. *Information*
    a) If first name only is given ask - Do you have another name too?
       First name, one point, first and last, two points. A middle name
       is acceptable in lieu of a last name.
    b) How old are you? Does not have to be correct age but response
       which recognizes years appropriate for the child. Responses such
       as four years old, four, fifth birthday are acceptable, responses
       such as I just had a birthday are questioned. Obviously incor-
       rect ages such as 2, 10 or 20 are not acceptable.
    c) If the response is the name of a town or city the question is re-
       peated. Children who live in rural areas or sections which do not
       have streets or numbers need to be scored accordingly. Child needs
       to indicate knowledge that the place he lives in has an identifying
       label.

2. *Vocabulary* (adapted from Stanford-Binet form L-M)
   If child hesitates, urge him to try by saying, "Just tell me in your own
   words. All I want to know is whether you know what a _____ is." or a
   similar phrase. If the child's meaning is not clear question him further by saying, "Tell me more about it." Any of the indicated definitions are given full credit.

a)	*hat*	put on you	on heads
		wear it	for your head
		material	it's round and it's got an opening
		wool	in the bottom
		straw	
b)	*ball*	to play with	round
		to play	kick
		to roll	catch the ball
		throw	like a balloon
c)	*stove*	cook	for dinner
		for boil eggs on	to put kettle on
		to burn	it smokes
		metal	to light it
d)	*orange*	a fruit	it's round
		tree	an orange is orange color
		a drink	a jello
		it's orange juice	a color
		what you drink	
		(eat, squeeze, cut,	
		suck)	
e)	*letter*	name a letter	to write
		to read	paper
		to mail	send to someone
			get from someone

3. *Language*
   A and B - child must point to the correct picture
   C and D - child must say word or a reasonable approximation

4. *Auditory Memory:*
   A child may have two trys; two points for first try, one point for second
   try. *Response must be identical.* In "b" contraction we're" is acceptable

5. *Concepts:*
   Only one try is allowed.

a) Child must count 1, 2, 3, 4, 5, 6, 7, 8, 9 consecutively and count the blocks in one to one correspondence, i.e. if child counts to nine but counts off six blocks it is scored incorrect.
b) child must point to group of nine blocks
c) child must pick up longer pencil

6. *Draw-A-Person:*
   Head - any clear method for representing the head
   Eyes - any method is satisfactory - a dot or a small circle is an adequate response
   Nose - any clear method of presentation
   Mouth- any clear representation
   Body - any clear indication of trunk (one or two dimensional)
   Legs - any method of representation clearly intended to indicate legs; unless in profile, two legs must be presented. Legs may be attached anywhere to the figure
   Arms - any method of representative clearly intended to indicate arms. Except in profile, two arms must be present
   Hair - any indication of hair, however crude
   Feet - feet indicated by any means; toes attached to the end of the leg are acceptable

7. *Copy Forms:*
   Say to child "Here is a piece of paper. Here is a shape (displaying figure) copy one just like this one on your paper."
   a. circle   The circle must be approximately round, a somewhat elliptical form is acceptable. Does not need to be completely closed
                Examples:

   b. cross   The lines must intersect and be relatively straight and not an X
                Examples:

   c. square   All lines must be connected and the angles preserved. The right angles may be formed by lines that intersect slightly but must not be decidedly round or have an ear. The lines of the sides must be relatively straight.
                Examples:

   d. triangle The figure should have three well defined angles. The lines should meet fairly accurately with little overlap and no ears for the corners.
                Examples:

   e. diamond   A satisfactory drawing must have four well defined angles, it must be more diamond shaped than square or kite-shaped, and the pairs of angles must be approximately opposite.
                Examples:

8. *Recall:*
   This is a visual memory task with a motor component. If the child names the shape even if it is not drawn correctly (see ques. 7) credit is given.

9. *Directions:*
   a. Circle must be in the general area of the back of the car.
   b. Line from bottom of paper up to the car doesn't have to touch bottom of paper. Credit is given if child draws reverse from car down if in appropriate place.
   c. Line must be on the left hand side of the paper and approximately touch the car.
   d. The X must be in the upper right quadrant of the paper. The X can be any crossed figure.

10. *Gross Motor:*
    a. If child does not seem to comprehend hop - you may demonstrate. Slowly and silently count to 5. Credit is given if the child does not put down the raised foot more than twice in the allotted time.
    b. Place masking tape in a straight line on the floor (about 5 ft.). Examiner demonstrates by walking with short steps one foot in front of the other staying on the line. If child holds arms or body very tensely or unusually rigid indicate in the comments. Credit is given if the child does not step off the line more than once.
    c. If child does not comprehend skip or seems uncertain, demonstrate. A well-coordinated skip, two points, a hop skip, one point. If child has difficulty, go right on to next item.
    d. May have two tries, may catch with one or two hands. May cup hands against body but must catch with hands not arms.
    e. This question is asked to see if the child can alternatively use both sides of the body. The examiner demonstrates by alternately opening one hand and closing the other and helps the child learn the task and get started. Let child try it with you while you are demonstrating then go it alone for six seconds. Credit if the child can do it without confusion to the slow, silent count of 6.

11. *Body Image:*
    The child should touch that area indicated. No approximations acceptable.

12. *Directions:*
    a. Make sure you have the child's attention before you start. If the child starts before the demonstration is over, ask the child to wait until you are finished and demonstrate again. After that do not repeat. Child should respond with mirror image (the opposite of what is demonstrated) and must touch all parts as demonstrated.
       1. Must do 1 and 2 correctly to get credit
    b. No part of the command may be repeated. Child must do all parts of the command as described to get credit.
       1. The child may take two steps forward, turn around to go back or just step backwards the one step.
       2. Credit is given if the child turns part way or all the way around as long as the direction is correct.

MATERIALS NEEDED:

Question 3 (see Figure 33)
   a) a strip of three pictures including a picture of a book
   b) a strip of three pictures including a picture of a cat
   c) a picture of an ice cream cone
   d) a picture of a truck

Figure 33.

Question 4
  a & b) Colored cubes of an equal size (1/2 to 1 inch) 9 of one color, 3 of
          a second color, 1 of a third color
  c) One long pencil (6") and one short pencil (3")

Question 5
  Sheet of plain white paper (8 1/2" x 11") and pencil with eraser.

Question 6
  Five small white cards each containing one shape: circle, cross, rectangle,
  triangle, diamond, drawn with a black magic marker. Two sheets of white
  paper (8 1/2" x 11")

Question 7
  Picture of car (see Figure 34)

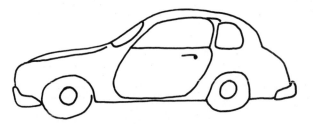

Figure 34.

Training Procedures:
   A test kit for each examiner should be prepared. Training should be done, if
possible, by someone experienced in individual test administration procedures,
i.e. a school psychologist. The goals and objectives of the screening program
should be described so the examiners can appreciate the relevance of administering the instrument. The ZEIS should be demonstrated either live or through video
tape or movie (which may be rented from the author). Each question should then
be reviewed as to procedure for administration and scoring. The examiners should
practice on each other to help raise additional questions. Most desirable is for
the trainer to observe one trial administration for each examiner. If more than
one training session is planned, the examiners might practice the test on children available to them who will not be part of the assessed population.

Scoring Suggestions:
   Individual questions should be checked __√__ or __X__ when administering. In
question 1, 2, and 4 the child's verbatim responses should be recorded. After
the test is over, scores should be totaled and transcribed on to the front. The
checklist should be used when the child displays a more than usual amount of that
characteristic. Observations are subjective and should reflect tester's judgment
based on a continuum of that behavior compared to other children of the child's
age range.

Figure Drawing:
   Excessive amount of time: If the child seems to be unable to stop, seems to go
off into a fantasy, or keeps scrubbing away at drawing.

   Refusal to do drawing: Child should be reasonably urged to do drawing. If he
refuses, one more attempt may be made at conclusion of test.

   Other indicators are self-explanatory (refer to Koppitz, E.) *Psychological Evaluations of Children's Human Figure Drawings.* Screening for emotional indicators
is difficult and not highly reliable. This checklist should be interpreted only
by the school psychologist.

   Comments: Any behavior that seems atypical should be noted, also any of the
following atypical speech or language patterns:

   · difficulty expressing ideas - does not converse well
   · points instead of using words
   · uses one or two word "sentences"
   · cannot answer a direct question
   · shrugs shoulders instead of verbal answer
   · shakes head yes or no instead of verbally
   · uses fingers to indicate numbers
   · speaks only when asked direct question
   · knows correct answers but cannot form verbal answer

   Irrelevant ideas: child brings into conversation something other than subject
at hand; uses unrelated known material to avoid answering unknown material; starts
to respond accurately, then loses track

   Speech problem: jumbles correct words into mess of words so cannot be understood; mispronounces words so they cannot be understood; mispronounces part of
word, but word is understandable; substitutes initial medial, or final sounds;
speech is unintelligible; immature speech pattern, "me" don't, baby talk

   Refusal to take the test: if a child refuses to take the test after encouragement, the testing should be discontinued. If possible, another time should
be scheduled. If the child still refuses, more needs to be known about the child
to understand the unwillingness to be involved. Children refuse tests for many
reasons, but in most cases it affects the way they begin school or function in
the classroom environment.

Media Available
A videotape (1/2") and movie of the administration of the ZEIS is available
for rental from the author.

Interpretation of the ZEIS

The ZEIS has been developed from age-normed materials as a screening instrument to detect children who may have special educational needs. It is the first
step of a screening program which includes diagnosis and follow-through with educational prescription and implementation. It is perceived as being most useful
if each school or district develops its own norms so that the results can be interpreted in relation to its own population, though normative data is included.

Individual items are too limited to predict or discriminate competence or lack
of it in a specific ability. The questions vary in difficulty so that even the
least competent child will experience some success (three-year-old expectations)
and that there will be a challenge for the most competent (seven-year-old expectations). No question is independent. The interaction of the various factors
gives an indication of the child's functioning in terms of those qualities which
are necessary to be successful in school. A child does not need to be competent
in everything.

To Develop Local Norms:
  A. Record the data
      Put results on class sheet (see Figure 35) highest score first to lowest.
      Total columns of subparts and total score.
  B. Compute for entire group:
      Mean and Standard Deviation; depending on the way the test is to be used,
      compute percentiles; i.e. 10 percent, 20 percent, etc.
  C. Children to be considered for diagnostic follow up:
      Each school develops its own cut-off point. The high risk population for
      your school can be defined as that percentage of children, who through the
      grades, seem to consistently meet with failure unless special help is given.
      1. Suggestions
          a. A school might initially consider diagnostic follow-through on the
              lowest 10 percent of the distribution or those children who are two
              or more standard deviations from the mean. Experience with the
              ZEIS and the educational specialists available to follow through
              will help determine how many children at the low end are most fruit-
              fully followed through.
          b. When resources for diagnosis are limited, start with the lowest
              score and work up.
          c. A rule of thumb is that scores of fifty-five and under warrant fur-
              ther examination of the child. Scores in the upper fifties should
              be considered in relationship as to where they are in the distri-
              bution of scores. If more than one standard deviation from mean
              they may be put in a "watch & wait" category to be followed through
              initially by teacher observation. Scores are influenced by time
              of year ZEIS is administered and the average chronological age of
              the group. The child we need to know more about is at the low end
              of the distribution.
          d. Graphing the results helps to see where the normal distribution
              curve flattens out indicating a potential problem population (see
              Figure 36).
          e. Those children who have a large difference in one subtest score.
              Example:

                    Language and Cognition   32
                    Perceptual motor   8
                    Gross motor and body image   29

          f. Characteristics checked, figure drawings and/or comments indicating
              atypical behavior or a unique problem.

Form for Report Data

ZEIS SCORES

Examiner _____

Date of Testing _____

List Scores From High to Low (Total Score)

Name	Sex	Yrs. Mos. at test time	Perfect Score →																		
			6	10	4	6	9	35	16	10	5	4	35	10	8	6	6	30	100
			Ques. 1	2	3	4	5	S U M	6	7	8	9	S U M	10	11	12 A	12 B	S U M	Total

Figure 35. Form for report data — ZEIS.

```
 9 --- *
 0 ---
 0 ---
 0 ---
13 --- *
 0 ---
 0 ---
 0 ---
17 --- *
 0 ---
 0 ---
20 --- **
 0 ---
 0 ---
 0 ---
 0 ---
 0 ---
26 --- *
27 --- **
 0 ---
29 --- **
30 --- *
31 --- *
 0 ---
33 --- ***
34 --- *
35 --- **
36 --- *
37 --- *
38 --- *
39 --- *****
40 --- **
41 --- *****
42 --- **
43 --- ******
44 --- ***********
45 --- ***********
46 --- ************
47 --- *****
48 --- **********
49 --- *****
50 --- *********
51 --- ************
52 --- ***********
53 --- **********
54 --- ****************
55 --- **************
56 --- ********************
57 --- ******************
58 --- ***********************
59 --- **********************************
60 --- **********************
61 --- ***************************************
62 --- ***********************
63 --- ********************************
64 --- ****************************************
65 --- **************************************************
66 --- *************************
67 --- **********************************************
68 --- ***********************************************
69 --- ****************************************************************
70 --- *****************************************
71 --- *************************************************
72 --- ************************************************
73 --- ***********************************************************
74 --- *****************************************************************************
75 --- ***********************************************************
76 --- ***************************************
77 --- **********************************************************************
78 --- ********************************************************
79 --- ******************************************************
80 --- ***********************************************************
81 --- ***************************************************
82 --- ***********************************************************
83 --- ****************************************************
84 --- ***********************************************************************************
85 --- *************************************************************
86 --- ***************************************
87 --- *******************************************
88 --- **************************************
89 --- *********************************
90 --- *****************************************
91 --- **********************
92 --- ****************************
93 --- ***************************
94 --- ****************
95 --- ************
96 --- ************
97 --- ********
98 --- *
99 --- **
 0 ---
```

Figure 36. Histogram of 1633 scores. Normative sample. ZEIS.

The Whole Group:

Scores give an overview of the entire group and may be used in some of the following ways:
  A. Initial arrangement of kindergarten classes. Suggestion: homogeneous-heterogeneous class if each class has one fourth of their children from each quartile.
  B. Curriculum planning based on strengths and weaknesses indicated by the total incoming group. The use of ZEIS data helps recognize the range of individual differences and the need for flexible programming.
  C. To initiate parent workshops and conferences.
  D. To compare kindergarten groups over a period of years.
The ZEIS may be duplicated and used upon notification of intent to the author. As this instrument is still in the research stage comments, reactions and suggestions relating to your experiences administering, interpreting and following through the ZEIS are greatly appreciated. The author may be contacted at the van den Berg Learning Center, State University College, New Paltz, New York 12561

Normative Data

The normative data is developed from a sample of 1633 children throughout New York State and one district in New Jersey. The children come from eight school districts which are a cross section of urban, suburban and rural. Socio-economic status includes lower, middle, and upper-middle class children. Approximately 25 percent of the children are from minority groups. Of this group 20 percent are Black and 5 percent Puerto Rican or with Spanish surnames.

The distribution of the scores is skewed (see histogram, Figure 36). Because of this, the nonparametric measure of central tendency and variability are also reported. Scores were computed to three places but are rounded off and reported as the nearest whole number.

Mean of all scores from raw scores
  N = 1633
  Mean is 73
  Standard deviation is 14

Median of all scores from raw scores
  Median is 75
  Semi-interquartile range (IQ) is 9

Composition and Mean of Sample Groups

Group	Number of Children	Mean	Time of Administration	Description of Group
1	187	72.13	May	Middle and lower middle class rural and small city
2	832	74.58	Sept-Oct	Upper and middle and lower class urban 35% minority population
3	192	76.17	Sept-Oct	Middle and lower middle class rural and small city
4	74	65.23	May	Middle and lower class resort community 20% minority population

Group	Number of Children	Mean	Time of Administration	Description of Group
5	126	76.95	October	Middle and lower class small town and rural
6	52	71.74	May	Middle and upper class suburban community
7	20	77.95	June	Middle class suburban parochial school
8	150	71.34	May	Middle and lower class small town and rural
Mean of sample means		73.90		

Percentile Rank of Scores

Score	Percentile	Score	Percentile	Score	Percentile
99	100	74	49	49	6
98	100	73	46	48	5
97	100	72	42	47	5
96	99	71	40	46	4
95	99	70	37	45	4
94	98	69	35	44	3
93	97	68	32	43	3
92	96	67	29	42	2
91	94	66	27	41	2
90	93	65	25	40	2
89	91	64	23	39	2
88	89	63	21	38	1
87	87	62	19	37	1
86	85	61	18	36	1
85	83	60	16	35	1
84	80	59	15	34	1
83	76	58	13	33	1
82	73	57	12	32	1
81	70	56	11	31	1
80	67	55	10	30	1
79	64	54	9	29	1
78	61	53	8	28	0
77	58	52	7		
76	54	51	7		
75	52	50	6	0	

Sex Difference

A sample of 324 males and 324 females were compared to determine if sex were a relevant factor.

Males Mean = 69.42
Standard Deviation = 26.47

Females Mean = 75.47
Standard Deviation = 28.62

A "t" test indicates that the difference between means is significant at better than .01.

Using nonparametric measures the results from the same sample are:

Males	Median = 71.7
	Q = 8.64
Females	Median = 77.5
	Q = 7.59

Time of Administration

The mean will vary depending on whether the ZEIS is administered in the spring or summer before kindergarten or early in the kindergarten year. Experience has shown the same rule of thumb for detecting potential high risk children described earlier exists at all times. The normative data for three-month age ranges shows the variation in means.

Age Differences

Age	Number	Mean	Standard Deviation
4.3 - 4.5	8	68.0	4.63
4.6 - 4.8	34	67.39	12.80
4.9 - 4.11	175	70.09	31.74
5.0 - 5.2	303	72.40	27.71
5.3 - 5.5	258	73.78	29.73
5.6 - 5.8	214	77.67	31.18
5.9 - 5.11	91	77.99	39.32
6.0 - 6.2	17	60.65	14.88
6.3 - 6.5	8	66.13	15.83
6.6 - 6.8	7	67.71	8.65

The scores at age six drop sharply. This may be due to the fact that children in this age range and older are mostly kindergarten repeaters and are probably an atypical population.

Subtest Scores

The subtest scores give an approximation of the child's functioning in three areas. Analysis of the data has shown the verbal part to be less discriminating than the pencil and paper and performance subtests. This must be taken into consideration when raising questions about a child's comparative performance in the three areas.

Verbal Subtest Percentile Rank of Scores

Score	Percentile	Score	Percentile	Score	Percentile
35	100	26	21	17	2
34	80	25	18	16	2
33	77	24	14	15	2
32	68	23	12	14	1
31	54	22	9	13	1

Score	Percentile	Score	Percentile	Score	Percentile
30	47	21	8	12	1
29	38	20	6	11	1
28	32	19	4	10-0	less than 1
27	25	18	3		

Pencil and Paper Subtest
Percentile Rank of Scores

Score	Percentile	Score	Percentile
35	100	19	29
34	100	18	25
33	99	17	20
32	97	16	17
31	95	15	14
30	91	14	11
29	88	13	9
28	83	12	7
27	77	11	6
26	70	10	5
25	64	9	3
24	59	8	2
23	53	7	2
22	45	6	2
21	39	5	1
20	34	4-0	less than 1

Performance Subtest
Percentile Rank of Scores

Score	Percentile	Score	Percentile
30	100	17	23
29	96	16	19
28	95	15	13
27	88	14	11
26	86	13	8
25	78	12	6
24	75	11	3
23	69	10	2
22	60	9	1
21	50	8	1
20	45	7	1
19	36	6-0	less than 1
18	30		

Validity

The validity of the ZEIS has been assessed in the following ways:
1. *Predictive*
   In three of the school districts, in the late fall, informal feed-back was received from the classroom teacher as to whether the children identified as being in the lowest 10 percent of the ZEIS were those that they were most concerned about. There was agreement that the ZEIS had identified those children.
2. *Concurrent*
   The ZEIS was compared to the VANE Kindergarten Screening Test. The Vane was chosen because in a survey of screening instruments most commonly used in New York State, the Vane was used most frequently. The Vane is reported in IQ scores and has some factors in common with the ZEIS, figure drawing, copy forms and vocabulary but has no performance,

information, memory, or concept tasks. With a sample of 45 children the results were r = .54. The sample is seen as too small and comparison with larger samples and other instruments is planned.

Content Validity

Each question of the ZEIS is drawn from developmental literature and normed measures commonly accepted in early childhood assessment. The developmental range is from age three to seven.

On a sample of 187 children (91 girls and 96 boys) the range of the average scores affirm the range of difficulty of the questions.

Reliability

The design of the test negated the possibility of testing for reliability by usual statistical procedures. The initial test-retest study was found to have too many contaminating variables, i.e. a test of inter rater reliability was not done and the period of time between tests varied too greatly due to factors beyond the control of the examiner. Additional research is planned in this area.

Average Scores for Each Question

Area	N=96 Male	N=91 Female	N-187 Total	Possible Scores
information	5.20	5.24	5.22	6
vocabulary	8.81	8.94	8.87	10
language (receptive & expressive)	3.98	3.97	3.98	4
auditory memory	4.85	4.89	4.87	6
concepts	7.64	8.20	7.91	9
draw person (visual-motor & cognition)	9.61	12.40	10.97	16
copy form (visual-motor)	5.84	6.18	6.01	10
recall (visual-motor & visual memory)	2.15	2.72	2.43	5
directions - directionality nonverbal concepts & auditory memory	1.48	1.60	1.54	4
gross motor bilateral integration	6.43	7.90	7.14	10
body image	6.89	7.36	7.12	8

Area	N=96 Male	N-91 Female	N=187 Total	Possible Scores
directions nonverbal - visual, memory & motor integration	2.77	2.88	2.79	6
directions verbal - auditory, sequential memory - concepts & directionality	2.94	3.49	3.21	6
TOTAL	68.68	75.75	72.13	100

DIAGNOSTIC TESTS — SUITABLE FOR PREKINDERGARTEN AND KINDERGARTEN CHILDREN

	Perceptual Motor	Cognition	Speech & Language	Social Emotional
Anton Brenner Developmental Gestalt Test of School Readiness	X	X		
Auditory Discrimination Test (Wepman)			X	
Basic Concept Inventory		X		
Bender Gestalt Test	X	X		X
California Test Battery	X			
Children's Apperception Test				X
Detroit Test of Learning Aptitude	X	X	X	X
Developmental Test of Visual Motor Integration	X			
Frostig Developmental Test of Visual Perception	X			
Goldman Fristoe Test of Articulation			X	
Goodenough Harris Drawing Test	X	X		
Illinois Test of Psycholinguistic Ability		X	X	
McCarthy Scale of Children's Abilities	X	X	X	
Parsons Language Sample			X	
Peabody Picture Vocabulary Test		X	X	
Primary Visual Motor Test	X			
Purdue Perceptual Motor Survey	X			
Stanford Binet Intelligence Scale-R	X	X	X	
Test for Auditory Comprehension			X	
Utah Test of Language Development			X	
Vineland Social Maturity Scale				X
Wechsler Preschool & Primary Scale of Intelligence	X	X	X	

*Addresses of publishers are at the end of this Appendix.

Anton Brenner Developmental Gestalt Test of
School Readiness (1964)
Brenner, A.
Western Psychological Services

The Anton Brenner is an untimed individually administered test which takes three to ten minutes to give. It has normative data for four- to seven-year-olds and has a Spanish edition. The Anton Brenner evaluates perceptual and conceptual differentiating ability. It can be used to identify both gifted and retarded children.

Auditory Discrimination Test (1973 revision)
Wepman, Joseph
Western Psychological Services

The Wepman, as this test is sometimes called, is used to determine the child's ability to recognize the fine differences that exist between the phonemes (the smallest unit of sound) used in English speech. The manual provides standardization scores for five- to eight-year-olds which is based on a five-point rating scale. It takes about five minutes to give.

Basic Concept Inventory (1967), Field Research Edition
Engelman, S.
Follett Educational Corp.

The Basic Concept Inventory is designed to detect deficiencies in basic learning skills. It is criterion referenced and covers basic concepts, statements repetition and comprehension, and pattern awareness. It is normed for children age three to ten years and is primarily intended for culturally disadvantaged preschool and kindergarten children, and other children with special educational needs.

Bender Visual-Motor Gestalt Test (1938)
Bender, L.
Western Psychological Services

The Bender Gestalt Test is used as a measure of visual perception. The psychologist also uses it as a tool to diagnose emotional disturbance and brain injury. The test is a series of nine cards with figures which are presented one at a time to be copied on a blank sheet of paper. It is untimed and takes approximately ten minutes to administer (see Chapter 4, screening instruments for the Koppitz version) and can be used for all ages.

Children's Apperception Test (1965)
Bellak, L. and Bellak, S.
Western Psychological Services

The CAT is a projective test used by psychologists to facilitate understanding of a child's relationship to important persons in his life and to his emotional drives. The test consists of a series of stimulus pictures about which the child is asked to make up a story. There are two versions of the CAT, one with human figures and one with animal figures.

Detroit Test of Learning Aptitude (1967)
Baker, H. and Leland, B.
Bobbs Merrill Co.

The Detroit Test is an individual test of mental functioning. There are nineteen subtests measuring various elements of mental processing. Each subtest yields a separate score allowing a flexible choice for the diagnostic process. It can be used for age four to adult. Some of the tests in the battery are pictorial and verbal absurdities, pictorial and verbal opposites, motor speed and precision, free association, memory for designs, oral directions, and number ability.

Developmental Sentence Analysis (1974)
Lee, Laura
Northwestern University Press

The Developmental Sentence Analysis is a grammatical assessment procedure for speech and language clinicians. It provides an overall plan for the assessment of grammatical structure in children's spontaneous speech. Normative data is presented for children age two through seven.

Developmental Test of Visual-Motor Integration (1967)
Beery, K. and Buktenica, N.
Follett Publishing Co.

The Beery, as this test is sometimes called, is a visual-motor test of the subject's ability in copying designs. It takes ten to fifteen minutes to administer and has normative data for ages five through twenty. Part of this test is often adapted for screening.

Frostig Developmental Test of Visual Perception (1961-1966)
Frostig, M., Maslow, P., LeFever, D., Whittlesey, J.
Follett Publishing Co.

The Frostig measure visual perception in five areas: eye-motor coordination, figure ground, constancy of shape, position in space, and spatial relationships. The test score is a perceptual quotient and has normative data for children three to ten. A remedial program is designed to follow the five areas of the test.

Goldman-Fristoe Test of Articulation (1969)
Goldman, R., Fristoe, M.
American Guidance Service

This articulation test assesses the child's ability to produce sounds in the initial, medial, and final positions. Articulation skill is measured both in the production of isolated words and in sentences. The test can be given by the classroom teacher. It takes thirty minutes to give and can be used for children age two and up.

Goodenough Harris Drawing Test (1963)
Goodenough, F. L. and Harris, D. B.
Harcourt, Brace and World Publishing Co.

The Goodenough test is devised around the human figure drawing. It measures abstract, spatial and quantitative concepts. It yields an IQ score and has normative data for children aged three to fifteen with different tables for boys and girls.

Illinois Test for Psycholinguistic Ability (ITPA) (1968)
Kirk, S., McCarthy, J. and Kirk, W.
University of Illinois Press

The ITPA is designed to identify the psycholinguistic abilities and disabilities of children five to ten years old. The test consists of twelve subtests from which both a total language age and a diagnostic profile may be obtained. The subtests provide information on the levels of organization, channels of communication, and psycholinguistic processes (receptive, expressive, and associative). Complex training is necessary to administer this text which takes from one to one and a half hours to administer. Much prescriptive material is available which follows the outline of the test.

McCarthy Scale of Children's Abilities (1972)
McCarthy, Dorothea
Psychological Corp.

The McCarthy scale assesses the intellectual and motor development of children

2½ to 8½ years of age. It yields scores of verbal ability, short-term memory, numerical ability, perceptual performance, motor coordination, lateral dominance, and overall intellectual competence. It takes forty-five minutes to an hour to administer by a trained psychologist.

Parsons Language Sample (1963)
Spradlin, J.
J. Joseph Spradlin

The Parsons Language Sample consists of subtests designed to sample both speech and nonspeech responses. It can be used with children four to five years of age.

Peabody Picture Vocabulary Test (1965)
Dunn, L.
American Guidance Service

The PPVT is an individual wide-range picture vocabulary test which measures receptive language. The examiner reads the stimulus word and the subject responds by pointing or otherwise indicating the best of four pictures illustrating the word. It takes ten to twenty minutes to administer and yields a score in mental age, standard score IQ or percentile. It is suitable for use with children age two years six months to adult.

Primary Visual-Motor Test (1970)
Haworth, Mary
Grune and Stratton, Inc.

The Primary Visual-Motor Test is designed to assess visual-motor development in the preschool and early primary grades and to evaluate deviations in visual-motor functioning during the developmental process; it has been standardized on children from various socioeconomic strata. Dimensions measured include rotation or reversal; line configuration, fragmentation, closure, omission, addition, distortion, directionality, and gross signs. It can be used with children aged four through eight.

Purdue Perceptual-Motor Survey (1966)
Roach and Kephart
Charles E. Merrill

This survey is used to evaluate the child's motor and perceptual-motor abilities. It assesses such areas as the child's ability in jumping, identification of body parts, stepping stones, and ocular pursuits. As it is based on a sample of thirty children, it is best used as a structured informal device. The Purdue relates perceptual-motor problems to a remedial program of educational methods and procedures. It is designed to be used with *The Slow Learner in the Classroom* (1960) by Dr. Newell Kephart as a therapeutic prescription for training.

Southern California Sensory Integration Tests (1974)
Ayres, J.
Western Psychological Services

This test battery includes a series of seventeen tests which measure visual, tactile, and kinesthetic perception in addition to several different types of motor performance. Entire battery requires about one hour to administer. There is normative data for children ages four to ten.

Stanford Binet Intelligence Scale, 3rd edition, Revised 1972
Terman, L. and Merrill, M.
Houghton-Mifflin, Co.

The Stanford Binet is an individually administered IQ test used for children aged two to eighteen years. Until age five, there are six questions at six-month age intervals and then at year intervals. IQ is derived from a mental age. Tasks up to age six are predominantly nonverbal. It is administered by a trained psychological examiner.

Test for Auditory Comprehension of Language (1973)
English/Spanish
Carrow, Eliz.
Learning Concepts

   This test is designed to measure a child's auditory comprehension of language structure. A series of 101 three-picture plates are used. No verbal response is required of the child. Instructions are provided in both English and Spanish. It is used for children ages three to seven.

Vineland Social Maturity Scale, Fourth Ed. (1965)
Doll, E.
American Guidance Service, Inc.

   The Vineland assesses progress toward social maturity, competence, or independence in subjects from birth to adulthood. Items are designed to elicit factual descriptions of the examinee's habitual or customary behavior as an established mode of conduct. The items are arranged in order of increasing difficulty and represent progressive maturation in self-help, self-direction, locomotion, occupation, communications, and social relations. The Scale is scored on the basis of information obtained in an interview with someone intimately familiar with the person scored, or the person himself.

Wechsler Preschool and Primary Scale of Intelligence (1967)
Wechsler, D.
The Psychological Corp.

   The WPPSI is an individual intelligence test similar to the WISC for children ages four to six and one-half. It contains five verbal tests (plus an alternate) and five performance tests. It yields separate verbal and performance IQ's and a full-scale IQ. It is administered by a trained psychological examiner.

Diagnostic Instruments for the Classroom Teacher

	Perceptual-Motor	Cognitive	Speech Language	Social Emotional
ADAPT				
Child-Diagnostic Inventory	X			
Circus	X	X	X	X
Handbook in Diagnostic Teaching	X	X	X	
Learning Accomplishment Profile (LAP)	X	X	X	X
Psychoeducational Inventory of Basic Learning Abilities	X	X	X	X
School Before Six - A Diagnostic Approach	X	X	X	X

ADAPT (A Diagnostic & Prescriptive Technique (1973)
Farrald, R. and Schanber, R.
Adapt Press

This handbook is subtitled: A Mainstream Approach to Identification, Assessment, and Amelioration of Learning Disabilities. Four areas are described: Learning Style - Psychological/Social Characteristics, Auditory Receptive Skills, Visual Receptive Skills, and Verbal Expressive Skills. In each area the types of disability are described, with observable behaviors and teaching strategies. There is an annotated bibliography of instructional materials.

CHILD - Childhood Identification of Learning Disabilities (1974)
Westinghouse Learning Corp.

The diagnostic inventory is part of a total program for early identification and treatment of children with learning disabilities. There are three individual diagnostic components: The Motor Perceptual Diagnostic Inventory evaluates gross motor control, balance and coordination, neural maturity, occular mobility, and eye-hand dominance.
The Fine Visual-Motor Screening Inventory evaluates fine motor control, perceptual and spacial organization, closure ability, and size discrimination.
The Perceptual Organization Screening Inventory evaluates visual perception, directionality, perceptual organization, form gestalt, and ability to follow verbal instructions. The kit includes a manual designed to assist teachers in relating inventory data to included curricular materials. The inventory can be used with kindergarten and primary grade children.

Circus (1974) (Preliminary Edition)
Educational Testing Service

Circus is a group-administered test which has sixteen diagnostic measures plus a measure of teacher program characteristics, and is developed around a circus theme. Each measure is a separate test and a school can choose whether it wants to use all or specific ones. It assesses children's competencies in various cognitive and social areas: receptive vocabulary, quantitative concepts, visual discrimination, perceptual-motor coordination, letter and numeral recognition and discrimination, discrimination of real-world sounds, auditory discrimination, aspects of functional language, comprehension, interpretation and recall of oral language, productive language, general information, visual and associative memory, problem solving, and divergent pictorial production, and has a behavior inventory. Circus can be scored by ETS, and reports to teachers are in the form of statements that describe each child's performance, directed primarily to diagnosis of individual strengths and weaknesses. Circus is for use with preschool and kindergarten children.

Learning Accomplishment Profile (LAP)
Sandford, A.
Chapel Hill Training-Outreach Project

The LAP is designed to provide the teacher of the young handicapped child with a simple criterion-referenced record of the child's existing skills. Use of the LAP enables the teacher to: identify developmentally appropriate learning objectives for each individual child, measure progress through changes in rate of development, and provide specific information relevant to pupil learning. The profile is in three sections. Section I is a hierarchy of normed developmentally appropriate behaviors which provide the basis for an evaluation of the child's existing skills in six areas of development: gross motor, fine motor, social, self-help, cognitive, and language. Section II provides guidance in sequencing skill development, and Section III records the child's progress in the curriculum units in the preschool curriculum manual which is part of the program.

Handbook in Diagnostic Teaching: A Learning Disabilities Approach (1974)
Mann, P. and Suiter, P.
Allyn and Bacon, Inc.

The book is a child-centered approach to diagnosis that is related to a pro-
cess-oriented curriculum. Chapter 4 (pp 63-114) in the book, entitled *Develop-*
mental Screening, is a compilation of screening devises to be used by the classroom teacher. The chapter has two sections. The first is a Primary Developmental Checklist which can be used to determine the presence or absence of pre-
requisite critical skills (readiness) for task level learning in children ages
four through six. The second section is the Developmental Screening which is
designed to supply supportive data accumulated through the use of other inven-
tories in the book. It helps the teacher to focus more specifically upon particular problem areas as they relate to language acquisition, and it becomes the
basis for the selection of more specific and sophisticated standardized testing
in each of the processing areas when deemed necessary.

Psychoeducational Inventory of Basic Learning Abilities (1968)
Fearon Publishers

The inventory is for the initial evaluation of children with suspected learning disabilities. It samples educational tasks from six major areas of learning:
gross motor development, sensory-motor integration, perceptual-motor skills,
language development, conceptual skills, and social skills for which remediation
tasks are described in the companion book, by R. Vallett, *The Remediation of*
Learning Disabilities: A Handbook of Psychoeducational Resource Programs, 2nd
edition (1974).

School Before Six: A Diagnostic Approach, Revised Edition (1974)
Volume I and Volume II
Hodgen, L., Koetter, J., LaForse, B., McCord, S. and Schramm, D.
The Cemrel Institute

These books are written to help nursery school and kindergarten teachers personalize each child's learning experience. It provides a simplified way of looking at each child which is also used to keep a record of the child's needs and
strengths. Volume I is diagnostic and Volume II is the activity book. Detailed
diagnostic procedures are presented in the developmental areas of large and
small muscle motor skills; perceptual-motor skills; language, social-emotional
skills, and conceptual skills.

Publishers Addresses

Adapt Press
608 West Avenue N
Sioux Falls, South Dakota 75104

Allyn and Bacon, Inc.
470 Atlantic Avenue
Boston, Massachusetts 02210

American Guidance Service
Publishers Building
Circle Pines, Minnesota 55014

Bobbs Merrill Co.
4300 West 62 Street
Indianapolis, Indiana 46268

Cemrel Institute
3120 59 Street
St. Louis, Missouri 63139

Chapel Hill Training Outreach Project
Chapel Hill, North Carolina
Can be ordered from:
Kaplan School Supply Corp.
600 Jonestown Road
Winston-Salem, North Carolina 27103

Charles E. Merrill
1300 Alum Creek Drive
Columbus, Ohio 43220

Educational Testing Service
Princeton, New Jersey 08540

Fearon
6 Davis Drive
Belmont, California 94602

Follett Educational Corp.
1010 West Washington Boulevard
Chicago, Illinois 60607

Grune & Stratton
111 Fifth Avenue
New York, New York 10003

Harcourt, Brace and World Publishing Co.
757 Third Avenue
New York, New York 10017

Houghton Mifflin Co.
111 Tremont Street
Boston, Massachusetts 02107

J. Joseph Spradler
1612 Morgan
Parsons, Kansas 67357

Learning Concepts
2501 N. Lamar, N. W.
Austin, Texas 78705

Northwestern University Press
1735 Benson Avenue
Evanston, Illinois 60201

Psychological Corp.
304 East 45 Street
New York, New York 10017

University of Illinois Press
Urbana, Illinois 61801

Western Psychological Services
12031 Wilshire Boulevard
Los Angeles, California 90025

Westinghouse Learning Corp.
P. O. Box 30
Iowa City, Iowa 52240

AUTHOR INDEX

SUBJECT INDEX